ENGLISH FURNITURE

Table desk, walnut, covered with painted and gilt leather, c1520. H10, W16, D11.

The interior of the table desk contains compartments and drawers, and the inner lid bears the royal arms of Henry VIII, encircled by the Garter Motto and supported by *putti* blowing trumpets. In panels either side stand figures of Venus with Cupid and Mars after woodcuts by the German engraver Hans Burkmayer. Further decoration includes the head of Christ in a roundel, St George and the Dragon, the profile heads of Paris and Helen of Troy, and the heraldic badges of Henry VIII and Katherine of Aragon — all on a background of arabesques and strapwork.

The desk's decoration shows Renaissance influence, and could be the work of an Englishman or of a foreign craftsman working in England. *Prov:* A. C. W. Dunn Gardner; Christie's 7 July 1932 (Lot 111); now in the Victoria and Albert Museum (No: W29-1932).

English Furniture 1500–1840

Geoffrey Beard
and
Judith Goodison

PHAIDON·CHRISTIE'S

OXFORD

Phaidon·Christie's Limited
Littlegate House
St Ebbe's Street
Oxford OX1 1SQ

First published 1987

British Library Cataloguing in Publication Data.

Beard, Geoffrey
    English furniture 1500–1840 (Christie's pictorial histories)
    1. Furniture – England – History
    1. Title   II. Goodison, Judith
    III. Series
    749.22   NK2529

ISBN 0 - 7148 - 8029 - 9

Design and typesetting by Gecko Ltd., Bicester, Oxon.

Printed in Great Britain by Blantyre Printing
and Binding Company Limited, Glasgow

NOTE: In the captions the width (W), height (H),
depth (D) and length (L) are
given in inches

CONTENTS

Bed, oak, c1530. H96, L86, W68.
The tester of the bed is made up of framed panels set with foliate rosettes and a frieze carved with male and female masks and acanthus scrolls. The pierced valance boards are designed as leafy dolphins, separated by cherub masks, and the built-in bedhead is constructed of carved panels divided by split columns. The upper panels show the arms of Wentworth and Dronsfield set in architectural niches in the centre, and male and female busts. St George and the Dragon before a Gothic castle are carved on the central panel of the middle row, with, on either side, David holding the head of Goliath, and Samson attacking a lion.
The lower panels are filled with portrait medallions above diaper work. The square foot posts have upper vase and baluster-turned sections, carved with acanthus foliage. The bed has been rebuilt several times, with some later additions.
Prov: Bretton Hall, built in 1530 by Sir Thomas Wentworth, Knight Marshal of Bretton. The Bretton estates descended by marriage from the Dronsfield family. Now at Temple Newsam House, Leeds (No: 3).

PREFACE

Books on English furniture often deal with a particular style, such as Regency, or with pieces fashioned in a particular wood, such as oak. To our knowledge this is the only book which attempts to survey a wide range of English furniture, dating from the early sixteenth century to about 1840, which has passed through a London saleroom. To construct the book, we have used only the archives of Christie's, but that distinguished firm has, in its long history, handled every category of English furniture, including pieces as important as the Badminton japanned suite, and chairs made to the design of Robert Adam for Sir Lawrence Dundas.

All researchers of English furniture, wishing to compare what they have found with what is already published, turn first to the seminal *Dictionary of English Furniture*. Published in three volumes in 1927 by the late Percy Macquoid and the late Ralph Edwards, it was followed by a revised edition by Edwards (with the assistance of the late Edward T. Joy and others) in 1954. A *Shorter Dictionary* in one volume spawned from it in 1964, and a reduced facsimile limited edition of the three-volume 1954 work was issued in 1983 and again in 1986. These volumes alone exceed the number of illustrations we have used here for a comprehensive coverage of English furniture.

In order to arrive at our final choice, we copied over three thousand photographs from Christie's archives, ranging in date of sale from the 1930s to 1986, arranged them in categories, and then reduced them to the six hundred illustrated here. Whilst it might be argued that this method only allows knowledge of a piece through a photograph and a catalogue description, it nevertheless provides the best and widest choice of the available material.

The prices realized in the salerooms fluctuate, and we have therefore provided a list of prices by date and lot number, cross-referenced to the illustration number, together with a glossary and bibliography. The salerooms are an unfailing indicator of taste, which is itself reflected in the balance of illustration in the book. Obviously the illustrative material is stronger in periods where the salerooms are strongest, and many of our best pieces are drawn from the eighteenth century onwards. For certain photographs which we considered necessary to balance the book we have stepped outside Christie's archives, and we are grateful to have been allowed use of the departmental files at the Victoria and Albert Museum and Temple Newsam House, both repositories of outstanding English furniture.

The assembling of so many illustrations, obtaining them in usable form, selecting and arranging, checking and captioning them, has been a time-consuming task. In it we have been well served by a number of people whom we wish to thank most warmly for their unselfish assistance. At Christie's, Hugh Roberts, Nicola Hassard, Charmian Baynham and Miranda North Lewis were essential to the completion of the book: they and their colleagues have over many years widened knowledge of furniture by scholarly cataloguing. We know that they were spurred on as much by the overall desire to see a useful book compiled as by friendship to us. At Phaidon Press, Roger Sears, Bernard Dod and Judy Spours (our Editor) smiled with indulgence at our frequent requests for even more illustrations, and coped ably with all the practical problems of making the book.

Geoffrey Beard
Judith Goodison
Bath/London, September 1986

Cabinet, oak, c1615. H46, W43.
Some of the pattern of the decoration on this cabinet may well copy
the engraved designs in Sebastiano Serlio's *Archittetura*, which had an
important influence on architecture and decoration throughout
Europe. The decoration comprises applied bosses, mouldings, vase-
shaped pilasters and inlaid panels of ivory and *lignum-vitae*.

CHAPTER 1

Oak and Walnut
1500–1700

1500–1600

By the time her major writer and poet Geoffrey Chaucer died in 1400, England was becoming independent from French thought and contemporary European literature. The country had recovered from the impoverishments of war, agricultural decline and the ravages of the Black Death. Its builders had turned to a cheaper form of linear decoration in cut stone—the Perpendicular style—than full-blooded French Gothic (so apparent in Henry III's Westminster Abbey), and timber, particularly oak, was plentiful. The knowledge of working it led to the creation of many fine roofs of hammer-beam type, and also to the formation of strong guilds of joiners and carpenters. Furniture-makers at the time made 'joined' furniture of simple sections nailed or joined together with pegs for medieval houses.

The most skilled furniture craftsman at the start of the sixteenth century was the cofferer. His trade had evolved to counter the vast number of coffers, or chests, which were imported via France. An Act of 1483 prohibiting this trade proved ineffective, and Flanders chests became a common possession in England. The travelling coffer, usually of oak covered in leather and tooled in gilt like an elaborate book-binding (a good example is the table desk illustrated in the *Frontispiece*), was an important object for the storage of papers, valuables and clothes. However, a sharp demarcation still existed between the oak furniture produced for church and small manor house, and the grander objects made for larger houses, decorated in exotic woods such as ebony, holly and box. There was also still an unresolved struggle between the use of Gothic and Renaissance forms of decoration.

The well-known desire of Henry VIII to have a male heir led to a rapid succession of marriages, deaths and divorce. The latter unholy state brought the King into direct conflict with Rome when the Pope refused to recognize the legality of the King's divorce of Catherine of Aragon, and his marriage, in 1533, to Anne Boleyn. England severed itself abruptly from Catholic Christendom, and any contact with the sophisticated repertory of Italian art and ornament ceased.

Early Tudor furniture therefore remained simple and close to medieval pattern, and no chance of amendment came until the King decided to build a great palace at Cuddington to rival the achievements of Francis I at Fontainebleau. The grand conception of Nonsuch was planned in 1538 by Nicholas Bellin of Modena, who acted as advisor to the chief officers of the King's works. Bellin provided the link by which the Renaissance style, in all its seeming jumble of Italian and French pattern, transferred to England. No effort was spared to make Nonsuch grand and enduring, though sadly it was pulled down in the seventeenth century.

The extant series of coffers—the so-called 'Nonsuch chests'—were not in fact made for the Palace. Heavily inlaid with marquetry panels representing formal architectural views, their association was a nineteenth-century fantasy created because of the superficial resemblance of the decoration to the elevations of Nonsuch. For the most part they represent later buildings in the 'antique' style and were created by continental furniture craftsmen settled at Southwark in the late sixteenth century.

From the mid-sixteenth century, furniture-makers were turning their attention to framed and panelled

Chest, oak, late 14th century. H29, W62, D22.
Oak chests of this form were used frequently for the storage of church
vestments, and an almost identical chest to this, but with applied
rather than carved tracery, is at Huttoft Church, Lincolnshire. This
example is panelled and carved with Gothic tracery and foliage. The
hinged top is secured with an iron lock, and iron handles are
mounted on the sides.

pieces of more sophisticated construction and comfort
than the simple joined furniture of previous centuries.
Some furniture incorporated decoration of interlaced
strapwork resembling cut and folded leather, an idea
that Rosso Fiorentino had taken from Italy to incorporate in plaster and wood in his Gallery for Francis I at
Fontainebleau. German and Flemish engravers used it
for edging cartouches and for surrounding panels.
With many other forms of engraved ornament to call
on, the Tudor age abandoned itself to a riot of robust
and vulgar styles. Nowhere was this more apparent
than in the swelled proportions and carvings of the
court cupboard, an open structure of three tiers which
resembled those in France and the Low Countries. It
was used for the display of plate and pewter, and at a
later stage, when enclosed, for the storage of these
items and of food.

Beds followed the Renaissance pattern of a richly
carved tester supported on a carved and inlaid headboard, frequently depicting bas-relief portraits
('Romayne' work). The posts, which first came into use
about 1500, were usually turned on the lathe, or made
up, in more elaborate examples, of combinations of
joinery and bulbous ornament—carved lion supports

and strapwork, small figures or animals, and arabesque
scrolls in box and holly. Biblical and mythological
stories interpreted in fifteenth-century wood-cuts were
the source of many carved panels. Whilst Tudor four-
post beds have usually been rebuilt on several occasions, with parts added, a number survive in which the
wealth of carved detail is of consistently good quality,
and the degree of restoration acceptable in furniture of
this early date. Despite domestic upheavals, the 'best
bed' of many inventories was held in family veneration,
particularly when it had a Royal connection, however
tenuous. That any survive at all is a demonstration of
the care taken to preserve them, as the small amount of
furniture which surrounded them has often disappeared or been altered almost beyond recognition.
The 1542 inventory of The Vyne, Hampshire, shows
that its fifty-two rooms contained only nineteen chairs,
of which seven were imports and described as 'Flanders chairs'.

A shortage of chairs was balanced by a profusion of
benches, forms and stools to sit on (joined with pegs at
simple joints), and more comfortable settles with backs,
arms and, often, box seats. Also popular was the chair
or table-bench in which a hinged back was lowered to
form a table top. Supremely, the wood in wide use was
still oak. From the 1530s armchairs often had panels
beneath the seats and arms, usually carved in linenfold
pattern, and some were formed from elaborate turned
elements. By 1600 it was becoming more usual to
attempt a lighter appearance by removing the panels or
excesses of bobbin-turning and carrying the arms forward over the simpler turned uprights to end in scrolls.

The back panel was often carved in low relief, and recent research in England and America has established that its decoration can show characteristics typical of the work of chair-makers of particular regions, for example, East Anglia or Yorkshire.

In summary, the Elizabethan age—the Queen reigned from 1558 to 1603—brought forward three distinct ornamental features: strapwork or arabesque ornament in low relief; bulbs on table legs and bedposts; and inlaying of woods such as poplar, box, sycamore, ebony and holly into a thin channel cut in the oak (or increasingly) walnut carcase. There was a concern with architectural detail, particularly of arcaded decoration, and even the occasional but precise imitation in coffered panels of plates in the Italian architect, Sebastiano Serlio's, fourth book of his architectural treatise (1537), available in many editions throughout the century, and in an English translation from 1611. Together with the Flemish, German and Netherlands pattern-books and engravings, the fruits of Antiquity could thus be studied with increasing ease, and amended and applied by artisans to many decorative schemes.

1600–1660

The early seventeenth century in England was characterized in artistic terms by the influence of the components of classical architecture—that is, arches, pilasters and columns. In furniture the demand for greater comfort was growing, and upholstery for the backs and seats of chairs came into widespread use. At the same time there was much that remained humble and practical. The university archives at Oxford contain hundreds of inventories of the 'goods and chattels' of university members. Some 700 survive from 1569 to 1699 and show the ways in which various rooms were furnished. The main wood in use was oak, with occasional pieces in walnut, elm, deal, cedar and sweet chestnut, which John Evelyn noted in his *Sylva* was, next to oak, one of the woods 'most sought after by the Carpenter and Joyner'. There were many varieties of table—including those supported on trestles and those designed for games—all framed and some with a swinging gate-leg to support a flap at each end. Most chairs were versions of extended stools, but the Renaissance form of 'X' stool, and a small low chair called a *caquetoire* (from *caqueter*, to chatter) were still popular. Carving was lavish; the bobbin-turned elements were used in profusion and settees with upholstered seats evolved from the earlier wood settle. In grand examples a fabric such as crimson velvet was fastened to a beech framework by gilt nails and trimmed with crimson fringe. Small wings were put at each end above the simple square-section arms and all the legs were connected with stretchers, sometimes of knobbed or bobbin-turning. Various leathers, turkey work (an imitation of carpets woven in the Middle East with a knotted woollen pile), baize and other fabrics, with rushes for wicker chairs,

Stool, oak, early 17th century. W18.
Joint stools were the commonest pieces of furniture in seventeenth-century interiors, but became more valued when upholstered in expensive fabrics. This is one from a set of six, with incised fluted friezes and ring-turned baluster legs joined by stretchers.

have been noted in the Oxford inventories. The trauma of the Civil Wars, however, sealed off the decorative impulses of the early years from those which followed the Restoration of the King and his Court in 1660. Up to that time English furniture-makers were certainly less sophisticated than their Continental counterparts and relied on Mannerist engravings and a casual demand from patrons to go on supplying rather outmoded designs, which had altered little for over a hundred years.

1660–1700

It was the experiences of Charles II, who had been forced to sojourn abroad in France and Holland before his Restoration in 1660, which brought about important changes in taste. He had been able to see the achievements of Baroque architects and to witness the fruits of the international trading connections of Antwerp, especially the products brought back in the ships of the Dutch East India Company, including elaborate lacquer and marquetry panels. However, these oriental pieces were difficult and expensive to acquire, so Dutch crafts-men imitated their forms, and improved on the rel-evant techniques in so doing. New ways of veneering allowed the creation of large Dutch cabinets with exotic veneers or with tortoiseshell backed with red foil. The work of the Dutch flower painters, acclaimed interna-tionally, also influenced the depiction of vases of col-oured flowers, which were painted or inlaid on drawers and the inner surfaces of doors. The Dutch East India Company had obtained a monopoly of trade with Japan in 1602 and set up a lucrative business, which included the carrying of furniture and porcelain to be decorated. Japanese 'verlakkers', keen to exploit new markets, travelled west and were soon working in Amsterdam making and delivering door panels for cabinets and tea tables, painted in gold and colours, as well as instruct-ing native workmen.

The East India Company (founded in London in 1599 and incorporated by royal charter 31 December 1600) was importing Chinese and lacquer panels into England by the late 1680s, and at the end of the century notices were appearing in the London Gazette advertis-ing 'Japan Cabinets', both Indian and English, for sale. 'Japan' as a term was used without implying any definite geographical area, following 'Indian', which since the end of Elizabeth's reign (1603) had been the term used for any oriental object imported into Europe.

English patrons had already become accustomed to Dutch and Baroque influences in the form of the robust naturalistic wood-carvings of Grinling Gibbons (1648–1721) and his team. Gibbons had come to England about 1664, and through recognition of his considerable talents by the diarist John Evelyn had been introduced to Charles II and his court. His work in soft wood, invested with a lively bravura, was followed but never surpassed by a few other carvers of English origin: their work resulted in some accomplished picture and look-ing glass frames, carved swags and table frames. In less obvious ways the aprons of tables and the stretchers of tables, chairs and settees reflected the input to English workshops of a blend of Netherlandish and French influence. The wood in wide use for furniture-making was now walnut, which had almost totally replaced oak as the principal timber.

The King's return and the consequent demand for luxurious furniture based on continental patterns led to almost continous improvement in furniture forms. The opportunities to rebuild following the Great Fire of 1666 further encouraged improvements during Charles II's reign. A second important phase of activity came about as the result of Louis XIV's intolerance of religious freedom—enjoyed in France since the Edict of Nantes in 1598. In 1685 Louis revoked the Edict and many talented artisans fled to Holland, and in turn to England. The replacement of the Catholic James II by the Protestant William of Orange and his Queen, Mary, in 1688 provided a certain refuge for them. In particular the work of one man, Daniel Marot (1663–1752), son of the French engraver Jean Marot and nephew of the cabinet-makers at the Gobelins, Pierre and Adrian

Gole, became important. In his position as William's court architect and designer he was able to introduce designs derived from the work of his master, the French engraver Jean Berain, to English patrons. In particular, the great towering State Beds, with furniture en suite, giving so much opportunity for the display of the skills of upholsterer, embroiderer and fringe-maker, were depicted in his Nouveau Livre d'Apparte-ments (1702) and created in many fine examples. They were of the so-called 'angel' tester form in which the superstructure does not rely for support on end-posts but is cantilevered from the back-board, albeit sup-ported occasionally at its upper forward edge by chains to the ceiling.

In 1688, the year of William III's accession to the English throne, John Stalker and George Parker, having gleaned some of their information from Dutch crafts-men (and perhaps from talented émigrés working in England, such as Gerrit Jensen) issued their Treatise of Japanning and Varnishing. Their patterns 'for Japan-work in imitation of the Indians for Tables, Stands, Frames, Cabinets etc.' were crude and bore a strong similarity to Dutch examples, particularly in the costumed figures. An important modification was that the finished cabi-nets were set on carved and gilded stands, whereas in China and Japan they stood on the floor. This improved the decorative appearance and the usefulness of a cabinet, thereby increasing its chances of sale. Unfor-tunately many imported lacquer screens were cut up for panels, but no consideration—as a contemporary writer explained—was given to 'the situation of their figures; so that in these things so torn and hacked to joint a new fancie, you may observe the finest hodgpog and medly of Men and Trees turned topsie turvie . . .' But the furniture still sold well.

This prosperous trade had aroused the jealousy of English furniture-makers, for their own work in walnut and olive wood was not being bought. They petitioned Parliament against the imports, but with pragmatic application also turned to imitate the 'Indian' lacquer ware. Stalker and Parker's manual gave a fillip to this, and also encouraged the skilled amateur to practise the art. They considered that their manual assisted readers 'to distinguish between good Work and Rubbish . . .', and they identified gums, metals and colours as the three elements of the craft. The gums, of which there were several, were used to form different varnishes by dissolving them in spirit of wine. The metals—brass-dust, with silver-dust, green-gold, powder tin and the coppers—were worked in as appropriate to the black or coloured varnish. The colours were laid on to make other coloured grounds: red, blue, olive or chestnut . In all cases after the surface was coated with the ground colour, twelve coats of best varnish were applied and polished with powdered tripoli and a damp cloth. The raised work of figures, birds, flowers and rocks was made of a thick paste of whiting bound with gum, and then cut, scraped and carved to model it to the required design. Craftsmen such as the Dutch Gerrit Jensen, who worked in England from the reign of Charles II and sheets of veneer would be arranged so that an attractive pattern could be formed from the figuring in the wood, either joining symmetrically or put as four pieces to form a quartered table top. Such panels were often 'framed' by a border of veneer in which the grain ran across the width. These 'cross-banded' veneers were decorative, and if 'feather-edged' (the cross grain of two lengths of veneer at an angle to each other) were even more so. Their popularity, on walnut furniture at least, extended into the reign of George I (1714–27).

A much richer effect was obtained with veneers by parquetry and marquetry. In parquetry (which was also often used to inlay ciphers and initials in the half-landings of great wooden staircases, e.g. at Beningbrough), the veneer was laid in small pieces cut to fit one another and produce a geometric effect. This suited the small pieces with 'oyster' markings taken from the branches of (in particular) the laburnum tree. The richest form of veneer was, however, marquetry, where extensive veneering was used to produce a pictorial effect. Confusingly, it was created by an 'inlayer', and the difference between inlaying and marquetry should be stressed. Inlay was employed on both oak and walnut furniture in the sixteenth and seventeenth centuries and denotes that the pattern of coloured woods was set into thin grooves, about ⅛ in deep, cut into the carcase to be decorated. By contrast, marquetry was formed into a thin panel of contrasting shapes, woods and colours, and laid in position over the carcase. A hot 'caul' was cramped down over it and the heat from it passed through the veneers liquefying the glue. As this became cold, after about thirty-six hours, the caul could be removed and the marquetry prepared for polishing.

Floral marquetry was in great demand in the last forty years of the seventeenth century. John Evelyn in *Silva* mentioned that the coloured woods used included 'Berbery for yellow, Holly for white . . . Prince and Rose wood for yellows and reds, with several others brought from both Indies'. We might add, sycamore, lignum vitae, coromandel, laburnum and figured and burr walnut, the latter cut from the large round burrs which often appear on a tree-trunk at the place where a branch has grown. This veneered furniture was often enriched by elaborate mouldings, sometimes ebonized, and in construction had drawers hung on runners fixed to the carcase. This was a development from the earlier method of the drawer moving on runners fixed to its underside, in itself an improvement over the period when the surface of the drawer bottom rubbed against the dust board which separated each layer of drawers from those beneath. This flush-bottomed drawer went out of use at the end of the seventeenth century. Much has been made of the fact that early walnut furniture usually has the boards of the drawer bottoms running with the grain from front to back, whereas those after, say, 1740, have the boards running from side to side. The rule, however, is not invariable, and the bottoms of long drawers with boards running from side to side also had the disadvantage of sagging in the middle, needing support by a muntin at the centre point.

Armchair, oak, late 16th century.
The skill of the turner was particularly English, and whilst his creations often seem to display this to excess, the forms were practical and acceptable for a limited period. The elaborate back has horizontal and vertical ring-turned splats, and turned legs support the solid seat. Now at Dunster Castle, Somerset (The National Trust).

died towards the end of Queen Anne's in 1715, were able to japan small rooms or closets (Chatsworth), as well as provide furniture decorated with marquetry or japan. In some cases pieces were inlaid with metal in a manner similar to that of the great French craftsman to Louis XIV's court, A.C. Boulle.

Until the advent of Charles II's reign wood had been largely regarded as a constructional material and little satisfaction was found in the figure of its grain, colour or texture. It needed to be carved, painted or inlaid with other contrasting woods or metal to render it pleasing to the eye. A wood such as walnut had, however, the attraction (common also to olivewood, laburnum and kingwood) of being rich in figure, especially when the small branches were sliced in thin sections producing a circular marking, similar to that of an oyster. These fine woods were too expensive to use as the carcase of a piece of furniture. Sawed into thin strips, a log could provide veneers which could be glued over a cheaper, common wood such as deal. The

Side Table, walnut and limewood, carved by Grinling Gibbons (1648–1721) w45, c1670.

This table was given to John Evelyn by the carver Grinling Gibbons who came to work in England from Rotterdam (his parents were however English) in the 1660s. It has a moulded walnut top and a deep pierced limewood frieze carved with oak, fruit and flowers. Evelyn's manuscript inventory of Wotton House (1702) records: 'A table of walnut tree curiously vein'd and vernished standing on a frame of lime-tree incomparably carved with 4 Angels, flowers & fruitages by that famous Artist Gibbons, & presented to me in acknowledgement of my first Recommending him to K. Charles the second, before which he was scarce known.'

Prov: John Evelyn; J. H. C. Evelyn; Major Peter Evelyn.

Whilst tables and chairs in which thin sheets of embossed and chased silver were laid over the carcase were always rare—they were among Charles I's possessions, and there are some of 1682 with the carcase by Jensen at Knole—ebony tables with silver mounts, sometimes with looking glasses and stands to match, were more common. There was little difference between centre tables and those intended to stand against a wall—a notable exception being that in limewood with a walnut top, carved by Grinling Gibbons and given by him to John Evelyn in the mid-1680s. Scagliola—an imitation marble formed from gypsum and stone dust—was used occasionally for table tops. The tops of occasional tables had hitherto relied for effect on the use of veneers, mostly walnut, but were more restrained than those in seaweed and foliated marquetry of the late seventeenth century.

Armchairs of carved beech or walnut frequently had cane or leather seats, with high interlaced stretchers carved with ribbon and acanthus motifs or trumpeting *putti*. The caned panels in the back were divided by carved and perforated splats. As noted, there was a lavish use of japanning and of upholstery, particularly in velvet and damask. On winged armchairs the velvet was edged with tasselled fringes, which extended to the arms. However, when the arms were of polished wood, their scrolling and termination in animal heads (lion, dolphin) on arm-supports of mushroom or gadrooned form, guaranteed a splendour which equalled that of upholstered chairs. Upholstery, lavish on the great beds, was also rich on day-beds, which had developed from benches with oak panelled ends to resemble a settle in construction, with one end letting down, or the long seat being supported on six or eight taper baluster legs, connected by serpentine stretchers. Cabinets, bureaux, scriptors, chests of drawers, corner cupboards, chests: the inventories abound with the various types of furniture. They evolved and multiplied and assumed varying forms and styles in later years, proportionate to the rooms they were created for.

The need for furniture to be light and portable, able to store papers and small objects and appeal to the eye, had led to innovations—the use of cane, pierced carving, thin veneers, and stamped and gilded gesso; and the proliferation of drawers and partitions, overlaid where appropriate with rich fabrics. Most pieces could be carried after use to more suitable positions. The dark spaces between windows were equipped increasingly with a table of suitable width, surmounted by a looking glass, and free-standing japanned or walnut toilet mirrors were set on heavily draped dressing tables. In fact by the time John Gumley petitioned Parliament concerning a glass-house set up by him at Lambeth in 1705, he could state that the trade in looking glass plates had so improved that they were 'likewise in great esteem in foreign parts; the Venetians themselves buying of these Plates, and preferring them to their own.' From 1694 the 'Joiners and Carvers' joined forces to pursue patrons, to their mutual advantage. It seemed that English furniture-making had at last achieved maturity and could hold its own against continental output in even the exotic woods.

Armchair, beech frame covered with appliqué of cloth of gold on a red satin ground, c1610-20.

The richly upholstered 'X'-shaped type of Elizabethan chair continued to be made in the early seventeenth century. However, only Knole has a considerable number. Every part of the chair is upholstered — the framework is covered with fabric edged with a cut fringe and fixed to it by gilt-headed nails. The back is divided into two panels by a cut fringe, and the fabric matches that on a contemporary bed in the house. The shield-shaped escutcheon at the intersection of the legs has been reversed at some date.

Prov: Knole Park, Kent (The National Trust).

John Evelyn noted that in hall and parlour long tables 'were as fixed as the freehold'. By this he meant that the early refectory tables, being heavy and difficult to move, descended through many generations in the same family. During the seventeenth century, the bulbous supports changed in character. They became less pronounced and were frequently refined by the turner. This may be studied in particular in the gate-legged tables, where many of the supports resemble contemporary staircase balusters. Dating can only be approximate due to the simple forms remaining popular among craftsmen over a long period.

1.   *Table, oak, c1600. L (fully closed) 81, L (fully extended) 154, H33, D35.* Many devices were in use to enable framed furniture to be adjusted. The earliest of importance was the sliding mechanism of tables with draw-leaves. This dining table, with its plank top and chequered frieze with a gadrooned border, extends by pulling the two leaves from under the top at each end. The top frame rests on legs with cup and cover supports, headed by Ionic capitals and joined at ground level by stretchers.

2.   *Table, oak c1655. W (open) 70.*
The simple form of this table is typical of furniture made during the Commonwealth period (1649-60). The rectangular top has semi-elliptical flaps, which, when open, are supported on hinged brackets. The plain turned legs are united by stretchers.

3.   *Table, yew, c1655. L72, H28, W61.*
The gate-leg marked a significant improvement in table construction, in which a movable frame supported one or more shaped flaps, to form an oval or circular top. In this example, the top is of solid burr yew, with the twin flaps so supported. The table has baluster legs joined by stretchers, and has turned feet.

4. Table, oak, mid-17th century. L93.
Various stylistic influences, from France and Italy in particular, affected both furniture and decoration. The pierced, tapering supports here are architectural in form, somewhat French, and could be imagined as finials on an Elizabethan 'prodigy house' such as Wollaton. However, less fancifully, the plank top rests on a fluted frieze and the base of the six supports is joined by robust stretchers.

5. Credence table, oak, 1655. w41.
The Italian *credenza* was a side table on which vessels were placed before being used to serve at table. As a form, it was rare in England, but those that survive are heavily carved, and some Elizabethan examples have canopies. Here the frieze under the trapezoid top is carved with simple lunettes and scrolls divided by applied split balusters; it conceals a central drawer.

6. Settle table, oak, c1655. w66.
Considerable ingenuity was used by furniture-makers across the years to make items which had two or more functions, and to see that each performed satisfactorily. An example is this settle with a triple plank top which can be lowered onto the turned arms of the panelled box seat to form a table.

7. Table, oak, c1655. w36.
The art of the turner matched to that of the joiner produced much satisfactory oak furniture, and even provided an opportunity for some lively carving. All three elements are blended in this oak table. The folding top, when open, forms a hexagon, the flap supported on a hinged gate-leg. The frieze is carved with stylized symmetrical foliage and scrolls in relief on a matted ground, and a platform base joins the ring-turned columnar legs.

1. Side table, painted, c1675. W48.
This design could have been made as a stand for a cabinet, but such pieces were also used as tables. The deep apron frieze, lavishly carved with billing birds, flanked by winged *putto* masks amidst scrolled acanthus leaves and fruit, supports a marble top. The scrolled legs, carved with pendant drapery, are bordered with overlapping wave ornament ending in flowerhead clusters.
Prov: Wateringbury House, Kent.

2. Side table, scagliola, gesso mounts, ebonized wood, c1670. W45, D30.
This rare Anglo-Dutch table incorporates imitation marble, *scagliola*, at several points — on the flower and bird bedecked top and frieze, in the simulated French red and white marble columns with gilt gesso mounts, and on the stretcher. At an earlier date the depiction of such ornament may well have been carried out in *pietra dura*, using semi-precious stones, but the refinement of techniques to simulate materials allowed this cheaper alternative.
Prov: Warwick Castle.

3. Side table, walnut and seaweed marquetry, c1690. W34, D23.
A number of craftsmen, escaping from religious persecution on the Continent, settled in England in the late seventeenth century. One such was the Dutch craftsman Gerrit Jensen, whose name is attached to a number of tables and chests of this form. The table top has ebonized borders, and the frieze, double scroll legs and stretchers are all inlaid with shaped panels of seaweed marquetry.

4. Side table, japanned, late 17th century. W37.
Through long and extensive trade with China and Japan, lacquer objects found their way to England. English craftsmen attempted to copy the form by applying successive coats of opaque colour in varnish to a wood carcase. An important treatise on the methods was published in London in 1688 by John Stalker and George Parker. This table alludes to the work of Gerhard Dagly, born in the early 1650s in Belgium. He entered the service of the Electors of Brandenburg in the late 1680s, and decorated furniture in all the bright palette of genuine oriental work. A craftsman familiar with his style fashioned this Anglo-Dutch side table.
Prov: Earl of Seafield, Cullen House, Scotland.

In the late seventeenth century the art of the furniture-maker reached a high point of achievement in the creation of small tables. Within a limited area he produced great variety in the scroll or spiral legs and connected these with elaborate stretchers, some of which had display platforms for oriental vases or were areas for marquetry tracery. The top surfaces, in marble or imitation marble (scagliola), gilded gesso, or with elaborate marquetry patterns were lavish and perhaps only outstripped by the fashionable use of black and coloured japanned surfaces. Continental craftsmen and stylistic influences were playing important roles in manufacture, and patrons were ever eager to support the trend and acquire the exotic items produced.

5. *Dressing table, elm and marquetry, c1690. W37, D26.*
When William III came to the English throne in 1688, he encouraged many Dutch craftsmen to work here as they had done for Charles II in the 1670s. In particular, they made fashionable seaweed marquetry furniture. Here the frieze patterns are set against the light background of boxwood. The top and centre of the stretcher were also good display points for more oval panels of marquetry. The table has attractive spiral and ball turned legs, which had come into use from about 1660 onwards.

6. *Centre table, gilt gesso and giltwood, c1695. W39.*
The gilt gesso top of this centre table is elaborately carved — rosettes, foliate scrolls and interlaced bands proliferate. There is a bold giltwood stretcher with circular platforms to display oriental vases. It is fashionable to think of all gilded gesso furniture as fashioned by James Moore the elder, but there were presumably many other London makers skilled in its creation.

1. Games table, fruitwood, c1690. w32.
Small tables, for a variety of purposes, were produced from the late seventeenth century onwards. Those for games usually had a folding top in order that they could be fitted into a small area when not in use, and to protect any relevant markings integral to the game. This games table has a leather-lined top inlaid with purpleheart lines. When open, it is supported by a hinged gate. The end drawers were fitted later, and the feet have been renewed.

2. Card table, walnut, c1690. w30.
A growing interest in a new vogue, taking tea or playing cards, could lead to many new forms of furniture made especially to serve such a habit. This card table has a folding top lined with velvet, enriched with metal-thread banding. Two drawers and two candle slides are fitted in the frieze at the sides.

3. Card table, walnut and seaweed marquetry, c1690. H29, w32, D11.
Architectural forms can often be most effective when transferred in miniature to furniture. Here, the arcaded front resembles the entrance to a grand *palazzo*, but it is all only 29 inches high. Two gate-legs swing out to support a folding top — almost all surfaces are covered with fine marquetry of scrolling foliage and strapwork.

4. Card table, burr walnut, c1700. H29, w30, D13.
Card tables were of many forms — square, oval, circular — but most had folding tops and gates of various forms to support them when in use. This semi-elliptical folding top is bordered with a herringbone band, and the frieze is fitted with three drawers and two candle stands. The attractive waved stretchers reflect the curved form of the frieze.

*Turning comprises the art of shaping
wood and many other materials by cutting into the substance with gouges and
chisels whilst it is revolving on a lathe.
It was a process familiar to the Romans,
but the trade seems to have established
itself in an organized way early in the
fourteenth century. Throughout the
seventeenth century the baluster form
for legs and spindles was produced in
great variety. It only became more sophisticated late in the century, being then
notable for its conformity to classical
models with a purity in proportion and
line.*

*Whilst chairs became more plentiful
in the Elizabethan period, the turner
was still much involved in the production of stools. These were distinguished
from the joined or joynt stools, which
were made and finished by a joiner (6.).*

5.   *Armchairs, oak, mid-17th century.*
The various bobbin-turned spindles and turned legs and stretchers produced (in this
case) by an unknown northern turner, look somewhat awkward when assembled.
However, the result was practical and inexpensive chairs, which were widely available.

6.   *Stool, oak, early 16th century.* H21, W20.
The joined stool was one of the earliest forms
of oak furniture, and it is frequently
mentioned in early inventories, although good
examples rarely survive. Here the frieze is
carved with vines in relief. Cusped arcading
reaches through the trestle supports.

7.   *Child's stool, oak, mid-17th century.*
Early oak furniture made especially for children
is rare, but needed to be robust and well constructed in order to be stable. This square stool
has a lunette carved frieze, and rests on heavy
turned baluster legs with square stretchers.

The panel back of various provincial chairs was an excellent space for the carver to fill with motifs, or to be inlaid with various woods. A further complexity was given to the outline by florid crestings and brackets carved with foliage (5). About the time of the Restoration of the King in 1660, the panel back was supplemented by a lighter type in which the space between the uprights was filled by a shaped rail (6. and 7). Upholstery was still comparatively rare, but also gained in popularity after 1660; walnut gradually supplemented oak, and caned panels on back and seat became common.

1. Armchair, oak, 1678.
Considerable research has been done in recent times to endeavour to sort out the various regional characteristics in such carved oak chairs. The names and date — 'Francis Heathcot Ellen Heathcot 1678' presumably commemorate a marriage in that year.

2. Armchair, oak, 1662.
This strong, well-proportioned armchair relies for its decorative appeal on a double panelled back which is incised with a common form of embellishment, lozenges, and carved with the initials 'H.H.' and the date '1662' above two stylized flowers. The sloping arms are supported on turned columns.

3. Armchair, oak and elm, late 17th century.
This chair is given considerable distinction by the careful positioning of the shaped arm rests, and the attractive flat relief carving of stylized foliage on the back and seat rails.

4.   *Armchair, oak, c1665.*
Research is being devoted to the difficult task of ascertaining in what area various chairs were made, on the basis of elements in the carved motifs common with those on church woodwork. The arcaded centre of the panelled back of this chair is inlaid with a flower spray, while the shaped cresting above is carved with roses and thistles. The initials 'IPN' appear on the uprights.

5.   *Armchair, oak, c1665.*
Early panel-back chairs are of massive construction, but relief was provided by the use of carved elements and often very flamboyant scrolled crestings and brackets attached to the sides. The carved motifs were, of course, often rendered without much flair, but they add to the overall decorative effect.

6.   *Chair, oak, c1665-70.*
One of a pair of Yorkshire oak dining chairs, this has rails carved with 'S'-scrolls and latticework with suspended acorns. The uprights are decorated with applied, split balusters. The solid seat is of later date than the frame.
Prov: Up Cerne Manor, Dorset.

7.   *Child's chair, oak, 1675.*
This chair is dated on the seat rail, but the arched back rails denote it as of North Country type. Bobbin-turned supports at the front legs lighten the design and support the footrest.

1. *Food cupboard, oak, late 15th century. w49.*
The title 'aumbry' (with variant spellings) was often applied originally to what later became known as a cupboard. It seems to have derived from being a receptacle for portions left after a feast, reserved as 'alms' to the poor. Without the pierced openings, which allowed air circulation, aumbries were used up to the Reformation for the storage of church vestments and ornaments.

2. *'Nonsuch' chest, oak inlaid with holly, c1620.*
Henry VIII's Nonsuch Palace, built in Surrey in the 1530s, was demolished in the seventeenth century. A type of inlaid decoration found on late sixteenth-century oak chests portrays conventional turreted buildings. The Palace bore some slight resemblance to the representations, but such chests were usually made by German craftsmen resident at Southwark from the last years of Elizabeth I's reign until the 1630s. The term 'Nonsuch' was in any case not applied to them until the nineteenth century. This chest is now in the collection of the Dedham Historical Society, Massachusetts.

3. *The 'Watford' chest, oak, early 16th century. w61.*
This distinctive oak chest belongs to a group originating from the Northamptonshire-Lincolnshire borders. It has a hinged lifting top and is carved across the front panel with three bands of decoration — crochets and rosettes, stylized leaves and a row of large spirally-fluted rosettes. Distinctive leaf motifs also embellish the feet brackets.

4. *Coffer, oak, incorporating 16th-century panels. w88.*
The influences of the depiction of scenes of medieval life on church misericords and within illuminated Books of Hours found a parallel in the carved depictions on various oak coffers. The Company of Coffer-makers, incorporated in the fourteenth century, produced chests to contain an owner's clothes and goods when travelling. This example is not typical of their work, but is attractive by the nature of the exuberant carving in arcaded panels.

The early sixteenth century was a time of change and gradual improvement to both houses and furnishings. There was much to achieve, because the traditional styles were more relevant to status than to comfort. Prudence necessitated the possession of a 'joined' chest for the storage of plate, and convenience required the possession of a food cupboard or 'aumbry'. All forms of cupboard developed, in which food, drink, candles and the contents of emptied pockets were stored with ease. The open shelves were gradually filled in by canted cupboards at the top and a full-width cupboard between the base uprights.

5.   Low cupboard, oak, mid-17th century. W44.
This low cupboard would have been made for the storage of plate and other possessions and was a useful piece of furniture. Two panelled cupboard doors were fitted below a carved arcaded frieze. The top was hinged and the lower stage of fluting conceals a long drawer.

6.   Court cupboard, oak, c1620. W47.
Putting together heavily carved elements, such as the two standing female figures and two dragons at the base, might have been sufficient to confer distinction on this oak court cupboard. It is, however, also richly carved, with representations of vines, birds, strapwork and flowerheads; there is even a drawer in the central section.

7.   Court cupboard, oak, 1610. W48.
The open form of court cupboard was developed by including a panelled cupboard in the upper or lower stages, or in both. This example is inlaid at the sides with vases of flowers, and a central convex drawer is flatly carved with strapwork. It is branded 'G.A' on the right-hand corner.
Prov: Sir Thomas Pilkington.

1. Court cupboard, oak, c1675. w39.
It is not possible to determine a precise definition for a buffet, but it was an early form of sideboard, often referred to in England as a 'court cupboard'. This one has parallel doors covering a cupboard. Dentil moulding is employed as unusual decoration overall, and the piece stands on fluted, turned baluster legs, joined by an open platform.

2. Food cupboard, oak, c1650. w36.
This simple, functional piece was made during the Commonwealth (1649-60), with three layers of cupboards, the upper one enclosed by a ventilated spindle door. Low relief carving of lozenges provides slight variation to the severe lines.
Prov: Avebury Manor, Wiltshire.

3. Food cupboard, oak, c1640. w31.
Various forms of Renaissance style decoration — the scrolled cartouches, strapwork carving and applied masks on the frieze — give this cupboard distinction. Ventilation to stored food is provided by spacing spindles in the doors.

Perhaps more than in any other wooden object, the large panels of a cupboard were able to show the skill of the carver and inlayer. Inspired by a wide variety of often misunderstood engravings, the craftsman isolated motifs to use, particularly those of architectual form—the arch, cornice, column, bracket and baluster. The use of oak and walnut predominated in the early seventeenth century, although there was a growing awareness of the contrasts which could be obtained by inlaying lighter woods against them. The use of bold gadrooning, and the depiction of acanthus foliage, were other decorative refinements.

4. *Press cupboard, oak, c1615. w48.*
Cupboards were used in many positions in hall, parlour or bedroom. When fitted with shelves for linen, or with pegs to hang clothes, they were known as 'press cupboards'. This one has doors inlaid in holly and fruitwood, with 'cup and cover' balusters supporting the frieze, which is carved with bold lunettes.
Prov: Mrs D. Hart.

5. *Press cupboard, oak, c1630. w66.*
In order to conceal linen or clothes, the upper and lower portions of the press are fitted with panelled doors, decorated with carved foliage borders and inlaid lozenges. The turned and carved balusters supporting the frieze, which has further decoration of acanthus leaves, is particularly attractive.
Prov: Up Cerne Manor, Dorset.

6. *Press cupboard, oak, c1640. w51.*
Considerable style is given to this press cupboard by the bold gadrooning at the top and bottom of the lower cupboard. The central upper door is attractively inlaid with birds and flowers.

1.   Chest on stand, oak, c1665. W36.
A chest of variously sized drawers, all set on a supporting stand, became a popular piece of furniture after the Restoration. This one has typical decoration of split bobbins at the sides of the four panelled drawers. The turned baluster legs are given strength by waved stretchers and heavy turned feet.

2.   Cabinet on stand, black lacquer, c1695. H67, W45.
The late seventeenth-century fashion for oriental lacquer soon produced makers willing to attempt copies. This cabinet does, however, have drawers of Japanese lacquer raised on an English stand. In 1692 in England, Edward Hurd and James Narcock petitioned the Crown that having brought the art of lacquering in the Japanese manner to a degree of perfection, they should be granted a patent.
Prov: Duke of Buccleuch and Queensberry KT.

3.   Cabinet on stand, walnut and elm, c1690. H56, W35.
This handsome cabinet on stand is well proportioned, but it is the veneers which give it distinction. It is veneered inside and out in oyster walnut, with the borders and precise interlaced lines done in holly. The doors conceal eleven drawers, and a central cupboard which encloses four more drawers. The stand with a long drawer is raised on spirally-turned legs with shaped stretchers. The brass drop handles are original.
Prov: Hampton Hall, Cheshire.

4.   Cabinet, oyster veneered laburnum on walnut stand, c1685. H69, W49, D22.
Great skill was used to select the veneers and set them into place to form oyster patterning over the doors, sixteen drawers and the mirrored, painted and ivory and ebony inlaid architectural centre of this cabinet. It is made the more useful by a slide which covers eight secret drawers. The cabinet is supported on six spirally-turned legs, joined by concave stretchers above turned feet.

Marquetry was introduced after the Restoration in conjunction with veneered furniture, usually in walnut. John Evelyn, writing in Sylva (1664), mentioned some of the coloured woods used: '... such as are naturally so: Berbery for yellow, Holly for white. Our inlayers use Fustic, Locust or Acacia, Brazile, Prince and Rose wood for yellow and reds, with severall others brought from both Indies'. To this might be added laburnum, (4), figured and burr walnut, lignum vitae, box and sycamore. There was also a growing interest in oriental lacquer and inserting Chinese or Japanese panels into pieces of furniture. Such panels were offered for sale in London shops, and soon led to attempts to produce them in England, as well as in France and Holland.

5.   *Cabinet on stand, ebony and marquetry, c1680. w45.*
The return of Charles II from exile on the Continent in 1660 encouraged decorative styles and craftsmen to come to England, and inlaid furniture with flowers and naturalistic foliage to become very popular. Set into black ebony grounds, cleverly balanced and stained in colour, the effect of the inlays is charming. They are here enhanced by the giltwood capitals of the stand, and the cutwork panels between the front legs. A central foot at the rear is missing.

6.   *Cabinet on stand, walnut and marquetry, c1690. w46.*
There are few parts of this William and Mary marquetry cabinet that have escaped the artist's attention. The floral panels centred by birds are counter-balanced by the even greater sophistication of the interior, and by the sinuous rhythm of the six spirally-turned supports, shaped stretchers and ebonized ball feet. The stand has been restored.

7.   *Cabinet, marquetry, c1690. w44.*
Inscribed as 'The property of King George I and II, George Spencer Duke of Marlborough and Rich Bartholemew Esq', this imposing marquetry cabinet is of workmanship commensurate with the importance of its owners. Panels of seaweed marquetry decorate the doors, the upper ones mirror backed, and gilt brass carrying handles are mounted on both sections.

1.   Cabinet, black japanned on giltwood stand, c1685. H61, W46.
Chinoiserie figures, exotic birds, scrolled acanthus,
engraved brass escutcheon, hinges and corners — all the
rich assemblage of late seventeenth-century ornament has been lavished on the black japanned cabinet; but it is almost
overpowered by the pierced and carved English giltwood
stand.

It is difficult to decide whether it is the black japanned panels or the splendour of the giltwood stand which is paramount in this first piece (1). The task is made easier by looking at the quality of the oyster veneered laburnum and the door panels of stumpwork which seem to dominate the less flamboyant turned stand of the second example (2).

2.   *Cabinet on stand, oyster veneered laburnum, c1690.* H56, W37, D18. The door panels of silk stumpwork (needlework in which much of the ornament is raised in relief) embroidered in silver and silk thread are an exotic accompaniment to a cabinet which already assails the eye. The brilliant display of oyster veneered laburnum over all the doors and drawers, and even in simulated form on the stand, guarantees yet more attention to this impressive cabinet. It stands on later bun feet.

1.   Chest, walnut, oyster veneered, c1700.
Careful choice of veneers and the use of geometric fruitwood
stringing on the top has lifted a simple chest to one of considerable
distinction. The bun feet are of a later date.

2.   Chest, laburnum, c1690. W42.
The striking veneer of this chest is made with characteristic brown
and yellow slice-cut laburnum to form radiating lobe and zig-zag
patterns. The contrasting radiating patterns are visually distracting to
some, but the display of talent is evident.
Prov: Hoveton House, Norfolk.

3.   Bureau, walnut, c1695. H37, W41, D25.
The bureau was not found in England until after the end of Charles
II's reign, and the word has never been clearly defined. Some form of
enclosing lid to the writing area seemed a prerequisite. This is inlaid
with shaped panels of arabesque seaweed marquetry. When open it
rests on sliding rails (lopers) at either side, and reveals a fitted interior
of drawers and pigeon-holes.

4.   Bookcase, oak, c1675. H98, W59, D19.
Bookcases of this form were made by Thomas Sympson for Samuel
Pepys for use during his tenure as Secretary to the Admiralty. This
oak bookcase was made for Charles Sergison (1654-1732), who
succeeded Pepys. It seems probable that he had seen and admired
Pepys's cases and decided to have one of the same pattern made.
There are others of the same pattern at Dyrham Park, and some
nineteenth-century copies.

The considerable attempts to make furniture which was useful and comfortable gained ground in the seventeenth century, and particularly after the King returned from exile on the continent in 1660. Various forms of cupboard and chest were refined to become writing bureaus or bookcases, serving a growing interest in literature. But even after the Restoration the chair still retained its function as the seat of honour. However, ornate forms of decoration found their way on to splats, arms and stretchers, cane seats were in vogue and upholstery gained in popularity. Some of the more elaborate examples (8) recall the designs of Daniel Marot, who spent some years in England in the service of King William III.

5. Armchair, walnut and beechwood, c1695.
Comfort is assured through the padded arm rests and seat of this late seventeenth-century armchair. It is, however, the back, arms and stretcher which command attention. The back is embellished with carving, and bears a foliate cresting with the initials 'M and L' and a heart-shaped trellised cartouche on the central splat.

6. Chair, walnut, c1680.
Seventeenth-century London furniture-makers made many chairs of unusual design. This has the top rail of the tall ladder-back carved with a crown flanked by *putti* and uprights topped by crown finials. The heavily-carved front stretcher echoes the back motifs and is decorated with a female mask. The chair is stamped 'R.W.'.

7. Armchair, walnut, 1687-88.
This very important chair has its associations stated firmly. The back, surmounted by cresting, is carved with the Royal Arms and Motto, flanked by the Lion and Unicorn. The splat and front stretcher are embellished with cupids supporting coronets amongst scrolling acanthus foliage. The seat frame is inscribed 'Febuary ye 20 Anno Do. 1687-8' and 'George Lewis' (Elector of Hanover, crowned George I in 1714.)
Prov: Sir Robert Hylton.

8. Chair, walnut, c1695.
This dining chair, in the manner of Daniel Marot (1663-1752), the French-born designer who entered the service of William, Prince of Orange, is part of a harlequin set of ten. The back, silhouetted almost like Marot's engravings, has a splendid arched and plumed top rail, and pierced back splat carved with foliage and baskets of flowers.
Prov: Halswell Park, Somerset.

1.　*State bed, pine with velvet damask hangings, 1692-1707. H162.*
Of beds based upon designs by Daniel Marot and other significant French designers of the late seventeenth century, only a few survive. They are grand statements of the art of the upholsterer and fringe-maker, and this bed from Melville House, Fife, is probably one of the finest of the type — high, imposing and richly decorated. It was made for George Melville, 1st Earl of Melville, a little after his elevation to the title in 1690. It bears his monogram 'C M G' on an escutcheon above the headboard. The openwork cornice is decorated with six coronets, covered with crimson velvet. The interior is lined with oyster-coloured damask of Chinese origin. The corner hangings or *cantonnières* are projected on curved iron supports. The bed is in the Victoria and Albert Museum (No: W.35-1949).

In 1685, Louis XIV revoked the Edict of Nantes, by which in 1598 Henri IV had granted religious toleration to Protestants. Many Huguenot (French Protestant) craftsmen fled to other countries, particularly Holland and England, taking with them advanced ideas and a complex array of patterns. One of these, of seminal importance to decoration and furnishing, was Daniel Marot (1663–1752). His designs, particularly for beds and chairs, were of a highly decorative Baroque character, and provided severe tests even for specialist craftsmen, many of whom were also adept at marquetry, inlaying and silver-mounting of furniture.

2. *Cabinet on stand, walnut and marquetry, c1685. w64.*
The oyster veneers, marquetry and ivory inlays have been put together by specialist craftsmen to form the exquisite decoration of this cabinet. Unlike some florid examples, a careful balance has been struck between the stained and engraved woods and the walnut ground of the cabinet. A further contrast is provided by the elm stand, with its spiral-turned legs joined by an inlaid under-tier.
Prov: Littlecote, Wiltshire; Leverton Hall, Berkshire.

In the early seventeenth century, the cargoes of the various East India companies often included lacquer artefacts, particularly screens (which could be packed flat), boxes and cabinets. While the majority of the surviving cabinets are lacquered black, others have coloured grounds of red, blue, olive-green, chestnut and (rarely) ivory.

Mounted on richly carved and gilt stands, they were surrounded by the infinite variety of upholstered chairs (some with lacquered frames), stools and small tables which still delight the eyes of all visitors to British country houses.

1. *Chairs, black japanned and leather upholstered, c1690.*
The type of chinoiseries popularized by John Stalker and George Parker in their *A Treatise of Japaning*, 1688 (Plate II), is seen to great advantage in these two chairs, from a set of four. The backs and seats are covered in contemporary leather, decorated with birds and flowers close in spirit to Stalker and Parker's engravings.

2. *Stool, painted and gilded, c1680. w16.*
The circular upholstered padded seat of the stool rests on four scrolled legs, joined by ring-stretchers ornately carved with seated *putti*. It is almost impractical to use — the carved relief on the legs and stretchers is an example of style outstripping function.
Prov: Warwick Castle.

3. *Stool, walnut, c1690. w17.*
Upholstered with a fragment of early seventeenth-century tapestry, the boldly arched stretchers give this stool a distinctive air of being able to do its job — to support any weight by strength of construction.

4. *Armchair, oak, c1690.*
By the clever use of a metal ratchet, this armchair has a reclining back. With its sumptuous upholstery and padded fringed arms, it was made to be strong enough to withstand being at a raked angle by turned legs joined by 'C'-shaped stretchers.
Prov: Up Cerne Manor, Dorset.

6.   *Cabinet, scarlet lacquered, c1695, on later giltwood stand. W47.*
Of the various colours of lacquered furniture, scarlet is one of the
most rich and attractive. The two cupboard doors are further
enriched by being mounted with pierced and engraved brass
lockplate, hinges and corners, and are decorated with chinioserie
figures and foliage and panels showing landscapes and figures. The
interior is similarly decorated.

5.   *Cabinet, cream lacquer on giltwood stand, c1700. Cabinet w26, Stand
w30.*
This cabinet demonstrates a richly decorated array, almost in
miniature, in its less than thirty-inch width and height of under five
feet. And yet the cabinet has been lacquered inside and out with
sprays of chrysanthemums and peonies in blue and white vases and
with borders of red and blue lotus flowers and foliage. The Régence-
style stand is ornately carved in relief with trellis and foliage scrolls
and rests on polygonal tapering legs.
Prov: Mrs D. Hart.

7.   *Cabinet, lacquer, c1695, on later 18th-century stand. H70, w44.*
The flamboyant exterior of the cabinet is dominated by a circular
design of Chinese landscapes in red and green on a cream ground
with green borders. The interior shows Chinese figures and flowers
on a red ground and the doors are mounted with fine engraved brass
escutcheon and hinges.
Prov: Major A. Breitmeyer.

1.   *Cabinet, painted and gilt, on giltwood stand, c1690. H33, W39, D19.*
This lavish cabinet is painted with vases and sprays of flowers and is also mounted with intricate engraved brass hinges and lockplates. French influence is seen in the stand, centring on the female mask, tapering square legs, and the acanthus-carved cross stretchers, which have a displayed phoenix at the centre.
Prov: The Duke of Buccleuch and Queensberry, KT.

It is fashionable, but casual, to regard most carved wood of superior quality as having some connection with Grinling Gibbons (1648–1721). Born at Rotterdam of English parents, he came to England in the early 1660s. He was 'discovered' by John Evelyn, who introduced him to Charles II, who appointed him Master Carver in wood to the crown. Certainly virtuoso carving in soft lime-wood was done by

Gibbons for many English patrons. We can, however, only attribute the picture frame (2) to him, and the carver of the stand (1) to the cabinet is unknown. However, the skilled maker, James Moore (c1676–1726), did work for the 1st Duke of Buccleuch, and some of the carved elements resemble his style.

2.   *Picture frame, limewood, c1680-85. H68, W49.*
This frame is crisply carved in the manner of Grinling Gibbons, who was carver to the Crown until his death in 1721. With its twin *putti*, exotic birds, pine cones, fruit, flowers and vegetables, it made a grand picture surround. It is now mounted as a mirror.
Prov: Sir John Ramsden, Bulstrode, Buckinghamshire.

It is a human characteristic—some might say failing—to look at yourself in a mirror. Necessary for toilet, frequent perusal in a mirror is narcissistic. In addition, the intricacies of the English language mean it is possible to 'look' for items lost in the multitude of drawers (some secret) and divisions of the handsome japanned cabinet (4). Its cornice developed from the hooded version first adopted about 1700, and when in black or red lacquer in the style of John Belchier (whose bill-heads announced that he made 'all sorts of cabbinet work, chairs, glasses and coach glasses . . . at reasonable rates') must have been difficult for any moneyed patron to resist.

2.   *Mirror, walnut and marquetry, c1680. H54, W30.*
The bevelled glass of the looking glass is set in a cushion frame inlaid with panels of seaweed marquetry. The delicate pierced cresting is made up of seaweed marquetry medallions surrounded by carved acanthus leaves.
Prov: Sir James Horlick.

1.   *Dressing table and dressing mirror, japanned, c1700. Table W32, D21; Mirror W18.*
The combination of small stand and toilet mirror was a particularly successful one. Here the mirror is decorated *en suite* with the dressing table with raised gilt chinoiserie figures and landscapes on a sage-green ground. The fitted compartments of the small bureau contain a brush, pincushion and two boxes.
Prov: Sir Thomas Carew.

3.   *Mirror, stained pine, c1680. H88, W65.*
The frame surrounding the bevelled glass of this mirror is pierced and lavishly carved in the style of Grinling Gibbons (d. 1721), with flowers and foliage surrounding *putti*.
Prov: The Duke of Buccleuch and Queensberry, KT.

4. Bureau cabinet, black lacquer, c1710. w39.
John Belchier (d. 1753) was a cabinet-maker in St Paul's Churchyard who specialized in lacquer work and in supplying pier glasses. However, this cabinet, in his style, cannot be firmly credited to him: it points up the hazards of stylistic attribution when there is no documentation. It is handsomely decorated and well fitted internally, combining a bureau and a place for ledgers and valuables in the upper stage.
Prov: Fonthill House, Wiltshire; Lord Margadale of Islay.

Bureau cabinet, burr walnut, c1710. w40, d23.
High-quality craftsmanship has resulted in this useful and finely-finished cabinet. Architectural motifs, fluted Corinthian pilasters, finials and sculptured figures have been successfully incorporated.

Close attention to detail is seen in the niches behind the gilt figures, which are worked in a parquetry star pattern reflecting that at the base.
Prov: Eleanor Medill Patterson.

CHAPTER 2

Queen Anne and Early Georgian 1700–1727

Early on the morning of Sunday, 8 March 1702, King William III died at Kensington Palace, and Princess Anne of Denmark was elected Queen. She inherited a country imbued with a sense of power and wealth derived from its leading position in European politics. Within the decorative arts, which owed no allegiance to the tidy pattern of succession, rule and death, a whole style combining 'beauty, comfort and practicality' was to be named after Queen Anne. The name was to live on to grace the Queen Anne revival of the late nineteenth century.

One of the prime manifestations of the new style was the introduction, *c.* 1700, of chair and table legs of cabriole form. Whilst *cabriole* is a French dancing term (derived from the Italian *capriola*—goat's leap), meaning to bound or leap, when applied to furniture it refers to the curved form of support adapted from a quadruped's leg. At first it was united to the chair seat rail at the knee by cappings, with the frame still strengthened by stretchers. As the knee became wider and stronger the stretchers were dispensed with, and the knee was embellished with carved ornament. This took the form of honeysuckle or scallop shells, and after about 1725 acanthus decoration and female, lion and Indian masks.

The demand for European walnut to supplement the native wood grown in the southern English counties remained constant. Often referred to in accounts as 'French walnut tree' or 'Grenoble wood', it was much prized by furniture-makers. The Great Frost of 1709, in which France faced famine, destroyed most of the walnut trees in central Europe. The timber became scarce in France and its export was prohibited in 1720. This problem was counterbalanced by imports into England of the darker Virginia walnut, but very soon

(by the late 1720s), ready supplies of mahogany were tempting furniture-makers to abandon walnut.

The first few years of the eighteenth century still saw, however, many fine pieces of walnut veneered furniture. Gerrit Jensen had popularized brass inlay in furniture supplied to William and Mary, but it was the elaborate forms of marquetry and burr figurings which characterized the many bureaux, bureau tables and cabinets fitted for writing or storage. Apart from many superb cabinets of red and gold japanning, surmounted by gilt pinewood crestings and on six-legged stands, a typical Queen Anne cabinet would have two doors enclosing an upper section (containing many drawers and pigeon-holes), which stood on a chest of drawers with two small upper and two longer drawers, supported by short cabriole legs. This was a variation of the earlier *scriptor*, in which the upper section was fronted by a large panel which, when lowered to the horizontal, provided a writing surface. It was also a built-up form of the chest of drawers itself, which stood on simple bracket feet or was elevated on a stand of turned legs and shaped stretchers.

Furniture-making for the Crown and other principal patrons during the reigns of Queen Anne and subsequently George I was in many competent hands—there were several hundred makers in London alone. A number have achieved greater significance because they labelled their work: for example, Coxed and Woster, from about 1700–20, made bureau cabinets veneered with burr elm, cross-banded with kingwood and inlaid with stringing lines of pewter. Their tradecard, noting them at 'the White Swan, against the south gate in St Paul's Churchyard, London', indicated that they made and sold 'Cabinets, Scrutores, Desks and Bookcases, Buro's, Chests of Drawers, Whisk, Ombre

Dutch and India Tea-Tables, all sorts of Looking-Glasses, Large Sconces, Dressing Sets and Wainscot-Work of all sorts at Reasonable Rates. Old Glasses New Polished and Made Up Fashionable'. Another important maker, who often labelled his work, was Giles Grendey (1693–1780), who exported furniture on a considerable scale, particularly in japan of a brilliant red sealing-wax colour finished with details in gold and silver, and resting on paw feet. His label noted him as able to make and sell 'all sorts of cabinet goods, chairs and glasses'. Service to the Crown was by those to whom a warrant had been given, and satisfactory service ensured that this often passed at death to a partner or successful master. John Gumley, who provided the great looking glasses for Hampton Court and to the 1st Duke of Devonshire at Chatsworth (1703) in the reign of Queen Anne, was in partnership with James Moore (c. 1672–1726), who specialized first in japanned and walnut furniture and then in gilt gesso furniture, on some of which he fortunately incised his name, amid the elaborate patterns and ciphers.

Gesso-gilding originated in Italy in the Middle Ages and was probably introduced into England from France. A thick whiting paste was applied in layers—allowing each to dry—over roughed out relief, and whilst wet formed into an agreeable pattern with brushes. It was tooled, punched with stamps and, to achieve a granulated effect, even sprinkled with sand. Then the item was passed to the gilder who decorated it with (at this time) oil-gilding. A mordant was applied, which whilst still tacky allowed the thin beaten gold leaf to be applied, smoothed free of creases, and polished with cotton wool or chamois leather. Much of what Coxed and Woster, Gumley, Moore, Grendey and others made was, however, somewhat old fashioned for the new Palladian houses which Colen Campbell and others were erecting from about 1715. As late as 1720 William Old and John Ody, 'Cabinet and Chair Makers at *The Castle* in St Paul's Churchyard' advertised on their trade-card that they made and sold 'all sorts of Cane and Dutch chairs, Chair frames for stuffing and Cane Sashes. And also all sorts of the best Looking-Glasses and Cabinet work in Japan, Walnut tree and Wainscot at reasonable Rates'.

One of the most significant changes in the appearance of chairs was the replacement of caned backs, and those with pierced frets, by splats of vase or fiddle shape. Many of the pieces of walnut furniture of the 1715–20 period, particularly chairs and settees, were also varied in appearance by covering the backs and seats with needlework of floral design. Wool needlework upon canvas had long been used as a durable material for seat covering, as the imported Italian velvets were extremely expensive and beyond the purses of country gentlemen living on small estates and smaller incomes. The source of many of the designs in the needlework panels was John Ogilby's *Virgil* (1658), which had large plates, easy to copy. Scenes from the great epic were often attempted, but several chairs are known with designs following the subjects of Aesop's *Fables*, and landscapes by Jan Brueghel and others. Turkey work was also employed for covering seats and backs of chairs, and, to a lesser extent, for rugs and carpets, into at least the 1730s.

After the Restoration oval and round tables, generally of the gate-leg type supporting two flaps, had been made in oak, walnut, or, more rarely, yew. Their popularity continued into the early eighteenth century, but when mahogany became more generally available in the 1720s cabriole legs were provided to swing out on either side to support the flaps. Even so, examples of the oak joined tables of the medieval hall are still found with dates as late as 1720.

Dressing tables completely enveloped in fringed fabrics were a feature of bedrooms in the late seventeenth century, and walnut or japanned swing toilet glasses on box stands were set on top of them. In due course, the glasses were placed on small tables with pillar or cabriole legs and two or three drawers to contain brushes, combs and other toilet necessities. This type of dressing table, and the later variation with a kneehole and drawers at the sides, remained popular in the first half of the eighteenth century, and was also used as a writing table.

The 1710 inventory of Dyrham Park, Gloucestershire, shows that William Blathwayt kept in his 'Gilt Leather Parlor' ten elbow chairs, five Dutch chairs, a couch, a gilt leather screen, two looking glasses with tables beneath them, one flanked by torchères, and three pictures. A pair of glass sconces gave scanty lighting, and the panelling was grained 'walnut'. Closets did not become a usual feature of English interiors until late in the seventeenth century: generally used for reading and writing, and also attached to bedrooms, they were part of a politer way of living. The closet at Dyrham had a japan writing table with a leather cover, two stools and three pictures. The floor was laid in walnut parquetry, and furniture was still sparse. Pride of place was given, as in any great house, to the State Bed. Dyrham's was made about 1704, and covered with crimson and yellow velvet with an interior of sprigged satin; it was fitted with case curtains of 'red cheney' to keep the dust and light off the valuable velvets.

Whilst the reign of Queen Anne still saw the creation of major pieces of walnut furniture, that of George I (1714–27) witnessed the increasing use of mahogany. Customs House ledgers first mention the import of mahogany to England in 1699–1700, but it had probably come in from the 1670s. Dr William Gibbons (1649–1728), a London physician, is said to have received one of the early consignments and to have made it popular when he commissioned the Long Acre furniture-maker Mr Wollaston to make him a candle box, and subsequently a bureau. Whatever the truth of this, we do know that mahogany from British plantations such as Jamaica was already well known. In 1672 Richard Blome wrote in his *Description of Jamaica*: 'Here are great variety of woods for Dyers as Fustick, Red wood, a kind of Logg-wood, etc., also Cedar, Mothogeney . . .' At first mahogany was imported as a veneer, and only

Toilet mirror, scarlet and gold lacquer, c1710. H68, W19, D12.
This colourful mirror is decorated in raised gilt lacquer and different shades of red lacquer, with summer pavilions, birds and flowers, framed by silver lines. The little bureau base is neatly fitted with a tiered interior of pigeon-holes and drawers, containing three boxes and two brushes.

1728 for the staircase and panelling at the Prime Minister's Norfolk house, Houghton Hall.

Mahogany was soon put to use to make furniture of dignified proportion and massive construction. The great libraries of the Palladian houses, Houghton among them, needed large mahogany tables, and in the 1720s versions were freely adapted from a style established in France at the end of the seventeenth century. As many as eight pillar legs were carved in low relief and united by flat, shaped stretchers. Most of these early examples were of open pedestal form and were well suited to architectural treatment. They occupied a position in the centre of the room, and had carved ornament applied which was calculated to accord with the general decorative scheme.

The bookcases made in Queen Anne's reign with figured walnut veneered over oak were characterized by excellent proportions. Within fifteen years, however, there were ready alternatives in painted pine with gilt enrichments and in mahogany with applied carving. Although walnut became less fashionable as it became less readily available from the Continent, it still had devotees for many further years. In country districts, oak and other indigenous varieties of wood remained popular. This was particularly true for all wooden chairs of the Windsor variety, which were used as indoor seats in taverns and as garden seats. However, the 1st Duke of Chandos had seven japanned Windsors in his library in 1725, and in 1729 Henry Williams supplied three in mahogany (two of them 'richly carved') to St. James's Palace.

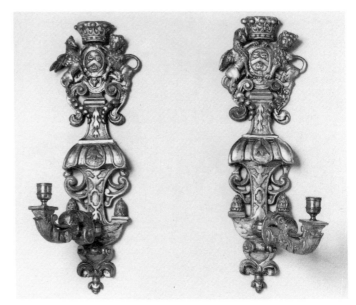

Sconces, giltwood, c1712. H22.
This pair of sconces was probably made for Thomas Wentworth, who was created Earl of Strafford in 1711. They are carved with the Strafford arms and supporters, below an earl's coronet, and are each fitted with one hinged candle-branch so that light may be directed as desired.
Prov: Wentworth Castle, Yorkshire; Godmersham Park, Kent.

became available in significant quantity in log and plank during the late 1720s. It might be said that during the period 1725–30 mahogany began to take precedence over walnut: the wood's first mention in royal accounts was in 1724. Furniture-makers liked the wood for the width of planks they could obtain, and for its good grain. It was adaptable for use for all parts of furniture, as it was stable and resistant to warping and attack from worm. It also carved supremely, and polished well. In order that it could be used without restriction, Sir Robert Walpole exempted Jamaican mahogany from duty, making it much cheaper than that from Cuba and Santa Domingo, which had duty imposed. In fact, Sir Robert was himself an early user of mahogany, for the joiner and carver James Richards (d. 1759) used it in

Armchair, walnut, c1725. H47, W34.
This fine, attractively-shaped chair combines both high-quality craftsmanship and comfort. The upholstery is of splendidly coloured silk and wool, worked in *petit point*; the cabriole front legs are carved with bearded masks with scallop shell headdresses and hairy paw feet.
Prov: Godmersham Park, Kent.

Chair, walnut, c1725.
This highly-mannered chair, sold with one other, is part of a set of chairs and settees, possibly made by Thomas How for the 4th Earl of Scarsdale, who started building Sutton Scarsdale, Derbyshire, in 1724. The unusual *verre églomisé* Earl's coat of arms is in a gilt-lead cartouche frame, applied to the shaped back splat; gilt-lead mounts are fitted to the hips of the cabriole legs and seat rail.
Prov: Sutton Scarsdale, Derbyshire; other pieces from the set are in the Metropolitan Museum, the Frick Collection and the Cooper-Hewitt Museum (all New York), and at Temple Newsam House, Leeds.

Chest on stand, yew, 1700. w38.
There is perhaps a certain awkwardness in the relationship between
the arcaded and heavily supported stand and the chest itself. This
example relies on the use of an unusual wood, yew; to give it
distinction. The legs are turned and joined by a shaped stretcher.

Windsor chairs were fashioned usually in a blend of beech (leg spindles) and elm (seats) with ash or yew for the bow. When used outdoors they were painted green, but yellow and red Windsors have been noted. Beech grew more plentifully in Buckinghamshire than in any other part of England, a fact noted by Daniel Defoe in his *Tour in Great Britain* (1725), which meant that High Wycombe became an important furniture-making town. Its craftsmen were typical of those who could both panel a room in deal and satisfy a continuing demand for small pieces of furniture, such as the profusion of small tables for cards and gaming.

Card playing had become very popular in the early eighteenth century, and an act of Queen Anne's reign sought to impose duty of sixpence on certain packs of cards, and five shillings on a pair of dice. The tables provided for the players were usually of multiple form, with extra flaps for games, and useful for writing and taking tea. The top, square or oval, was supported by a swing-leg hinged to the back framework. Circular corners were dished for candlesticks, with recesses for money or counters, and swing-out-drawers to store both were common. In Queen Anne examples, the walnut frame supported a top which was often covered with cross-stitch needlework, and some were in softwood which was japanned in black and gold. The 1st Duke of Chandos had in his closet at Cannons in 1725 'a red japan'd Card Table with doors and drawers, the top

lined with green velvet'. Whilst a table with doors was exceptional in construction, many were versatile enough to be triangular in form with tripod supports and folding tops, or to include rising flaps for ease of drawing or reading.

In 1711 a Dutch maker resident in London advertised (*The Postman*, 5 March) that he made 'and sells all sorts of fine painted Tea Tables with new fancies and that can endure boiling water'. This implies that they were japanned and that tea drinking was increasing in popularity. In fact the Joiners' Company at the end of the seventeenth century had petitioned against imports from the East Indies, indicating that within four years 6,582 tea tables had been imported. None seems to have survived, but walnut tea tables on slender cabriole legs with a tray top are known, and several carved and gilt ones of Baroque robustness are shown with silver equipage in the paintings of William Hogarth: for example his *Assembly at Wanstead House* (1729, Philadelphia Museum).

Vast numbers of tables for special and general purposes were produced from the Restoration onwards, serving a pleasure-loving society and veneered in all the exotic woods, or decorated with carved gesso or black and gold japan. Carved stands also supported tops inlaid with various marbles, particularly those which were made by furniture craftsmen near the circle of the talented architect and decorator, William Kent.

Side table, gilt gesso, c1715. H31, W36, D20.
It is fashionable to credit all gilt gesso side tables of the early eighteenth century to the London maker James Moore (c 1672-1726), who undoubtedly produced a great number. The gesso is carved in low relief with pairs of female masks with plumed headdresses, eagles' heads, foliage enclosed by strapwork and a scallop shell centre to the concave frieze.
Prov: Godmersham Park, Kent.

Bureau cabinet, scarlet japanned, c1705. H104.
A number of London makers, such as John Belchier and
Giles Grendey, specialized in making japanned cabinets
early in the eighteenth century. Those in scarlet are the most
flamboyant in appearance. This richly-decorated cabinet is
gilt with chinoiseries, except for the exterior of the cupboard
doors, which have bevelled mirror plates above candle
slides.

Bureau, walnut, c1715. H36, W25, D18.
This type of bureau was derived from the seventeenth-century writing cabinet, in which a flap enclosed the contents. This type developed further with the introduction of the sloping front, which allowed space to show skill in veneering. The interior, of chequer-banded drawers and pigeon-holes, centres on a small cupboard, the door of which is also veneered with marquetry.

1.   Tea table, walnut, c1710. w30.
The fashion for drinking tea, and all the consequent provision of equipage in wood, metal and ceramic forms, grew in popularity in the early eighteenth century. The semi-elliptical top can be folded out to be supported on one of the tapered club legs with paw feet.
Prov: Godmersham Park, Kent.

The small table was one of the most useful of all the productions of the furniture-maker. As habits and rooms changed in function and appearance, there was need to provide surfaces on which tea could be taken, games played, letters and drawing prepared and beneath which an infinite variety of small objects could be kept available but out of sight. Decoration was rife, and made easier when the carcase was covered with gypsum, which could be incised, raised, punched and carved into elaborate patterns. It was far easier than the time-consuming effort of selecting and glueing veneers on to tables, but these also abound, and are especially attractive when laburnum was used.

2.   Card table, walnut, c1720. w33.
Within a small compass, the lively curves of this table hide its ingenious parts. When the folding top is needed it its opened and supported by the back legs, which pull out through a concertina action of the hinged frame. All the parts are enhanced by the lobed top and the deeply-carved cabriole legs.

3.   Card table, laburnum, c1710. w33.
The naturally-striped laburnum veneer provides all that is needed to enhance the simple lines of this games table. The legs are moved through a concertina action to support the top, when open. This is baize-lined and carved with indentations on which to rest candles and to hold coins.

Writing table, walnut, c1705. H29, W36, D20.
hilst the tapered octagonal legs, joined by the saw-edged cross
etchers, give this table a 'busy' appearance, it functions well.
nen raised, the table top is held in place by a push-up rest, and
des for candles are fitted each side at the top of the arcaded frieze.

5. *Side table, gilt gesso, c1700. W44.*
Gesso, a paste of gypsum and size, made a useful medium for
carving, allowing more spontaneity and variety than could be
achieved in wood. The top of this table, with its projecting gadrooned
edge, is incised with scrolled foliage and strapwork on a marbled
ground. The frieze is flatly carved with scrolls and geometric
patterns.
Prov: Hampton Court, Leominster, Herefordshire.

Side table, gilt gesso, c1715. W29.
oulding in relief, and carving and punching the background with
ecial tools, were two techniques used to decorate gilt gesso tables.
his side table, one of a pair, has a moulded low-relief top, with
rolled foliage and flowers, and a central foliate medallion on a matt
round. The frieze and legs are treated in a similar manner.
ov: Mrs Diane Gubbay.

7. *Side table, burr walnut, c1720. W33.*
Walnut does not lend itself so well to carving as mahogany. The main
feature of this table is therefore the attractive finish produced by the
careful choice of burr walnut veneers.

1.   Bureau, walnut, c1715. W37.
The sloping front of the bureau opens to rest on sturdy sliding
supports, revealing arcaded pigeon-holes, drawers, fluted columnar
narrow drawers and a small panelled cupboard door. Below, the
piece is fitted with three long drawers and stands on bracket feet.

The arrangement of a bureau allows the writer to have his paper and envelopes arranged neatly in pigeon-holes before him, a writing surface to use and the whole kept out of sight when closed. By contrast, working at a desk requires books and papers to be taken out of drawers, used on the top surface and moved back after use. The one was a development of the other, with the desk used extensively in libraries, to both read and write thereon. At the start of the eighteenth century walnut was used for making both.

2.   Kneehole desk, walnut, c1720. H33, W39, D24.
Careful attention to detail characterizes this desk of unusual form. The lift-off upper section has a hinged sloping flap, which encloses a fitted interior with drawers. No space is left unused: a cupboard is even fitted in the kneehole, as well as numerous drawers.

3.   Kneehole library desk, walnut, c1715. H30, W48, D29.
The desk was an important feature in any library. This one is primarily functional, being fitted with drawers on both sides, but with a central cupboard and a top drawer opening only on one side. These are represented on the other side by false drawer fronts and a false cupboard door.

Upholstered furniture satisfied the demand for comfort, relieving the hardness of an unyielding wooden seat. In simple terms, padding materials were placed beneath a cover, which was then nailed to a wooden frame, or were supported by webbing stretched across and nailed to the frame. The beginning of the eighteenth century was marked by a rise in the popularity of needleworked upholstery. This coincided with the introduction of the winged armchair (3), which offered an ideal surface for covering with finely executed scenes. The most durable material for this was wool needlework on canvas, but various velvets, plain or cut, were in use.

1. Armchair, walnut, c1715.
It should not be argued that all furniture from the past was of outstanding design. This armchair is of an uncommon character, with shaped back, concave seat rail at the front and an 'X'-form stretcher which represents 'a figure of a lady in contemporary costume'. This illusion is helped by the upholstery of needlework in coloured silks.
Prov: Percival D. Griffiths; Dowager Marchioness of Cholmondeley.

3. Armchair, walnut, c1715.
By the 1720s, chair-makers were able to produce chairs of outstanding quality and comfort. They pulled, stuffed and nailed the finely worked *petit point* needlework into position, and set it all on a sturdy frame with large acanthus leaf decoration carved on the legs. The eared padded rectangular back, scrolled arm supports and cushion seat enfolded the user.

2. Armchair, gilt gesso, c1710-15.
Important furniture was provided to the Dukes of Leeds, of Kiveton and Hornby, including this high-quality gilt gesso armchair. The shape is carefully calculated to support at back, arms and seat, and the heavy gilt gesso frame has both rigidity and attractive decoration. The padded arms end in scrolled eagle heads, and the legs are carved with acanthus on a punched ground. The waved stretchers bind the design together.
Prov: The Duke of Leeds; Col. H. H. Mulliner; Godmersham Park, Kent.

4. Armchair, walnut, c1715. H40.
This combination of unusual shape and striking arabesque decoration is extremely rare. The legs of the chair, of hipped outline, inlaid, are seldom found, even on chairs with inlaid backs. Here the upholstery, in differing floral *gros* and *petit point* needlework, almost dominates: it is worked with exotic birds, urns and strapwork. But the stretcher is also particularly mannered, centred by an up-turned lotus leaf. One longs for exact documentation to move it beyond its attribution 'unknown maker'.

5. Armchair, walnut, c1715. H41.
There are a number of chairs of this form which have been given great sophistication by the use of gilt gesso lining on legs and seat rails. Whilst this chair, one of a pair, falls a little below that quality, it was primarily designed for comfort, with its high raked back and broad seat, padded and upholstered in green velvet. It is still a chair of some distinction.

6. Armchair, gilt gesso, c1725. H (back) 41, W (seat) 27.
The chair-maker has exercised skill in the proportions of this chair, one from a set of eight. The shape of the arm and rake of the back are particularly satisfying. All four legs are elaborately carved with masks and acanthus leaves, and the back and seat are upholstered in needlework with centrally-placed medallions.

1.   Chair, black and gold lacquer, c1720-33. H (back) 46, W (seat) 19.
This chair is one from an important set made for William Heathcote, who had married Elizabeth Parker, daughter of the Earl of Macclesfield in 1720. He was himself created a baronet in 1733. The back bears a polychrome armorial cartouche, with the arms of Heathcote impaling Parker, and the chair is decorated in raised gilt with chinoiserie landscapes, all edged by a moulded parcel-gilt border.

2.   Chair, walnut and marquetry, c1720. H42.
The blending of walnut, partly gilding it and incorporating marquetry, has produced a chair of fine craftsmanship. The back is decorated in stained and engraved woods with a foliate cartouche above flower-filled urns. Carving and gilding of shells and foliage is used to decorate the front cabriole legs.

The chair-making trade in the early eighteenth century was dominated by the use of walnut (often part gilded), red or black lacquer and by the application of upholstery to the frame. The back was usually vase or fiddle-shaped, although examples with a more complex outline are known. In the finest chairs the splats are veneered with figured burr walnut and the junction between veneer and carving is hardly perceptible to the naked eye. Sometimes the splat was enlivened with the painted arms of the owner. By Queen Anne's reign stretchers were dispensed with, and soon after 1710 the claw-and-ball was adopted as the usual terminal for the cabriole legs, although the hoof form (1) was in use, and the club foot (4) continued to be employed from time to time over the next forty years, to c1750.

3.   *Armchair, mahogany, c1720.*
Many mahogany chairs of George I's reign are scarcely distinguished in design from Queen Anne models. However, the growing use of mahogany allowed a solid concave back rather than a veneered one, and for the upholstery to be confined to the seat alone. Some authorities regard these as 'writing chairs'; the cabriole legs are carved with honeysuckle.

4.   *Stool, walnut and parcel-gilt, c1720. H17, W21, D17.*
The acanthus leaves carved in low relief on the legs of this stool are brought out by the gilding, which enhances this piece of very simple form but good proportion. The eighteenth-century *petit point* seat is worked in colours with flowerheads and leaves.

1. Chair, walnut, c1715.
Canework was less popular at this period than it had been at the end of the seventeenth century. However, it had the continued advantage of being cheap and comfortably resistant, as well as having attractive decorative qualities. This chair comes from a set of four, and two of the back splats are stamped 'G.B.R.' and 'I.A.'.
Prov: Cornbury Park, Oxfordshire.

2. Chair, gilt gesso, 1725.
The unusual form of this velvet-upholstered chair leads us to hope that eventually we will learn the identity of its maker. It is from a set of six chairs and two stools, obviously influenced by Continental engravings. The elaborate frame is of strongly curved members, gilt and carved with a central mask, acanthus foliage and scroll brackets.

3. Chair, black and gold lacquer and giltwood, c1715. H44, W22.
We would willingly know much more of the origins of furniture supplied to Sir Robert Walpole at Houghton Hall, Norfolk. This striking chair, which is one of a pair, has the seat and back lacquered in black and decorated in shades of gilt, with orange highlights, and depicts groups of Chinese buildings and landscapes.
Prov: The Marquess of Cholmondeley, Houghton Hall, Norfolk.

4. Chair, giltwood, c1718.
The desire to mount the panels of exotic needlework on to a large suite (eight chairs, two settees, two pole screens) has outweighed other considerations and dictated a little to the shape of the chair. The heavy nailing and heavy giltwood legs are not to all tastes, but quality overall is evident, and the carving is done with vigorous style.
Prov: Gilbert, 4th Earl of Coventry (d. 1719).

In constructional terms, it is only necessary for a chair to have three or four legs, a seat, back and perhaps arms to be immediately functional. However, that did not, fortunately, satisfy a good chair-maker. He was anxious to embellish the basic frame with an interesting shape and good decoration and upholstery. He could introduce mannered front legs (2) or think of the demands of writing and reading (7 and 8). Whilst he may not have contributed anything which helped these processes, the results were invariably interesting. Furthermore, the ample space of many chairs allowed excellent display of needlework and other covers.

5.   *Armchair, walnut, c1715.*
A seat-covering of wool needlework upon canvas was in wide use in the late seventeenth and early eighteenth centuries. It was fixed to the frame by close-set nails, and frequently depicted scenes from John Ogilby's *Virgil* or from Aesop's *Fables*. Here the ambitiously designed contemporary needlework in *gros* and *petit point* shows the 'Toilet of Venus' in a landscape.

6.   *Chair, mahogany, c1724, attributed to Giles Grendey.*
This is one from a splendid suite of twelve chairs and a settee, probably made by Giles Grendey (1693-1780) of Clerkenwell. He had a large workshop and an active business in producing good middle-class furniture for the home market and japanned pieces for export. The fine needlework, depicting figures in a landscape, is in colours on a white ground.
Prov: Col. E. J. Wythes, Copped Hall, Essex.

7.   *Writing chair, walnut, c1720.*
This type of chair was introduced in the early eighteenth century. The seat projected but the arm rests were set back, continuous with the top rail. This ensured that the chair could be drawn close up to a desk or table for ease in writing.

8.   *Reading chair, walnut, c1720.*
The padded back top rail of this chair, with its adjustable reading flap fitted behind, spreads into two arm rests, so that the reader can sit astride, facing the back, with elbows supported. A drawer is slotted into the front seat rail for pens and inkwells, or even to support a candle on a shaped section. Such chairs were chiefly used in libraries, but are frequently misnamed as 'cock fighting' chairs.
Prov: The Earl of Feversham.

It is suggestive of slow change in the furniture trades that lacquer furniture, popular in the seventeenth century, should enjoy continued support from patrons in the early eighteenth. The piece was immediately attractive visually—the raised gold decoration on a coloured ground and the continuance of the decoration throughout the interior. There was much storage space in the various cabinets and chests on chests. The latter, however, relied on walnut veneers and the occasional mannered piece of decoration such as an inlaid demi-star in a contrasting wood for their appearance.

1. *Bureau cabinet, black and gold lacquer, c1705. H91, W41, D23.*
The black and gold lacquer cabinets, with double-domed cornices, became very popular in the early eighteenth century. The exterior of the doors of this example are glazed with mirrors. The cabinet is richly decorated both inside and out with chinoiserie figures and landscapes, and the sides with peonies and other flowers. The turned feet are of later date.

2.   *Chest on chest, walnut, 1710. W43.*
Apart from the fluted, chamfered corners, it is the skilled use of
veneer that provides the decorative effects on this chest. The well-
figured walnut on the drawers is framed with feather banding: the
lower one has the veneered concave demi-star to enhance it.

1.   *Settee, walnut, c1710. w60.*
This settee is part of an important suite, which also includes four chairs and two armchairs. The elaborate needlework shows 'The Fall of Phaeton' set amidst landscape and flowers. Unusual scroll brackets joining the legs to the seat rail lead the eye towards the marquetry crests.
Prov: Denham Place, Buckinghamshire.

It is perhaps the complex mythological stories told on needlework panels which play a part in commending early Georgian settees to the onlooker. Whilst they might not have understood all the details of 'The Fall of Phaethon', the usual classical education enjoyed by an eighteenth-century aristocrat would have given some knowledge of Greek and Roman mythology. Writing in 1747, Robert Campbell, in The London Tradesman, *confirmed what had been obvious for many years: he regarded the 'upholder' or upholsterer as being in charge, with the cabinet-maker as his right-hand man. Campbell regarded the 'stuffing and covering a chair or settee-bed . . . the nicest part of this branch' but stated, loftily, that the skill 'may be acquired without any remarkable genius'. These examples prove him to have been understating the case.*

2.   *Settee, giltwood, c1718. w72.*
This is a very handsome settee, with shaped back and outward scrolled arms. It forms part of a well-known suite of eight chairs, two settees and two pole screens. The *gros point* needlework of massive vases of flowers is firmly contained within a broad border outlining the forms.
Prov: Gilbert, 4th Earl of Coventry (d. 1719).

3. *Settee, mahogany, attributed to Giles Grendey, c1724. W79.*
The needlework on this settee, part of a suite which includes twelve chairs (see page 61) is particularly handsome. It is worked on a white ground. The suite was probably made by Giles Grendey of Clerkenwell. There are sophisticated touches: the knees of the legs are prolonged to form brackets beneath the seat rail. It is all done in rich Cuban mahogany, rendering the birds' head terminals to the arms and the lions' heads very striking and realistic.

5. *Stool, giltwood, c1720. W25, D18.*
Gilt and carved wood decoration can always be used to pleasing effect when the forms are strong. Here the cabriole legs (which finish in claw-and-ball feet) support a frame which is edged with scrolls and has a drop-in seat upholstered in brocade.
Prov: Godmersham Park, Kent.

4. *Settee, walnut, c1710. H41, W54.*
This elegant, high-backed piece of furniture is covered in contemporary *gros* and *petit point* St Cyr needlework in well-preserved coloured wools and silks. The subjects depicted are chinoiserie figures, some playing instruments. The sides and back are upholstered in plain velvet.

2.   *Bureau cabinet, walnut, by John Belchier, c1720. H80, W33.*
This well-made, functional cabinet bears the trade label of 'John Belchier at the Sun in St Pauls Church Yard'; he is recorded at that address until 1753, the year of his death. The cabinet has two shelves behind the glazed door, and a sloping bureau front which opens to form a writing surface and to reveal a fitted interior with a well and drawers.

1.   *Bureau cabinet, walnut, c1725. H84, W25, D20.*
This small, slim cabinet, with its graceful swan neck pediment and carved parcel-gilt border surrounding the mirror plate, is fitted inside the upper section with three shelves above pigeon-holes, drawers and a candle slide. The bureau below contains more pigeon-holes and drawers, some with removable toilet boxes.
Prov: Percival Griffiths; General and Mrs Micklam.

The placing of a looking glass plate in a bureau cabinet, or surrounding it with a carved and gilded frame, was a specialist task. The trade-cards of many early eighteenth-century London and provincial makers testify to the range of both their abilities and their stock. One of John Belchier's trade bills states that he 'Grinds & Makes-up all sorts of fine Peer & Chimney-Glasses and Glass Sconces' and his London contemporary, Henry Bell, advertised that he followed the practice of his predecessors in business, Coxed and Woster, in 'altering old looking glasses to the latest fashion'. Topped and flanked by pierced crests, winged masks and plumed acanthus, and when possessed of their original silver-blue, slightly mottled plates, they are among the most satisfying pieces of English furniture.

3.   *Looking glass, giltwood, c1710. H43, W19.*
This looking glass, one of a pair, is of handsome architectural form. The arched plate is surrounded by carved leaf-tip mouldings, which secure the sectional mirror borders; the pierced cresting is boldly carved with plumed acanthus and scrolled foliage.

4.   *Pier glass, gilt gesso, attributed to John Belchier, c1725. H88, W34.*
The glass, one of a pair, has a handsomely carved frame. The cresting is topped by a dolphin crest, and the winged *putto* mask below is on a punched ground with incised strapwork. Apart from the crestings, these pier glasses are almost identical to two which were supplied by John Belchier to John Meller in 1723 and 1726 for the two best bedchambers at Erddig in North Wales.

There is a fine dividing line between the chest and the bureau—both offer storage in their many drawers. However, the bureau top lowered to be supported on wooden slides and to provide a writing surface, with paper, ink and pens neatly kept in the facing pigeon-holes. London firms, such as that of William Old and John Ody, specialized in such case furniture, and they frequently affixed their paper trade-label (5) to pieces they had made. It announced that they made and sold 'all sorts of Cane & Dutch Chairs, Chair Frames for Stuffing and Cane-sashes. And also all sorts of the best Looking-Glass & Cabinet-work in Japan Walnut Tree & wainscot'.

1.   Bureau, walnut, c1710. H35, w23.
The figure of the veneered burr walnut already gives a decorative effect to this bureau, but each panel and drawer front is also surrounded with herringbone bands. A cupboard is fitted within the narrow kneehole arch of this small piece, which is only twenty-three inches wide overall.

2.   Bureau, walnut, c1710. H36, w24, d18.
The top of this bureau, with its projecting lower edge which visually separates it from the chest, is particularly reminiscent of the sixteenth-century table desk, from which pieces like this are derived. It has a fitted interior and drawers; the feet have been restored.

3.   Bureau, walnut, c1725. H32.
The sloping lid of this bureau, which encloses the usual fitted interior of pigeon-holes and drawers, is decorated with chequered lines. This attention to detail is continued in the form of the ogee bracket feet.
Prov: C. H. St. J Hornby Esq.

5.   The trade label on the bachelor's chest: 'William Old and John Ody at the Castle in St Pauls Churchyard . . .' (London).

4.   *Bachelor's chest, walnut, by William Old and John Ody, c1725. w31.*
The description of this chest, with its folding top that converts into a table, may be contemporaneous. It is lavishly cross-banded, and care has been taken to choose veneers of almost burr type. The original brass handles and lockplates have punched decoration. The makers may have entered into partnership in 1723, when John Ody became free of the Joiners' Company.

7.   *Chest on stand, walnut, 1705. w41.*
The stand, with its arcaded frieze and cup and baluster turned legs, forms the main decorative feature of this useful chest. There is ample storage space in eight drawers set between the dominant top and centre mouldings, or in the frieze.
Prov: North Mymms Park, Hertfordshire.

6.   *Chest, walnut, c1720. w31.*
This dressing chest has good storage space, but also has a brushing slide fitted above the drawers. This may be pulled out to form a shelf on which clothes may be brushed. It is veneered in walnut, the quartered top and well-figured drawers decorated with cross-banding.

1. *Secretaire cabinet, mulberry, by Coxed and Woster, c1715.*
The materials and design of this cabinet, with inlaid pewter stringing, are typical of the work of Coxed and Woster, whose label appears on one of the drawers. The firm is known to have flourished in St Paul's Churchyard, London, between 1700 and 1736. The lower section of the cabinet is fitted with a top secretaire drawer containing small shelves, drawers and pigeon-holes.

The London makers Coxed and Woster probably made the fine secretaire cabinet with its multiplicity of drawers, shelves and pigeon-holes both in the lower section or hidden behind the two upper doors (1). Within and without there is excellent attention to detail in working the golden-brown mulberry wood: hard, heavy, streaked dark, it was used as a veneer in the Queen Anne period, and never fails to please the eye. Almost as highly coloured was the variety of rosewood known as padouk, reserved for exceptional pieces and given added interest here (2) by being banded with the yellow-tinted laburnum.

2.   *Cabinet on stand, padouk and other woods, c1715. W38.*
The two doors of the cabinet are ingeniously decorated with basketwork parquetry, banded with laburnum. They enclose a mahogany and laburnum interior of drawers and cupboards. The carved stand is made of richly-coloured padouk (a variety of rosewood), ranging from dark crimson to brown and red. The back of the cabinet is inscribed 'E. Countess of Warwick 1773'.

3.   *Bureau cabinet, walnut, c1735. H80, W25, D19.*
This thin, attenuated cabinet is perhaps not well served by the unusual concave form of the drawers in the lower stage. But it is lavishly fitted: the mirror-plated cabinet door is framed by fluted Corinthian pilasters and conceals shelves, a central cupboard, drawers and holes above candle slides. Similar fittings are enclosed by the sloping flap on the lower bureau.
Prov: Mrs E Guy Ridpath.

It is fitting that the last two illustrations of this chapter show pieces of furniture which well represent the high achievements of the Queen Anne and Early Georgian years, 1700–27. The walnut used in the bureau cabinet was soon to be eclipsed by the growing use of mahogany, and had in any case become scarce after depletion of trees in the Great Frost of 1709. And a State Bed in the Marot style, a *tour de force* of the arts of the upholsterer and fringe-maker, over twelve feet high; opulent, slightly old-fashioned, but one of the glories of the Huguenot tradition in English furniture-making.

1. Bureau cabinet, walnut, c1720. H100, W47, D25.
The architectural forms dominate this handsome cabinet. The two doors contain mirror-panels headed by spiralling star medallions. Straight lines complement concave shapes, and chequered patterns combine with walnut veneers; in addition, a profusion of drawers and cupboards of all sizes form a piece of furniture with good overall design.
Prov: J. Michael Wood Esq.

2.   State bed, c1710. H152, W76, D100.
This splendid bed comes from Leeds Castle, Maidstone, Kent. It is not mentioned in an inventory carried out there for Thomas, Lord Fairfax, dated 9 November 1710, but appears in the next inventory, dated 9 June 1719. The bed was originally upholstered in yellow damask, and the interior is shaped as a lobed dome. This type of bed was popularized by the designs of Daniel Marot for *lits de la duchesse*, but for its date this example is somewhat old-fashioned.

Chair, scarlet lacquer, by Giles Grendey, c1735-40.
Giles Grendey (1693-1780) established himself as 'Cabinet-Maker and Chair-Maker' in St John's Square, Clerkenwell, London, specializing in furniture for export. He supplied an exceptional suite of furniture, of which this chair, one of eight, is a part, to the Duke Infantado for his castle at Lazcano, Northern Spain. The frames are enriched with slightly differing chinoiserie designs in gold and silver with black details. The back splats each show an oriental figure holding a festooned umbrella against feathery landscape.

CHAPTER 3

Mahogany and Gilded Pine 1727–1754

t had taken about 150 years for a safe classical form of decoration to become established in England. It was first introduced by Inigo Jones (1573–1652), the English architect, who had visited Italy in the early seventeenth century to study the Italian villas of Andrea Palladio. By about 1715, England had also seen a literary revival of Palladianism with publications by Colen Campbell and others. Then in 1719 the 3rd Earl of Burlington, who had visited Italy twice to look at Palladian villas and buy any drawings by Palladio he could trace, returned from his travels. He brought with him William Kent (1685–1748), who had completed nine years study in Italy. Burlington's patronage of Kent established Palladianism as a firm style, which resisted for a considerable time inroads made by the new French rococo style. Kent was an exact contemporary of the French engraver Nicolas Pineau (1684–1754), but the wide divergence between the French and English styles—asymmetry versus rigour in proportion—allowed little decoration on furniture in England until fashion forced the change in the mid-1730s.

Furniture-making in the early years of George II's reign—he succeeded to the English throne in 1727—was therefore characterized by the use of mahogany as the staple wood and by the importance of William Kent as the principal designer. From the early 1750s, during the last decade of the King's reign, it was in turn dominated by the ascendancy of Thomas Chippendale the elder (1718–79) as the leading maker.

At the risk of being simplistic, it must be stressed that Kent (or for that matter Robert Adam) did not actually make furniture: he provided designs. Morover, the furniture-makers Kent used provided furniture directly to patrons, many of whom were employing Kent, in a style we regard as Kentian but without following a specific design by him.

The principal sources for Kent's furniture are to be found in Italy—in the work of certain Baroque artists such as Foggini, Parodi, Giardini and (to a lesser extent) Brustolon—and, seminally, in the work of the Frenchman André Charles Boulle (1642–1732), as later interpreted in the published designs of Daniel Marot. In particular, many of the face masks found in Boulle furniture seem to reappear, albeit in gilded wood rather than ormolu, on Kentian furniture. When Kent was ready to return to England in 1719 he had sent ahead two boxes of 'wax boys and heads, legs and arms'. Although these found little tangible expression in his furniture designs, the memory of the scrolls, conch shells, sea horses, dolphins, eagles, palm branches and merfolk of the Baroque tables and chairs he had seen in churches, *palazzi*, and sculptors' workshops in Genoa, Florence, and elsewhere certainly did.

Furniture-making for the Crown during Kent's first few years in England was in the hands of the Gumley family, and of their partner James Moore the elder. When he died in 1726, the warrant passed to his apprentice, Benjamin Goodison, who led a talented group. Principal among the members of the group were James Richards (who carved the enrichments of the Royal Barge Kent designed for the Prince of Wales, 1731–32), Moore's son, also James (d. 1731) and John Boson (d. 1743). Matthias Lock and the frame-maker Paul Petit were also ready to follow the stylistic lead set by the leading craftsmen, and commissions came to them from George II, his estranged son, the Prince of Wales, and their leading courtiers. Kent's appointment in 1725 as Master Carpenter to the Crown brought him

Pier glass, walnut and parcel-gilt, 1730. H57, W29.
One of the best combinations of texture and colour is that of walnut enhanced by gilding. Here it is done well, and the pier glass is further enriched by an elaborately carved architectural cresting with scrolled broken pediment and central cabochon cartouche.

into constant touch with both patrons and craftsmen.

Kentian furniture may be characterized as follows, albeit with many variants:

Tables These are marble-topped, with pine frames that had coupled consoles and corner blocks, the whole painted white with gilded details. The consoles are panelled and have pendants in the form of joined plant husks. The frieze contains Vitruvian scrolls, and the apron garlands within flank a centrally placed mask, *putto* head or shell. Side elevations contain, frequently, great shell forms borne on solid base-runners which unite the front and rear scrolled feet. Other tables are gesso-covered and gilded overall and have as supports either console legs with fish-scaling down the sides (sometimes derived from engravings by Nicolas Pineau and others, as in Kent's early ceiling paintings) or stylized eagles heads; or female sphinxes; or *putti* seated on scrolls or in front of shells.

Settees These are of two kinds: hall settees with solid backs and seats of mahogany with carved scroll arms; or settees upholstered in cut Genoa or Utrecht velvet or figured damask. The frames of the upholstered settees are of parcel-gilt mahogany or of gilded gesso. The hall settees usually have a tripartite panelled back with a heavy scrolled pediment enriched with fluting, Vitruvian scrolls and a central shell. A later type of mahogany settee, *c.* 1740, has four turned baluster legs in front and two at the back. Acanthus leaves are carved on the shoulders of the legs.

Chairs Apart from the architectural form mahogany hall chairs—there are several at Chatsworth which were formerly at Devonshire House, London—the most magnificent of Kent's chairs are allied to designs by Daniel Marot and are covered in gilded gesso and upholstered in cut velvet or figured damask. Variants, with arms terminating in serpents' heads, masks or satyrs, and with carved shells or foliage below the seat, are also found.

Other forms include items as varied as the green velvet State Bed at Houghton (1732), and a looking glass frame Kent designed for Frederick, Prince of Wales—a similar one was sold at Christie's in 1984 (28 June, lot 91). Several of these designs were published in 1744 by John Vardy in *Some Designs of Mr Inigo Jones and Mr William Kent*, which includes some even more varied—drawings for an organ case, gold cups, silver épergnes and a Gothic pulpit for York Minster.

Whilst Vardy faithfully copied Kent's Palladian style in his own drawings, he was also prepared to reflect French inventiveness in spritely engravings. The rococo fashion began to spread to England in the 1730s, and it was not long before engraved suites of designs of ornament began to be printed here. William De La Cour's *First Book of Ornament* was one of the first dated sets (1741), and it was about this time that the ubiquitous pattern-book publisher Batty Langley inserted six projects for tables, pirated from Pineau without acknowledgement, in his *Treasury of Designs* (1740). Whilst there had been architectural pattern-books with English texts for many years prior to the eighteenth century, the decorative arts had fared badly. De La Cour, Batty Langley and others therefore deserve credit for trying to widen the range of designs, although the first to do so with really good observation of the French manner was Matthias Lock, a carver of rare ability. His *Six Sconces* (1744) and *Six Tables* (1746) were among the earliest English furniture designs in which the rococo style was used competently. It is obvious that Lock had looked at French engravings from a knowledgeable standpoint of what, amid the riot of sprite-like curves, it was possible to carve and gild. He may be credited with the introduction of a delicate form of girandole, in which episodes from *Aesop's Fables* were carved against a light *rocaille* background, with candle-branches writhing outwards in twig-like forms.

As a contrast to carved and gilded wood, or partly gilded mahogany, English patrons in the 1730s and 1740s still found pleasure in setting embroidered and woven fabrics on appropriate frames. Such upholstery

ide table, mahogany, c1730. H30, W29.
his is a well-shaped table, one of a pair, with all four legs clearly
arved with scallop shells and claw-and-ball feet.

vas well understood in the late years of the seven-
eenth century and in the time of Queen Anne (1702–
4). The most elaborate of the later suites is the twenty
hairs, four settees and a day-bed made in 1746 by
ames Pascall for Henry, 7th Viscount Irwin, and now
t Temple Newsam House, Leeds. The wool needle-
vork of a floral design, in *petit point* on canvas, was
vorked in England. One of Lord Irwin's neighbours
vrote in March 1745 from Cambrai in France to tell him
hat seat covers there were obtainable at half the
.ondon price: a hazard of competitive trading and one
till current. Fastening the needlework to the wood
arcase was done by brass-headed nails, often used in
louble rows, with the heads gilded. Blended with a
avish use of heavily carved and gilded mahogany,
hese rich fabrics were mounted by the upholsterer, the
:ading craftsman in the furniture trades in the reign of
George II.

Some indication of this skill is evident in the bill of
732 from 'Turner Hill, and Pitter in the Strand' sent to
ir Robert Walpole for the State Bed William Kent had
lesigned for his Norfolk house, Houghton Hall. 266¾
ards of double rich gold clouded lace with 305 yards of
Gold Vellum Rivicea', 36¼ yards of cord and 16¾
ards of 'double rich gold bullion fringe' were amongst
he items charged, and show that the gold embroidery
vas worked on a vellum ground and that much was
lued to the framework. Thorough cleaning was there-
ore difficult and always led to the troublesome bed-
ug extending its territory. As a result, panelled maho-
any backs and fluted posts in place of those covered in
often) red silk damask quickly came into fashion. In

place of fabric the frieze was carved with Vitruvian
scrolling, or gadrooned, until the gradual adoption of
the sinous and flamboyant rococo style.

From about 1745 the rococo style dominated the
design of English chairs. The use of the strong mahogany allowed the creation of a light and fanciful fashion
in subtle curves and delicate carving. At this time a
significant change occured in the treatment of chair
backs. The solid shaped splat was opened out into a
symmetrical arrangement of scrolls, often headed by a
shell motif, with lion decoration on arms and feet or
finely carved with acanthus on the shoulders and
apron. The uprights of the back became almost straight,
tapering slightly outwards to a scroll as they met the
top rail. There were, however, still many heavy near-
Baroque forms in manufacture in the 1730–40 period,
particularly in the so-called 'writing chairs', often with
two strapwork splats and scrolled arms, with a shaped
seat on three massive cabriole legs at the front and one
at the centre of the back. At this time a chronological
sequence is difficult to establish as the solidity of the
Baroque persisted in some models, whilst others
yielded to rococo styling. Cabinet-makers had little in
engraved form to guide them, and what there was had

Exercise chair, walnut, c1745. W29.
Exercise chairs, with deep leather boxes containing boards and wires
which bounced one up and down, were popular from the mid-
eighteenth century. This one, on its strong base and with six legs, is
fitted with a pull-out step to help the user reach the high concertina
seat.

Mirror, gilt pine, c1735. H69, w28.
This mirror is attributed to the London cabinet-maker Benjamin Goodison (d. 1767), who was in royal employment from 1726 (when his master James Moore died). This also included service to Frederick, Prince of Wales. A mirror of almost identical design to this is in the Victoria and Albert Museum (No: W. 86-1911). It relates to a design by William Kent for the stem of the Prince's Barge (1731-32), which was included in John Vardy's *Some Designs of Mr Inigo Jones and Mr William Kent* (1744, Plate 52). It may well be that, as in the carving for the Barge, there was some involvement by the talented carver James Richards (d. 1759), who was well known to Goodison.

Cabinet on stand, ebonized, on giltwood stand, c1740. H83, W56.
This fine cabinet has a central cupboard surrounded by ten drawers inset with mosaic plaques of various Italian coloured marbles, depicting figures with classical buildings, ruins and landscapes.

These are divided by columns veneered with *Porta Santa rara* marble. The stand is in the style of William Kent, and centres on a mask face above a shell, flanked by reeded floral swags.

Side table, giltwood, c1735. W60.
William Kent (1685–1748) patronized a number of furniture-makers who were capable of realizing his designs: others worked in the 'Kentian' style he had made popular. This heavy Kentian table, with a *verde antico* marble top, is strongly supported by massive console-shaped square legs carved with large-scale acanthus leaves, fruit and flowers. A black cartouche surrounded by scrolled acanthus forms the apron.
Prov: HRH The Duke of Kent.

not been produced to be of assistance to the trade. In the *London Magazine*, November 1738, a writer exhorted that 'the ridiculous imitation of the French taste has now become the Epidemical distemper of the Kingdom', but enough of Baroque form was still being produced under Kent's influence to hold the sway, with patrons busy redesigning their rooms and collections.

This was certainly true of bookcases, where the architectural form was present in fluted columns with Corinthian capitals (which were used as late as 1762, when William Vile made his famous bookcase for Queen Charlotte) and with a pediment, either of triangular shape or broken at its centre. The panels of the lower doors allowed mahogany with a fine 'figure' to be selected, and this was quartered to obtain an even richer decorative effect. The glazed doors were divided by plain bars into six panes and the pediment had urns at each corner. In his *Treasury of Designs* (1740), Batty Langley illustrated several bookcases which used elements taken from any of the five architectural orders. It was but a short step in style and years to produce a centre section which projected forwards of two wings—a 'breakfront' bookcase. Large bookcases of this kind were often surmounted by a plaster bust of one of the classical worthies.

When Sir William Stanhope's effects were sold at his house in Albemarle Street in St James's on 25 April 1733, the highest assessment was reserved for 'a mahogany desk and Book-case of the most curious workmanship and ornamented with brass work finely graved and glass Doors, £50'. The Channon family of Exeter and London are the probable makers of an impressive group of brass inlaid furniture made in the 1740s—there is a pair of signed bookcases by them at Powderham Castle, Devon—and the considerable skill they displayed has been found present in at least three other contemporary firms. However, whilst brass can be cut to thin sinuous forms and sparkles as the light catches it, the vogue for such inlays did not become general until the early years of the nineteenth century. This is perhaps surprising in view of their popularity in France and England in the late years of the seventeenth century. However, gilded metal was used to enrich the delicate capitals of the small, architectural-shaped elements within cabinets, set as part of an array of pigeon-holes and shelves, or for the mounts, handles and classical figures on fine examples of cabinet-making in the early rococo years.

The tallboy bureau had developed from the 'chest on chest' and incorporated a top drawer in the lower portion of the cabinet, which let down on a quadrant to reveal an interior fitted as a small desk. At this time, in the late 1740s, the use of mirror glass in door fronts was still common—it was due to the adaptation of Chinese railings in the 1750s which allowed clear panes of glass to be easily used in attractive patterns for bookcases and china cabinets.

A number of attractive collectors' cabinets, made to hang on a wall, were also made, and occasionally fine examples such as that made for Horace Walpole or Thomas Brand grace the salerooms. Walpole wrote about his cabinet to his friend Sir Horace Mann in July 1743: 'I have a new cabinet for my enamels and miniatures just come home, which I am sure you would like; it is of rosewood, the doors inlaid with carvings in ivory'. The growth of interest in writing, books and collecting had understandable effects on the forms of furniture made. Large library desks of pedestal form were made from about 1725 onwards; the richest were of mahogany with carved and gilt decorations, with panels divided by lions' head terminals, dominant ovals in the centres and elaborate mouldings at each edge. They occupied a position in the centre of the library and their ornament was calculated to be integral to the general decorative scheme. After about 1740 the massive terminals—an attractive example produced in 1735 for Lady Burlington featured the owl crest of her Savile family—were rare, but refinements such as legs pulling forward to support the top drawers and vertical divisions for folio books were more frequent.

Amongst the most common in designs in the 1730s and 1740s were console tables with marble tops resting on a wood eagle or dolphin support, carved with striking realism: such tables were generally made in pairs and set against walls under looking glasses. Many have been mutilated and regilded in Regency and Victorian times, and only a few now retain the carved apron ends which concealed the metal or wooden struts which secured them to the wall.

In books published by the architectural designers, console and side tables figure well. They are set below the large pier glasses they were made to accompany. William Jones in his *Gentleman's and Builder's Companion* (1739) shows no other form of furniture. The console

Pedestal table, painted and gilt, c1730. W49, D35.
This solid pedestal table, one of a pair, is massively carved with huge acanthus leaves and garlands, eagles' and rams' heads in the style of William Kent — all gilt on a white ground. A veined marble slab forms the top.

Pole screen, mahogany, 1750. H59.
The delicately carved rococo frame surrounds a panel of *petit point* needlework to form the screen of this piece. The screen can be adjusted up or down the pole, which has a scrolled tripartite base and flaunts an elaborate flowering finial at the top.

Wall brackets, giltwood, c1750. H15.
Asymmetry was one of the characteristics of the rococo style. Here it is well displayed in light and frivolous wall brackets, with finely carved 'C'-scrolls and busts emerging from volutes. They are the perfect brackets for displaying delicate porcelain.

tables shown a few years later by Thomas and Batty Langley followed foreign models: Italian, French, and particularly those engraved by Nicolas Pineau. From 1740 the heavy Baroque models declined in favour, although many later rococo examples with a less robust shell are nevertheless of massive construction, with acanthus similarly repeated on the plinth.

Every inventory of a country house at the start of the eighteenth century listed a considerable number of tables. Some had tops of stone or marble, others were japanned, and many veneered in a conscious reaction against the marquetry enrichments of the previous generation. The long mahogany table was much more elegant, often eight feet in length, with legs carved with a male mask finishing above in acanthus leaves hipped on to a frieze, and a central pendant consisting of a finely-modelled female mask set within a shell and flanked by more acanthus.

Tables fitted with toilet requisites for use when dressing begin to occur in inventories and accounts in the 1740s. In 1745 the leading maker, William Hallett (1707– 81), supplied to the 4th Earl of Cardigan 'a mahogany Dressing Table on casters, the top to lift up with a Glass and boxes, a shelf underneath with the sides and back cut open'. The first of these Georgian examples were of knee-hole pedestal form, with a top drawer divided into compartments and a small hinged glass at the centre. The heavy burr walnut top was supported when open by a brass stay, and the construction was robust, with pilasters fluted and carved in the solid. A sophisticated form of dressing table was japanned in black and gold, but at its simplest might merely be a draped toilet table: Hogarth illustrates one in the Countess's dressing room in *Marriage à la Mode* (1745).

For dining, the gate-leg table was still in use in the early eighteenth century until those with swinging legs to support the flaps appeared in the 1720s. Most could be extended by an extra leaf, but in 1731 Sir Robert Walpole reported the common practise of the company dining at several tables: 'we were generally between twenty and thirty at two tables'. A variant enabled the semicircular ends to the square centre table to be detached and used as pier tables. It was also becoming customary for friends to take tea at each other's houses, and furniture-makers turned their attention to making suitable tables with accompanying tripod mahogany stands to accommodate the silver tea and coffee equipage. The fashion for tea-drinking had spread rapidly

Settee, mahogany, 1750. W56.
The 'X'-framed chair form of this settee was widely adopted on the Continent, particularly in Italy, in the fifteenth and sixteenth centuries. The form was occasionally revived in England in the eighteenth century, notably by William Kent. Here the form is used rather awkwardly in the shape of a double chair with buttoned leather upholstery. The front supports are carved with ribbon-tied acanthus leaves and joined to the back cabriole legs by curved stretchers — an odd combination. The set also includes six armchairs.
Prov: Langley Park, Norfolk.

from the 1660s to all classes of society: in 1745 a contributor to the *Female Spectator* wrote that 'the tea-table costs more to support than would two children at nurse', a late reference to the constant high price of tea. The highest point of design for the tea table came after Chippendale had published two designs for tables in the 1754 edition of the *Director* (Plate XXXIIII), in which slender legs were united by a delicate form of stretcher in the rococo style. It was but a short step to those on tripod stands with a carved and perforated gallery. However, few remain that have not been amended in later years.

A small but attractive item which architects like Kent introduced into Palladian houses was the gilt stand of term and pedestal form. It was used to support heavy objects such as candelabra, vases, lamps and marble or plaster busts. The use of terminal figures was common in Continental furniture from the sixteenth century onwards: when later used as portable stands they were frequently capped by the bust of a child or woman supporting a capital of (usually) Ionic form, with a tapered lower portion ending in scrolled feet or a square plinth. Several handsome examples attributed to Benjamin Goodison are further enriched with fish-scale carving and are festooned with leaves. Those made to support porcelain cisterns or oriental vases were, in the early Georgian period, of mahogany in the fashion of contemporary stools, but had a slightly raised rim to the top to prevent items from slipping.

At the end of the 1740s London furniture-makers had to take account of a new rising talent, Thomas Chippendale the elder (1718–79). The pervasive influences of the Gothic and Chinese styles, seemingly incompatible, were soon to dominate patrons' choice of furniture. With no special knowledge of Chinese work, cabinet-makers looked at late seventeenth-century lacquer cabinets and the painting on Chinese porcelain and set out to make furniture of a bastard Chinese type for uncritical clients keen to be in fashion. It was a mood which suited Chippendale's new London business.

Bureau cabinet, mahogany, c1735-40. H87, W43.
This cabinet has a slightly archaic appearance, caused by the use of three heavy, fluted flat Ionic pilasters in the upper section, beneath an attractive swan-neck pediment. The bureau base encloses a well-fitted interior above three long drawers. Fluted half-round pilasters are set on the canted front corners, above ogee bracket feet.

Mirror, beech, scarlet japanned, by Giles Grendey, c1735-40. H47, W24.
This mirror is part of a large and important suite of furniture supplied by Giles Grendey to the Duke of Infantado's Castle at Lazcano, Northern Spain. The shaped frame, which surrounds an original bevelled mirror plate, is delicately gilt at the crest with a crowned Chinaman flanked by attendants and hounds, and at the sides with latticework and architectural landscapes including figures and birds. Three candle brackets are fitted at the base, with two late candle arms. Other pieces from this suite are at the Victoria and Albert Museum, Temple Newsam House, Leeds, and the Metropolitan Museum, New York.

There is a temptation, in writing short notes about dissimilar objects, to compare and contrast them. There may well be reasons to do so with this scarlet japanned mirror and giltwood chair. Both are of similar date, and the mirror is by an accomplished maker, Giles Grendey, and intended for export. The chair is by a good, but unknown, maker, working for a patron who employed both the accomplished architects and decorators, William Kent and Henry Flitcroft, at Ditchley. The fabric, whether new or old, is in the tradition of the cut velvets long imported from Italy. Both had to please the patron and both attempted to capture something of an exotic style in doing so.

Chair, giltwood, c1730. H42, W27.
This heavily-built chair is one from a set of six, with back and seat upholstered in boldly-designed crimson cut velvet on an ivory satin ground. The solid front supports of 'broken' cabriole form are headed by lions' masks with bared teeth, and the splayed back legs are carved with acanthus leaves on a punched ground.
Prov: The Earls of Litchfield, Ditchley Park, Oxfordshire; The Lady Anne Tree, Mereworth Castle, Kent.

Wherever white and gilded furniture of the 1730–40 period, heavily and dramatically carved with mask faces, foliage and scrolled legs, is found it is connected with the architect and decorator, William Kent (1685–1748). He, of course, made no furniture, but after nine years training in Italy returned to England and had soon an extensive patronage, and a number of important jobs for the Crown as its Master Carpenter. Many of his designs were published by John Vardy in 1744, and there is no doubt that they inspired many carvers, in particular of the calibre of Matthias Lock, James Moore the Younger and James Richards, to make furniture to their own version of Kent's designs, or to work directly for him.

1.   Console table, white painted and parcel-gilt, design attributed to William Kent, c1730. H33, W47, D19
This is one of an important pair of tables which, in its use of the central female mask, scrolled bracket supports and flamboyant design, resembles a pair of console tables designed by Kent for Chiswick House (now at Chatsworth, Derbyshire). The Kent design was published by John Vardy in *Some Designs of Mr Inigo Jones and Mr William Kent* (1744), Plate 40).

2.   *Side table, ebonized and gilt, c1730. W45, D24.*
An alternative to contrasting gilded ornament with walnut was to put it on wood which had been blacked to simulate ebony. The foil between the two colours was dramatic, and seen to good advantage in the scrolling acanthus, double shell and ball-and-claw feet of this table.
Prov: The Lady Anne Tree, Mereworth Castle, Kent.

3.   *Side table, walnut, c1730. W45, D22.*
This table has an exotic flavour. The heads of the griffin monopodia supports have bared teeth, and their wings form part of the ornate frieze, which is centred by an asymmetrical cartouche carved with a Medusa mask. The *verde antico* scagliola top is later, but presumably replaces one that was similar.
Prov: Godmersham Park, Kent.

4.   *Side table, white painted and parcel-gilt, c1740. H34, W50.*
By the 1740s, lighter forms for tables were becoming fashionable, as
this side table shows. It is one of a pair, and is unusually decorated
with an apron carved with a basket of flowers and trellis pattern, and
legs headed by basketwork panels.

5.   *Side table, white painted and
parcel-gilt, attributed to William
Kent, c1730. W62.*
This heavily-ornate table is said
to have come from Raynham
Hall, Norfolk, which was
remodelled by William Kent
between 1720 and 1730. Elements
in its design are characteristic of
Kent; the unusually scrolled
cornucopiae would seem to
originate from a design for a table
by Kent published finally by John
Vardy in 1744. The same 'S'-scroll
supports and central mask
flanked by swags are found on a
table formerly at Chiswick and
Devonshire House, at both of
which Kent was much involved.
The marble top has been
replaced.

1. Side table, giltwood, c1730. H32, W54, D29.
This very important table presents many problems. It is perhaps too
simple to say it was probably designed by William Kent and executed
by James Moore the younger, assisted by the carver James Richards.
The relevant archives — the table was formerly at Ditchley,
Oxfordshire — also contain five designs for table frames by Henry
Flitcroft, who worked with William Kent and succeeded him as
Master Mason. There is also a pair of tables now at Temple Newsam
House, Leeds (also from Ditchley) which compare closely to an
autograph design by the carver Matthias Lock. So we have the
hazards of attribution present in full measure. The table frame
supports a veined Siena marble top with moulded white marble
border.
Prov: Made for George Lee, 2nd Earl of Lichfield, Ditchley,
Oxfordshire.

*It is easy to forget when looking at very accomplished pieces of
furniture of the 1740s—perhaps no finer table exists than that shown
here (1)—that there was much also created in modest format. The
carver was an important member of any shop, and enough workshop
bills survive to show that he was paid considerably more than those
responsible for the basic carcase. The design might be one plagiarized
from the French, but it was still done with great competence. There is
slight reason to think James Moore the younger and James Richards
might have been involved in the table, formerly at Ditchley.
However, that is of little consequence; whoever it was who did any
carved and gilded table had rare skill and ability.*

2.   *Pier table, white painted and gilded, c1740-45. H34, W56, D31.*
The design of this table originates from an engraved plate in Nicolas Pineau's *Nouveaux Desseins de Pieds de Tables*, which was plagiarized by Batty and Thomas Langley. Pineau was a leading designer and creator, with Juste-Aurèle Meissonnier (c1693-1750), of the *genre pittoresque*, or the French rococo style. This was soon taken up in England, as seen here, although the form of this table is still basically symmetrical.

3.   Design for the table, Plate CXLIII, dated 1739, from *City and Country Builder's and Workman's Treasury of Designs* by Batty and Thomas Langley, published 1740. This design derives from an engraved plate in Nicolas Pineau's *Nouveaux Desseins de Pieds de Tables*, published between 1732 and 1739.

1.   *Side table, painted white and gilt, c1735. W69, D35.*
There seems to be good contemporary evidence that some side tables used in dining rooms were painted white. Gilding was the additional ornamentation. The displayed eagle and twin dolphin supports of this table are well worthy of the skills of the London carver, James Richards (d. 1759). He carved dolphins in profusion on the Royal Barge, designed 1731-32 by William Kent for Frederick, Prince of Wales (now at the National Maritime Museum, London).
Prov: Lady Anne Tree, Mereworth Castle, Kent.

It is easy to assume that all furniture of seemingly asymmetrical form is based on the French rococo style. Whilst the Huguenot silversmiths who came to England at the beginning of the eighteenth century did introduce the early manifestations of rococo, much of the carved furniture of the 1730s still has overtones of Baroque, dictating to its appearance. The intermesh between Baroque and rococo cannot be defined in a few words. The spread of engravings from the continent and the familiarity of many patrons and architects like Gibbs and Kent with the Italian Baroque, however, encourage us to recognize its many robust flourishes, stated, and even over-stated, in many fine pieces of furniture.

2.   *Side table, giltwood, 1740. W55, D29.*
The pierced frieze, carved with scrolls and shellwork, lightens an otherwise heavily-designed table, bearing a shaped top of Sicilian marble. It is one of a pair.
Prov: The Earl of Feversham.

3.   *Card table, walnut, c1750. H28, W34, D17.*
This is an elegant and useful table, which relies on the beauty of the wood and good proportion for effect. The craftsman only makes use of restrained carving to complete the lower edge, with gadrooning, and to cover the knees. When unfolded, the velvet-lined top rests on the movable back legs, which pull out through concertina action, and are attached to a hinged frame.

4. Side table, pine, c1745. W72.
The form of this table may have been inspired by a design by William Jones published in the *Gentlemen's and Builders' Companion* (1739), which is clearly influenced by engraved designs in Nicolas Pineau's *Nouveaux Desseins de Pieds de Tables* (1732-39). This table shows the effect of the lighter French influence.

5. Console table, giltwood, c1745. W52.
A console table only has legs at the front, but derives strong support from the wall to which it is fixed. It is therefore most suitable for flaunting the extravagant curves of the rococo style. Often made in pairs, like this example, the tables stood between windows, with a mirror above.

6. Side table, giltwood, c1740-45. H33, W72, D35.
The conjoining of console brackets, connected at the base by heavy square section stretchers and with swags below, is a feature of furniture in the style of William Kent. The elements are not too well handled here, but the table was supplied to an important collector, the 4th Earl of Shaftesbury, who employed the architect Henry Flitcroft to supervise alterations at his home, Wimborne House, St Giles, Dorset, from 1740-44. Further, the table is similar to one at Wimpole Hall, Cambridgeshire, where Flitcroft also worked. They were probably all carved to his designs by Matthias Lock, although many of the carved masterpieces at Wimpole are by the equally talented London carver, Sefferin Alken (d. 1783).

Four front legs, four elephants' heads, an elaborate carved stretcher, the many 'running feet' of carved Vitruvian scroll on the seat rail, seven shells at each point of the scrolled back, make for a lavish statement of Kentian-style furniture, some twelve feet wide. It would not be to every taste, one argument being that there is not enough sophistica-tion and superb quality of carv-ing to justify the size. However, there is ample furniture of the 1740s, particularly mahogany-framed upholstered armchairs, or those richly gilded, to stand as the exemplars of what was needed for the new Palladian houses.

1.   Settee, pine, c1730. H41, W144, D30.
This settee, in Kentian style, is part of an unusual suite comprising two settees, five chairs and a pair of stools, and comes from Castle Hill, Devon. It was presumably made for Hugh, 14th Baron Clinton, who built the new Castle Hill from 1725–33. Lord Clinton employed the leading Palladian architect Roger Morris, who, according to documentation, was directed in this commission by Richard Boyle, 3rd Earl of Burlington, the mentor and friend of William Kent. The scroll legs are linked by oak-leaf swags to carved elephants' heads with upturned trunks.

2.   Armchair, walnut, 1745. H39, W28.
This spacious armchair is handsomely covered with contemporary *petit point* needlework in wool and silk, showing roundels of country scenes. The curved arm supports are carved in shallow relief with acanthus leaves and rosettes, and the splayed, hairy paw feet provide a steady base.
Prov: Percival Griffiths Esq.

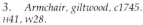

3.   *Armchair, giltwood, c1745.
H41, W28.*
This is one of a pair from an
important suite of Soho tapestry
chairs from Wentworth Castle,
Yorkshire. They may be the
chairs seen by the 1st Duchess of
Northumberland on her visit to
the Castle in 1760, and described
by her as 'French chairs emb'd
with flowers upon Brown by the
famous Mr Wright'. A bill dated
1746 exists for sofas and chairs
made for Wentworth Castle from
Richard Wright and Edward
Elwick who, as partners, became
the pre-eminent firm of cabinet-
makers in Yorkshire during the
second half of the eighteenth
century. One of these chairs is
now in the Victoria and Albert
Museum (No: W.36-1964).

1. *Chair, giltwood, c1740.*
The chair is part of an important suite, which includes four chairs and a settee (*see* page 100). The carving of the legs closely parallels that on a large set of seat furniture at Holkham Hall, Norfolk, made by Benjamin Goodison, who had supplied furniture to the royal palaces, and designed by William Kent. Another group of chairs of similar style, formerly at Chiswick House, were designed by Kent for Lord Burlington.
Prov: The Hon. Edward Keppel Coke, Longford Hall, Derbyshire; The Viscount Leverhulme; Wateringbury House, Kent.

2. *Armchair, giltwood, c1740.*
This broad chair, one of a pair, is of a grand design suitable for use in a saloon. The 'broken' cabriole legs and outward-turned scrolled arms are carved with large acanthus leaves.
Prov: General Sir Francis Davies.

3. *Armchair, mahogany, c1745.* H38, W31.
This armchair, one of a pair, is part of a large but distinguished group, now scattered to the Metropolitan Museum, New York, the Philadelphia Museum of Art and elsewhere. It is upholstered with floral *petit point* needlework. The arm terminals are well carved with lions' masks, which match those on the knees.

4. *Armchair, pine, walnut, oak, gesso and gilt, c1750.* H40, W29.
This chair is one of a set, now divided, of which examples are in the Victoria and Albert Museum (No: W.99-1978) and the collection of Mr and Mrs Gordon P. Getty in San Francisco. They have a slightly unusual pattern worked in the gesso on a punched ground of flowerheads framed by a key pattern. The chair is in The J. Paul Getty Museum, Malibu (No: 85 DA 120).

The increasing use of mahogany from the 1720s onwards at first hardly affected taste. Chairs were still made in walnut to an identical design, according to the purchasers' wishes, and the stuffed-over or upholstered back was a ready alternative to the shaped or carved wooden splat. The carving was, however, of a high order, and many motifs were put on the knee of the cabriole legs or rendered in the

various forms of foot—the claw-and-ball, the scroll and the paw. As the carver worked largely by invention and not from measured drawings, little was of a stereotyped nature. Much invention was shown in the subjects of the various pieces of needlework and tapestry applied to back and seat. And finally the heavy, near Baroque, styles gave way to the lighter, sinuous rococo forms in leg and seat rail.

5. *Chair, walnut, by William Hallett, 1735.*
This is one from an important set of eighteen chairs and a settee, supplied by William Hallett (1707-81) to Arthur, 6th Viscount Irwin, in 1735 for his London house. After his death in 1736, they were removed to his country seat, Temple Newsam House, Leeds. They were sold from there in 1922. The set was fully described in *Connoisseur* (December 1964).

6. *Chair, walnut, c1740.*
This chair has a back splat carved with a strong shell motif, and is in the manner of the London maker, Giles Grendey (1693-1780), who possibly originated the inverted shell design.

7. *Chair, mahogany, c1750.*
The mid-eighteenth-century Soho tapestry, woven with birds within broad naturalistic flower borders, provides the dominant feature of this ample-framed chair, one of four.
Prov: Warwick Castle.

8. *Chair, mahogany, c1754.*
The chair represents a form of rococo furniture made popular by Thomas Chippendale after he had published his *Director* in 1754. It is one from a set of four, with the waved back and seat upholstered in contemporary *gros point* needlework. The seat rail and legs are carved with scrolling acanthus foliage and 'C'-scrolls. One of the chairs is stamped with a journeyman's signature, 'R'.

1. *Armchair, giltwood, c1740. H42, W30.*
This is one of a pair in the French taste. It has a curved back and oval drop-in seat covered in contemporary needlework, showing Venus and Vulcan. The tightly-scrolled arm rests and legs are carved with acanthus leaves.
Prov: Spye Park, Chippenham, Wiltshire.

3. *Chair, walnut, c1735.*
This chair, one from a set of six, is of distinctive shape, in the manner of Giles Grendey (1693-1780). The central splat of pierced lyre form is surmounted by a carved fan motif and scalloped cresting.

2. *Writing chair, yew and mahogany, c1735.*
This is a chair of strong design, with shepherd's crook arms and boldly carved and shaped front cabriole legs. The figure of the mahogany is well displayed on the cartouche-shaped back.

4. *Chair, walnut and parcel-gilt, attributed to Giles Grendey, c1745.*
A set of virtually identical chairs are at Stourhead, Wiltshire, where Giles Grendey worked for the Hoare family. This is one of a pair stamped 'R' and 'TT' respectively ; other chairs by Grendey bear the journeyman's stamp 'TT'. If we allow for slightly indistinct punching, this could read 'JT' for Grendey's apprentices John Tudgey, James Tomlyn or James Turney, working for him in 1737 and 1741 (latter two) respectively.

certain amount of confusion invariably arises when one is dealing with the career of a long-lived furniture-maker, in this case, Giles Grendey (1693–1780). We know something of his early work through his concern to put labels on what was made. He had one of the largest workshops in London, and an extensive export trade for his furniture. He was also described in 1755 as 'an eminent Timber

Merchant' in the year that his daughter married the upholsterer (and partner of William Vile) John Cobb (d. 1778). But did he make the walnut chairs illustrated here (3 and 4)? It is also perhaps more frustrating not to know which one of, perhaps, six makers provided the superb gilded settee to William Kent's design. Such pieces are among the finest of English Georgian furniture.

5.   Settee, giltwood, attributed to William Kent, c1735-40. H43, W58, D27. This is one from a set of six settees 'covered with crimson Genoa velvet' and almost certainly commissioned by the 9th Earl of Pembroke for the Double Cube room at Wilton House, Salisbury. Lord Pembroke was a great admirer of Kent's work, and undoubtedly met him at Houghton and elsewhere. The sphinx supports on this settee are very similar to ones on the great side table in the Saloon at Houghton, and both seem to derive in form from an engraved tail piece Kent made for Pope's 1725-26 edition of Homer's *Odyssey*. The settee is still at Wilton House.

1. Hall settee, giltwood; design attributed to William Kent, c1735-40. w65.
This is part of a suite comprising four side chairs and a settee. The carving of the legs is closely paralleled on a large set of seat furniture at Holkham Hall, Norfolk, made by Benjamin Goodison (who had supplied furniture to the royal palaces) and designed by William Kent. This settee is covered with contemporary crimson cut velvet and silk damask.
Prov: The Hon. Edward Keppel Coke, Longford Hall, Derbyshire; The Viscount Leverhulme; Wateringbury House, Kent.

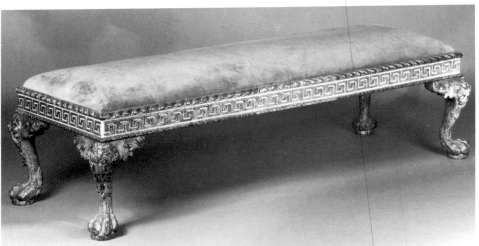

2. Long stool, white painted and parcel-gilt, c1740. w69.
The closest parallel to this handsome long stool are those attributed to Benjamin Goodison (d. 1767) in the Long Gallery at Longford Castle, Wiltshire, His name appears in the Longford accounts for significant sums between 1737 and 1745, with one entry 'Gallery at Longford £400'. This surely relates to the chairs, day-beds and stools therein. However, whilst this stool is painted white, those at Longford are in carved mahogany and parcel-gilt, have six legs and carved scrolls to the apron.

3. Stool, pine, c1730. w25.
The stool is part of a set which includes two settees, five chairs and two stools; the seat rail, carved with Vitruvian scrolls and holding an upholstered drop-in seat, is supported on scroll legs linked by oak-leaf swags to carved elephants' heads.
Prov: The Lady Margaret Fortescue, Castle Hill, Devon.

Settee, walnut, c1730. w61.
The chair-maker never quite resolved the dilemma of having to make the splats of the double-back settee a little wider than was visually attractive. But he has tried to compensate with the elegant scrolled uprights, which reflect the curved design of the slender arm rests, terminating in lions' masks. The good cabriole legs are headed by acanthus.
Prov: Percival Griffiths Esq.

It is easy to accept the statement that mid-Georgian upholstered settees are one of the best creations of the period. The eye accepts the colour of the coverings, their warmth and padded comfort more readily than the florid carving of a pine stool (3). Furthermore, the upholstery prevents us noticing that the settee is basically two chairs side by side, usually amended to hide the fact, and perhaps a little awkward when not (4). Nevertheless, there was still enough space for the carver to demonstrate his skills on the carcase before it was sent to the upholsterer. And if the last was not a requirement, he could be bold to the point of flamboyance.

5. *Settee, mahogany, c1740. w63.*
The rectangular back and seat of the settee are covered in contemporary *gros* and *petit point* needlework, with a procession of oriental figures on a black background. Open-mouthed lions' heads terminate the arm rests, and Vitruvian scrolls are carved on the seat rail. This is very much the kind of furniture that the London maker, William Bradshaw, was providing when he was in partnership with the tapestry artist, Tobias Stranover.

6. *Settee, mahogany, c1740. w70.*
This settee, which is one of a pair, is finely carved with lions' masks holding flowerheads in their mouths, acanthus, *guilloches* and poppy heads. It formerly came from Kinfauns Castle, Perth, and bears the coronet of the 8th Earl of Moray. It has been re-upholstered. Another of identical design exists bearing the coronet of the 2nd Baron Conway of Ragley Hall, Warwicks.

1.   Bureau bookcase, mahogany, c1745. W43.
This workman-like bureau bookcase, although partly restored, is set up
well on large paw feet below a carved base. Above the rectangular
mirror-glazed doors is a broken pediment decorated with octagonal
fretwork. A fitted interior is concealed behind the sloping front.

The long continuity of some London furniture firms perhaps inhibited a ready flow of design innovation. Elizabeth Bell carried on her husband Henry's business, and he had succeeded Coxed and Woster, and all at the same St. Paul's Churchyard address. She labelled the kneehole desk (2), as her predecessors had consistently done. Giles Grendey, as we have noted (see page 98), also labelled his furniture—at least his export pieces—regularly, and the mahogany chest (3) has two. Alas, the bureau bookcase has none, and deserves a maker's name attached, rather than mere anonymity (1).

2.   Kneehole desk, walnut, c1740. H30, W30, D18.
This is a useful small desk, with a recessed cupboard in the kneehole and a small drawer above. It bears the trade label of Elizabeth Bell: 'Elizabeth Bell at the White Swan against the South Gate of St Pauls Churchyard, London'. She was there from 1740 to about 1758, and was almost certainly the widow of Henry Bell, who had succeeded Coxed and Woster at this address.

3.   Chest, mahogany, by Giles Grendey, c1750. H33, W33, D20.
This is a simple, functional chest, with a brushing slide fitted below the top, which pulls out to form a surface on which to brush clothes. The piece bears two trade labels inscribed 'Giles Grendey, in St John's Square, Clerkenwell, London, makes and sells all sorts of Cabinet-Goods, Chairs and Glasses'.

The names of William Hallett (1707–81) and William Vile (d. 1767) are linked frequently together as makers. This is because Vile referred to Hallett in 1749 as 'my master', and Hallett backed him financially when he set up in partnership with John Cobb in 1751. In 1762 Vile supplied some important furniture to the Royal family, George III and Queen Charlotte, some of which has applied carved foliate ovals. It has become a tradition to credit all such furniture to Vile. It is necessary to bear in mind it might have originated with Hallett or be the work of a specialist carver supplying several makers. We have two pages of illustrations here which show the perils of attribution for what they are—uncertain. The fine owl desk formerly at Chiswick (1) was attributed for convincing reasons to Benjamin Goodison. The bill recently came to light in the Chatsworth archives proving it to have been supplied in 1735 by John Boson, probably to a design by William Kent.

1. *Pier table, mahogany, c1735. H35, W59, D31.*
This is one of a pair of pier tables (*en suite* with the pier glasses) which were provided in 1735 to Lady Burlington by the carver John Boson (d. 1743). Lady Burlington refers to them in a letter written from Bath in 1735: 'I hope the Signior [William Kent's usual nickname] has remembered about my tables and glasses', implying that Boson was working to a design by Kent. Boson submitted his bill in September 1735, listing: 'two mahogany tables with Tearms folige and other Ornaments' as well as 'modles for ye Brass work', charged at £20.
The owls were intended as a reference to the crest of the Countess' family, the Saviles.
The carving of the tables (and mirrors) is of the highest quality. They stood in the Summer Parlour at Chiswick House; they are now at Chatsworth.

2. *Commode, mahogany, c1750. W50.*
The oval medallions on the doors of this commode have been treated as a characteristic of furniture supplied by William Vile (d. 1767), due to his supplying furniture to Queen Charlotte so ornamented in 1762. However, Vile trained under William Hallett (1707-81) and was supported by him financially from c1751. It would therefore seem reasonable to attribute this piece, supplied to the 4th Earl of Shaftesbury, to Hallett, as his name occurs in the relevant accounts, although without details of what was supplied.
Prov: The Earl of Shaftesbury, Wimborne House, St Giles, Dorset.

3.   *Secretaire-cabinet, mahogany and burr yew, c1750. H88, W44, D23.*
This well-finished cabinet has been attributed to William Hallett (1707-81) on the basis of its overall similarity to a group of cabinets, one of which was signed on the carcase. The two mirror-plated doors are framed by fluted Ionic pilasters and enclose shelves and small drawers. There is a fitted section behind a fall front. Large carrying handles are mounted on the sides.
Prov: The Dowager Marchioness of Cholmondeley.

4.   *Reading stand, mahogany, c1740. H45.*
The arched book rest of the stand is supported on a turned shaft with a tripod base. This may well have been adapted to serve this functional piece.
Prov: The Earl of Shaftesbury, Wimborne House, St Giles, Dorset.

5.   *Library table, mahogany, c1750. W68.*
The unusually-patterned frieze of this table, applied with latticework, is fitted each side with three drawers, the central one divided into compartments. The sizable top is covered with leather with a tooled gilt border.

1. Mirror, walnut and parcel-gilt, c1735-40. H56.
The frame of this mirror, with its fine architectural broken pediment, is embellished with a pierced shell cartouche, suspending acanthus and pendant oak branches. The gilded carving stands out against the plainer surfaces of the burr walnut to make a very handsome object.

2. Torchère, white painted and parcel gilt, c1735. H49, Diam 15.
The circular top of the torchère, with gadrooned border, is raised on a baluster stem, the lower part of triangular form, carved with acanthus foliage, pendant bell-flowers and tassels. The cabriole tripod base ends in claw-and-ball feet. The torchère may be compared with those in a celebrated suite of George II giltwood furniture, traditionally thought to have come from Stowe and erroneously associated with James Moore.

We are apt to forget that the Georgian house needed many candles, and candle chandeliers and candelabra to hold them, in order to provide light in the hours of darkness. This inevitably led to the provision of many torchères. Many of those whose ornament was worked in gesso, subsequently gilded, have been attributed to James Moore the elder. However, he died in 1726, his son in 1731, and perhaps the best maker to continue the form was Moore's apprentice Benjamin Goodison (d. 1767). But again attribution is not fact—the mirror (1) is merely 'worthy of a craftsman of the skill of Matthias Lock'. Such are the hazards of English furniture research, more acute when quality is undeniable.

3. Mirror, giltwood, c1740. H68. This mirror is of the highest standard of carving, worthy of a craftsman of the skill of Matthias Lock. The large frame is fitted with a shaped mirror plate, dramatically surmounted with a carved female mask — surrounded by scrolled acanthus leaves, wave pattern, 'C'-scrolls and pendant laurel leaves.

1.   *Bookcase, walnut, c1740. w68.*
The intricately-carved classical borders to the cornice, frieze and base
provide the restrained decorative detail needed to complete this
well-proportioned bookcase. The shelves are adjustable and enclosed
by well-glazed doors with fine, gilt metal, asymmetrical escutcheons.

The architectural forms of pilaster, brackets, broken pediments and glazing, matched to decorative frets found on buildings, may not seem the likely elements for furniture manufacture. It is, however, the large bookcases which can carry them off well. Whilst there is some awkwardness in the formation of the base (2), the upper section is handsome, and more so when filled with the colourful bindings of many books. The walnut bookcase (1) is more restrained—almost old-fashioned—but its size, and that of all bookcases, was such that they could dominate in Palladian rooms, which were made to be large, impressive and indicators of proud status.

2. Bookcase, walnut, c1740. H106, W96.
The lower portion of this vast bookcase is of uncommon design, with a bowed central cupboard door framed by scroll corbels, and the horizontal frieze above it carved with rosette medallions and key pattern. Ample storage space has been provided in drawers, cupboards and on the shelves in the upper section.
Prov: The Earl Cadogan.

Armchair, mahogany, upholstered in silk damask, c1750.
H (of back) 39, W (of seat) 28, D (of seat) 26.
This armchair is one of the superb pieces of furniture made for the Earl of Shaftesbury at St. Giles's House, Dorset. His collection of rococo furniture was one of the most important in England. Some of the furniture, which incorporates Chinese motifs and is carved in high relief, is documented as by William Hallett, but the records are incomplete.

CHAPTER 4

Chippendale and the Rococo 1754–1765

Thomas Chippendale was born in 1718 at Otley, Yorkshire, and after training under his father and the York joiner, Richard Wood, left the north in the early 1740s for the wider opportunities of London. We know little of Chippendale's early years, apart from his first recorded comission from Lord Burlington in 1747 and his marriage on 19 May 1748 to Catherine Redshaw. By 1753 the young man had prospered enough to take up premises in St. Martin's Lane, and a year later in 1754 to publish his important pattern-book, *The Gentleman and Cabinet-maker's Director*. Part of the title bears repetition in order to show his intentions:

> . . . Director, being a Collection of the most Elegant and Useful Designs of Household Furniture in the most Fashionable Taste . . . calculated to improve and refine the present Taste and suited to the Fancy and Circumstances of Persons in all Degrees of Life'.

The first edition, followed by two others in 1755 and 1762, shows Chippendale incorporating Chinese decoration for his 'household furniture': chairs, beds, sofas, tables, bookcases and firescreens. He shrugged away in the Preface to the 3rd edition that 'some of the Profession' had represented his efforts 'especially those after the Gothic and Chinese Manner, as so many specious Drawings, impossible to be worked off by any Mechanick whatsoever'. He stated firmly that every design in the book could be 'improved, both as to Beauty and Enrichment in the Execution of it, by their Most obedient servant, Thomas Chippendale'.

The chairs were given their 'Chinese' character by the fretwork backs in which a central panel was formed of diagonal bars surrounded by rectangles and squares. All was set under a curved top rail, and whilst the seat rails, legs and stretchers were decorated with low relief frets and piercings, there was a robust and practical framework underpinning the excess of decoration.

The first of these engraved designs for Chinese railings used as fretwork on furniture had not appeared until 1750 in William Halfpenny's *New Designs for Chinese Temples*, but he had already been copied by George Edwards and Matthew Darly (*A New Book of Chinese Designs*, 1754) and of course by Chippendale. The lattice of fretwork in chair and settee backs was very suitable for use in china cabinet and bookcase doors, and was used supremely in William and John Linnell's japanned bed, 1752–54, for the 4th Duke of Beaufort (sold at Christie's, 17 February 1921) which, with some supporting pieces, is now in the Victoria and Albert Museum. The bed has a canopy of pagoda form with, at the four corners, gilt dragons of carved wood, and a red and gold japanned bedhead of fretwork panels.

Fifty years ago it was assumed that the carver Matthias Lock, in company with one 'H. Copland' (his first name remains elusive), had ghosted drawings for the first edition of the *Director*. However, a considerable amount of evidence now supports Chippendale's own fluent draughtsmanship, and the new styles, particularly rococo, gave splendid opportunities for the entrepreneurial furniture-maker of more than ordinary ability to make his name. The designs in the editions were widely circulated, and were readily accepted by craftsmen and also by those working at the bench in eastern American towns such as Philadelphia. To the more casual searcher of design ideas or merely a Gothic seat to set in a landscaped vista, Chippendale's pattern-book was the one to plunder. By 1760 its author was sufficiently recognized to be listed as a member of the

Breakfast table, mahogany, c1755. w (open) 44.
Thomas Chippendale illustrates similar designs to this in his *The Gentleman and Cabinet-maker's Director* (1st edition, 1754, Plate XXXIII), and describes them in his 3rd edition (1762) as follows: 'One hath a Shelf, inclosed with fretwork. Sometimes they are inclosed with Brass Wirework. In the Front is a Recess for the Knees, &c'.

Society of Arts and Manufacturers, which had Hogarth, Walpole, Reynolds, Garrick and Sir William Chambers as fellow members.

Chambers was one of the few whom Chippendale would have known who had a first-hand knowledge of the Orient. As a young man he had visited China in the service of the Swedish East India Company. He had sketched and studied, refined what he had seen by comparing it with the scene in Rome, and returned to England in 1755. In 1757 Chambers published his *Designs of Chinese Buildings, Furniture, Dresses, Machines and Utensils* with a short preface by Samuel Johnson, who asserted that a concern for the 'highly individual type of civilization' of the Chinese was 'a matter of general interest'. It kept demand for Chinese-style furniture high.

Chippendale's success with the *Director* enabled him in 1754 to move into larger premises in St. Martin's Lane. He had at least twenty-two men working for him,

and notwithstanding the problems of a fire in April 1755 was fulfilling large and important commissions with his advanced rococo furniture for such patrons as the youthful Earl of Dumfries. What the pieces showed was 'a richness of detail unsurpassed by English designers', and they confirmed Chippendale's position 'as the most skilful and imaginative all-round interpreter of the Rococo style in the London Cabinet trade'. His book also had 'six new designs for Gothic Chairs', and the *Director* engravings obviously sustained the demand for such exotics until the early 1760s.

The publication of the *Director* had given chairmakers a useful source of ideas. Chippendale aimed at the latest fashion: he eschewed the ball-and-claw foot, and had one engraving that showed a scrolled foot in conjunction with the cabriole leg, a feature of French furniture. William Ince and John Mayhew adopted the same form in their *The Universal System of Household Furniture* a few years later, in 1759–63. Chairs in the Gothic and Chinese styles were fashioned either with square straight legs with small block feet, or less often with a tapered leg with a pierced and moulded foot.

Perhaps the best-known form of Chippendale chair of the 1750s was the 'ribband-back', which he illustrated in the 1754 *Director* (Plate XVI). His explanatory notes show he was proud of it, but he had used a French design by Jean Bérain in 1710 as his source. The lower part of surviving chairs after the Plate have strong rococo characteristics, with scroll terminations to the legs. The top rail and the framework of the splat are formed of 'C'-scrolls, the uprights are fluted and the carving is of superb quality.

Few chairs or tables of the mid-eighteenth century can, nevertheless, be traced to any particular pattern-book. The variations from the published designs were endless, and evidence only of fertile imaginations. One chair-maker who had a style eccentric enough to make chairs following his patterns distinctive was Robert Manwaring. In 1765 he published a small book, *The Cabinet and Chair-Maker's Real Friend and Companion*. Later, in 1791, Thomas Sheraton was dismissive of the book and noted it contained only 'what a boy might be taught in 7 hours'. One design was frequently copied, spawning chairs with splats formed of interlaced loopings with rococo foliage at the centre of the top rail and on the shoe above the back seat rail.

No fashionable eighteenth-century drawing room was complete without at least one commode, and Chippendale had included them as a new form, but referred to them as 'commode tables' in the *Director*. He envisaged their use in bedrooms, fitted with sliding shelves for clothes. He also produced designs for 'Commode-clothes-presses' and Ince and Mayhew referred to 'a commode chest of drawers'. It is not easy to sort out Chippendale's terminology, as to him a chest of drawers and a commode divided with drawers in a similar manner were synonymous: in fact he misses the appellation 'chest of drawers' from the title-page of the *Director* in all three editions. The craze for French

Tripod table, mahogany, c1755. H29, W26.
The pierced gallery of the table top is carved with scrolled foliage and medallions, and the fluted baluster support stands on tripod legs.

fashion enabled him to use 'commode' instead, and his readers to know what was meant. The French shape always had two doors hiding the drawers or shelves within, and that defines the difference to some degree.

Whilst the early chests of drawers were made in walnut up to about 1750, the early commodes were fashioned throughout in mahogany. No inlay was attempted, and the only decoration was the metal handles and escutcheons. Commodes are usually of four types—the earliest were in mahogany or japanned, whilst those which were painted or decorated with marquetry belong to the mid-1760s onwards (see Chapter 5). There are some splendid example of commodes attributed to Chippendale in which the front and sides are shaped and divided by flat pilasters with legs and aprons carved boldly in the rococo taste. Each of the three front interspaces formed between the pilasters has two drawers within it. A design of 1753 in the *Director* (Plate XLIII) for a commode shows sinuous cabriole legs, a delicate gadrooned edge to the top, and four drawers within a gentle, swelled front, separated by interlaced patterns of carving.

Close attention was paid to library and writing tables in both the first edition of Chippendale's *Director* and Ince and Mayhew's *Universal System* (1759–63). Chippendale illustrated six library tables in 1754 and eleven in 1762. They are all of the open pedestal type and indicate his care over ornament and convenience with open compartments for folio books and drawers from 'front to front' for holding maps and prints. He also designed a number of sideboard tables, to be made of

Centre table, mahogany, c1760. H31, W34, D23.
A pierced, waved gallery surrounds the rectangular top; cluster column legs with pierced, scrolled angle brackets form supports.

Mirror, giltwood, late 1750s. H62, W34.
The pierced mirror frame is carved with naturalistic birds and branches, 'C'-scrolls, rocaille ornament and scrolled acanthus. When gilded and in good condition, there are few finer evocations of the spritely rococo style than the English looking glass.

mahogany, with cabriole legs carved with floral pendants ending in paw-and-ball feet. However, the ornamental side tables in the Gothic and Chinese styles had straight legs. Where they were joined to a perforated latticework frieze, the attractive feature of pierced brackets was used. Some of the rococo console tables were examples of the carver's skill rather than functional designs. In those carved and gilt examples with marble tops following the designs (c 1755–60) of Thomas Johnson, branches of trees, birds, animals, and flowers are introduced in bewildering complexity. Enough survive to indicate that whilst fancy had run riot they were taken seriously and used, albeit with difficulty.

In the lesser categories of furniture were screens. Eyes were shielded from firelight by the *cheval* (horse)

screen. Chippendale illustrated *cheval* screens in the 1754 *Director* (Plate CXXVII). He explained that those standing on four feet were commonly called 'Horse Fire Screens' and that the woodwork 'should be gilt in burnished gold'. He also illustrated the folding and tripod types. Finally, the candlestand, fashionable from the early seventeenth century, enjoyed a new popularity when Chippendale illustrated no fewer than seventeen in the 3rd edition of the *Director*, (for example, Plate CXLIV), with a recommendation that between 3ft. 6ins. and 4ft. 6ins. was a convenient height for them. Gothic and rococo latticework could be used effectively in the shafts and trays and they stood sturdily on any form of tripod base.

Among the most accomplished examples of *Director* period furniture are the mirrors and girandoles. Both

Armchair, yew, c1755.
This is one from a set of seven Windsor chairs in the Gothic style, with pointed arched back and splats pierced with tracery. This style may not be easily adapted to furniture forms, but it is practical enough for robust pieces which might be used outdoors.

the first edition of the *Director* and Ince and Mayhew's pattern-book include them. There were many serious competitors in the 1750s to Chippendale, and we might start here with William Hallett, and his later partners William Vile and John Cobb. None of them had subscribed to the *Director*, so as to avoid any charge that they had copied (as many of lesser status did) its attractive designs. They had sufficient ability in any

case to survive by their own merits. Their senior partner, William Hallett (1707–81), had been successful enough with his accomplished mahogany furniture, and by an advantageous marriage to an heiress, to buy the site of Cannons, the 1st Duke of Chandos's great house at Whitchurch, Middlesex, and to build himself a house on its centre vaults. William Vile trained under Hallett, and in 1751, together with a Norfolk-born upholsterer, John Cobb, he set up in partnership near to Chippendale in St. Martin's Lane. Hallett acted as their financial backer and continued to support them for the rest of their lives. He outlived Vile, who died in 1767, and Cobb, who died in 1778. Examples of oval beads on furniture attributed to Vile in the early 1750s show the hazards of crediting authorship without documentation. The mahogany table press made by Benjamin Goodison for the Earl of Leicester at Holkham in 1751 also has applied ovals on each side. There are indications that the freelance carver Sefferin Alken supplied them to several makers, including Vile. The latter does seem to have made some furniture with elaborate pierced frets; here again the attribution rests on comparison, this time with the fret top to the bureau-secretaire he made for Queen Charlotte in 1761.

There were other able contenders for a patron's purse and interest—in particular, William and John Linnell, William Ince and John Mayhew, the carver Thomas Johnson (at least for his designs) and the French *ébéniste* resident in London, Pierre Langlois. We have noted that in the 1750s the Linnells secured one of their most important commissions, to provide the 4th Duke of Beaufort with a japanned bed, eight armchairs, two pairs of standing shelves and a commode *en suite* for the Chinese bedroom at Badminton House, Gloucestershire.

When Ince and Mayhew had established the outline of a business, they decided, in 1759, to issue designs 'in weekly numbers'. They imitated Chippendale's *Director* both in the intended number of plates (160) and in the use of Matthew Darly as engraver. Unfortunately they underestimated the amount of work required, and they had to compete with the build-up by Chippendale to his third edition; the venture foundered in the autumn of 1760 after the appearance of Part 21. The astute Robert Sayer, one of the most successful eighteenth-century print-sellers, not averse to plagiarism when it suited him, then issued about 90 of the engravings in a large folio titled *Universal System of Household Furniture*. It was dedicated to George Spencer, 4th Duke of Marlborough, for whom the firm were later to work at Blenheim Palace. Rococo, with Gothic and Chinese overtones, formed the main style of the designs. Some were unashamedly copied from the 1754 edition of the *Director*, but explanatory notes were printed in both English and French.

As one of the most accomplished carvers of his generation, if the suites of engravings of the late 1750s

Armchair, mahogany, c1755.
This chair is one from a set of four in the Chinese taste, the back and arms filled with latticework and other designs. The drop seat is covered with needlework. Contemporary critics castigated the creators of the style in which 'all was Chinese', but designs in Chippendale's *Director* (1754) encouraged the demand.
Prov: Ingress Abbey, Kent.

Chair, mahogany, c1755. H39, W26.
One from a set of four, this chair has the back splat carved with riband bows and 'C'-scrolls. The seat is upholstered in contemporary needlework. This design is taken almost exactly from Plate XVI in Chippendale's *Director* (1754). The chair is in the Victoria and Albert Museum (No: W.56–1926).

Girandoles, giltwood c1755–60.
h40. w17.
The gilt mirror frames are carved with scrollwork and wave ornament motifs typical of the rococo style. Such spirited creations owe much to contemporary engravings by talented carvers such as Thomas Johnson (b. 1714)., and also plagiarize French engraved ornaments.
Prov: Fountains Hall, Ripon.

bearing his name are any guide to his real abilities, Thomas Johnson (1714–*c* 1778) was teaching carving, drawing and modelling. He had already published several suites of engravings in a flamboyant rococo style in the 1750s, and his name is associated with a small range of highly mannered furniture. Not least in this connection is a set of four candlesticks, *c* 1758, which correspond closely to a 1756 design in his *One Hundred and Fifty New Designs* (which was freely adapted by Chippendale in the 1762 edition of the *Director*, Plate CXIV). Two are now at the Philadelphia Museum, one at the Victoria and Albert Museum and one at Temple Newsam House, Leeds. They have lobed tops supported on an irregular shaft of clustered columns, entwined by a pair of dolphins mounted on an intermediate triangular base of piled rockwork. Made for George, 1st Lord Lyttelton, of Hagley Hall, Worcestershire, they are in the vanguard of all rococo furniture of the 1750s.

Many of Johnson's designs, unlike those of Lock, were, however, marred by an excess of ornament blurring the structural outlines. Circular and oval mirrors were also given in every pattern-book, with carved squirrels perched on the crestings and long-beaked birds, rush fronds, bulrushes, central heads of Apollo and floral sprays. Among the most attractive mirrors are the overmantel examples, in which a rectangle would be surrounded by a froth of exuberant carving, with paintings often incorporated in an upper or lower stage, and brackets provided to display oriental porcelain. A lively imagination was a first requirement for a carver, and in those examples which incorporated depictions of architecture and ruins Chippendale urged that the ornament 'must be carved very bold, so that the ruins may serve as bas-relief'.

The French *ébéniste* Pierre Langlois, born in Paris about 1738, had settled in London by the late 1750s and is known only by furniture completed within a very short period of time. His trade-card recorded 'all sorts of fine Cabinets and Commodes made and inlaid in the Politest manner with Brass and Tortoiseshell . . .' His first known commission was for the 4th Duke of Bedford in 1759, and suggests that by that year his reputation was established in London.

Commodes were Pierre Langlois's speciality. He created them in bold serpentine form in the early 1760s, with doors or drawers, and decorated with coloured marquetry of flowers and musical instruments set against light-coloured herringbone-pattern backgrounds. The tops, inlaid with brass or marquetry, were set on deal carcases. The inexpensive deal was used in chamfered panels at the back, and painted black to hide its cheapness. The corner ormolu mounts, wreathing down the curved legs and terminating in a scroll foot and volute, were presumably imported from France—some examples have a crown 'C' mark, showing that tax has been paid—or were cast from French examples.

It was at this stage of his career, the early 1760s when he was turning forty years old, that Chippendale demonstrated the extent of his mature abilities and business acumen. The rising star in the architectural firmament was Robert Adam (1728–92), fresh back in 1758 from four years' training in Italy and bent on introducing English patrons to a refined form of the antique-classicism adapted in a linear and elegant way to a new style of decoration. Any furniture-maker who wanted to be in on the profitable vogue had to change his whole output from rococo, Gothic and Chinese, intermeshed as they were, to precise neo-classical shapes. This subject was addressed by Chippendale in the 3rd edition of the *Director* (1762). The tide of opinion had been turning slowly throughout the 1750s, lacking focus and impetus, but accepting the archaeological designs found in the publications of Robert Wood and James Dawkins, *Ruins of Palmyra* (1753) and the *Ruins of Balbec* (1757), and in Piranesi's etchings of the remains of ancient civilizations. James Stuart, William Chambers and Robert Adam had all returned from studying in Italy and embarked on neo-classical projects. However, it has been suggested that, important as these books and events were, the percipient Chippendale had started to design furniture which revealed neo-classical precepts 'at least three years before Robert

Adam's first essay in this style'. He 'experimented with fluted term legs, combined with rails treated as a Doric frieze; he used caryatid supports united to a Doric entablature and employed classical demi-figures on the open lower stage of a cabinet and stand.' (Christopher Gilbert, *The Life and Work of Thomas Chippendale*, 1978.) Elegant ovals were made to serve for looking glass shapes, girandoles incorporated picturesque classical ruins, lions' masks, rams' heads, husks in festoons and swags, paterae, square tapered legs—all these elements and more were blended into the 3rd edition *Director* designs. The clients were even more eager to see them made than they had been half a dozen years before when 'all the world was Chinese'.

In the transitional period in the early 1760s, when rococo was giving way slowly to neo-classical styling, Chippendale was asked to supply furniture to Sir Lawrence Dundas of Aske Hall in north Yorkshire, who also had homes at Moor Park, Hertfordshire, and 19 Arlington Street, London. The latter is best known through Zoffany's enchanting portrait of Sir Lawrence and his grandson sitting in the library at Arlington Street. Chippendale worked for many patrons of Robert Adam, but is firmly documented as working to Adam's precise design when he executed a suite of furniture, including three sofas, for Sir Lawrence. This remained in the possession of Sir Lawrence Dundas's successor, the Marquess of Zetland, until four armchairs were sold by Christie's on 26 April 1934—when they offered the major contents of 19 Arlington Street for sale—and more furniture was sold on 5 July 1963 at Sotheby's. Some pieces are now at the Victoria and Albert Museum, some at Temple Newsam House and some at Aske Hall. The whole story of the documentation and furniture of this rich collection has been recorded (*Apollo*, September 1967).

By the mid-1760s the classical style was beginning to affect design and decoration and to oust the exotic and sinuous styles. Whilst in analysis the 3rd edition of the *Director* contains only a few designs in the new mode, Chippendale's workshop and those of his competitors were adapting to meet the demand for classically-inspired furniture from the imperious and knowledgeable patrons of Robert Adam and his many architect rivals.

China cabinet, mahogany, c1764. H37, W34.
The form of this cabinet could be derived from the lower part of a design for 'A China Table and Shelf' in Ince and Mayhew's *The*

Universal System of Household Furniture (1762, Plate XLVI). As cabinet-makers they rivalled Chippendale.
Prov: The Earls of Dysart, Ham House, Richmond, Surrey.

1.   Side table, giltwood, c1758. w61.

On the stretcher of the table, an elaborate waterfall issues from a ruined wall, alongside drinking deer and a male figure. The composition is hardly practical, but it undoubtedly pleased patrons fascinated by the rococo and Chinese styles. Tables of a similar design were published by the carver Thomas Johnson (1714–c1778) in his various collections of designs, published in and around 1758.

The intermesh and counterpoise between two of the four dominant styles of the eighteenth century—Palladian, rococo, Chinese, neo-classical—is here apparent. The spritely rococo style merges almost imperceptibly into that of the Chinese, which is made obvious only by the two unwinking Mandarin figures. A further subtle feature of the obsession with things Chinese was the use of stylized blind frets which were used to decorate, in particular, the friezes of tables. Legs varied between those of sinuous rococo form with entwined tendrils to more precise curves, and square ones, delicately enriched with raised patterns in shallow panels.

2.   Console Table, giltwood, c1755. w48.

Whether tables should be supported by representations of rockwork flanked by seated and standing Mandarin figures wearing straw hats is arguable. The situation arises because the unknown maker is committed to the chinoiserie style, rife in England in the mid-1750s. It attracted equal support and abuse, but produced, at least to many eyes, pieces which were lively and innovative, if almost impractical.

3.   *Side table, mahogany, c1765. w58.*
The frieze, with egg and dart moulding, is applied to the table with blind fretwork, and the legs are similarly decorated to include rosettes and bell-flowers. The elements combine to form a practical and well-proportioned whole.

5.   *Centre table, mahogany, c1760. w38.*
The serpentine top of the table has a brass gallery of interlaced Gothic arcading, and a frieze with blind fretwork in the Chinese manner. Cabinet-makers such as William Vile achieved high quality in such tables, with strong construction of delicate components and superb carving on the cabriole legs.

4.   *Pembroke table, mahogany, c1765. w24.*
Here is a practical table with two robust flaps, but one in which style has not been lost sight of. The deeply-moulded legs of almost cabriole form, with over-scrolled tops and in-scrolled rococo feet, may be compared with the legs of a writing table in Chippendale's third edition of the *Director* (1762, Plate LXXII). The rectangular platform has a kneehole recess.

The curve was a familiar element in mid-eighteenth-century design, and was given additional emphasis when William Hogarth (1697–1764) published his The Analysis of Beauty in 1753. He tried to vindicate the undulating line, the 'S'-curve of so much rococo furniture, as the 'line of beauty'. He failed because he could not really define the exact degree of curvature necessary for such a line. Nevertheless, his discussion of linear values, whilst perhaps little understood by furniture-makers intent on making a living, were arresting in an age of formalism. Waving lines were meant in Hogarth's words to lead the eyes on 'a wanton kind of chase'. These tables do just that.

1.   Side table, giltwood, c1755. H34, L68, D31.
A fluted table frame bearing a marble top seems restrained enough, but high-quality asymmetrical carving, with deep-cut mask faces and disporting *putti*, show to what lengths a carver would go to satisfy a patron, such as the 4th Earl of Shaftesbury, fascinated by the rococo style.
Prov: The Earl of Shaftesbury, St Giles's House, Dorset.

Side table, mahogany, by William Gomm; 1764. H33, W49, D31.

he table was supplied to the 5th Lord Leigh by William Gomm & n of Clerkenwell Close, for the Chapel at Stoneleigh Abbey. The voice, dated 30 June 1764, ran as follows: 'An Exceeding handsome ahog^y Communion Table the feet very neatly Carved with Flowers & foliage, the Frame very richly Carv'd, on the Front a Cherubims Head, Foliage & Flowers a Solid Mahog^y Top, the edge neatly Carv'd . . . £31 10s.' The old-fashioned design was probably dictated by the existing rococo decoration in the Chapel. By 1786 it had been moved and was being used as a side table.

1. *Tripod table, mahogany, c1760. Diam 24.*
The delicate turned spindles and lozenges of the pierced gallery of this table are practical, allowing spaces for the fingers to lift the top from the tripod base for use as a tray.
Prov: Earl of Brownlow, Belton House, Lincolnshire.

2. *Tripod table, mahogany, c1755. Diam 26.*
Such tables are often referred to as 'in the Chippendale style', through loose association to patterns in his *Director*. The pierced gallery has a railing pattern, but it is the deep carving on the baluster support, the knees of the cabriole legs and the spirited scroll feet which satisfy the eye.
Prov: The Mount Trust.

3. *Kettle stand, mahogany, c1760. Diam (top) 12.*
The spirally-fluted baluster shows the turner's skill, and the fretwork gallery is pierced with a delicate variation of Chinese railing. Together with the splayed tripod base, the piece forms a stable and pleasing stand for a silver tea-kettle.

4. *Tripod table, mahogany, c1755. Diam 24.*
Different types of decoration were used for such tables: this one has an octagonal tip-up top with canted fretwork, supported on a robust tripod.

A design is at its best when it does not allow stylistic embellishment to hinder function. The galleried tops of the small tripod tables, whilst illusive in appearance of Chinese open fretwork, are designed to prevent objects falling off. The tops of the rectangular or square tables are designed to be neat and useful when folded over their supporting curved legs, but to function additionally when opened out on expanding sections, stays, or, in some cases, extra legs or gates. In the fully opened position, design and function perhaps transcend appearance, but some attempt is made to have all three with the use of the deep Gothic fret.

5. *Card table, mahogany, c1755. w34, d17.*
This is one of a pair of tables in the full Chippendale *Director* manner. The table top opens on a concertina action, whereby part of the frame is hinged and moves to support the fold-over top. The carving on the cabriole legs is well accomplished: rosette and ribbon ornament snake down to the French toes.
Prov: The Earl of Sefton, Croxteth Hall, Liverpool.

6. *Card table, mahogany, by Thomas Chippendale, c1760. h28, w37, d18.*
The legs of this superb table, one of a pair, flow in assured style into the tablet-centred frieze at the front, and are enhanced by very delicate carving. The tablet bears a marquess's coronet, framed by a laurel and wheatear swag.

7. *Dressing table, mahogany, c1760. w (open) 43.*
This piece incorporates a mixture of styles—the blind fretwork on the frieze and legs is in Chinese taste, and the open tracery at the front and sides is Gothic. The centre of the top lifts to reveal a mirror, fitted trays and compartments. The moulded feet conceal castors. The design is an adaptation of Thomas Chippendale's 'Breakfast Table' in the *Director* (2nd edition, 1755).

1.   *Armchair, mahogany, c1760.*
This is one from a set of twelve chairs, including two armchairs, in the Gothic style, with back and arm rests filled with tracery and cluster column legs. This set was probably ordered by William Fitzherbert of Tissington Hall at the time he made Gothic improvements to the house around 1760. His friendship with Horace Walpole undoubtedly inspired his interest in the style.

The Gothic chair almost seems to employ ecclesiastical window-tracery as a pattern for the back and arm supports. However, this was dictated by a mid-eighteenth-century fascination with medievalizing objects for which no prototype existed in the Middle Ages. In spite of its Gothic trimmings, it would have bewildered 'the doughtiest knight that ever strode within an ancient castle' and the late Lord Clark even described such medieval designs as 'monsters' and 'unusually misbegotten'.

The French style of the armchair was, however, seen by Chippendale and his contemporaries as highly acceptable to those of their patrons who were fascinated, by contrast, with 'rococo work of high quality' of the late 1750s.

2.   *Library armchair, mahogany, c1765. H38, W29.*
The controlled rococo form of this chair, one of a pair, derives from two designs for 'French Chairs' included by Chippendale in the 3rd edition of the *Director* (1762, Plate XXIII). In this edition Chippendale was gradually coming to terms with the fact that he would need to turn to neo-classical forms. There is every evidence that whoever carved this chair had no such inclination: here is rococo work of high quality.

The mid-eighteenth-century armchair was at the forefront of the chair-maker's skill, demanding a careful concern for style, balance, upholstery and, lastly, comfort. The mahogany frames provided ample opportunity for the display of the current styles and of needlework, took carving well, and by the inherent strength of the wood gave years of service. Several examples here reflect the importance of Thomas Chippendale's pattern-book, the Director, which went into three editions (1754, 1755 and 1762) in eight years. As the various editions reflected the interplay of rococo and Chinese, it was inevitable that the furniture itself incorporated the relevant motifs. But as much is owed to patrons who had the courage to buy it.

1.   *Armchair, mahogany, c1755. H38, W24.*
The back of this chair, with its waved top rail and pierced interlaced splat carved with foliage, corresponds almost exactly to a design included in the 1st edition of the *Director* (1754, Plate XII). This does not imply that Chippendale made it: merely that some competent maker with access to his pattern-book did so.

2.   *Armchair, bamboo, c1760.*
One of four, this chair, with its octagonal shape and openwork panels, is in the Chinese style made popular in England by the architect William Chambers (1723–96). Bamboo furniture originated in the East, and Chambers would have seen examples when he travelled to the Orient as a young man with the Swedish East Indies Company.

3.   *Armchair, mahogany, attributed to Thomas Chippendale, c1760.*
This armchair is one of a set of ten, including its pair, which are similar to a documented set by Chippendale. They are close to patterns in his 1st and 3rd editions of the *Director* (1754, 1762), and might be held as a late manifestation of the Chinese style, with pierced pagoda top rails and moulded backs filled with Chinese paling.
Prov: The Dixon-Johnson family of Aykley Heads, Co. Durham.

4.   *Armchair, mahogany, c1760.*
One of a pair in the Chippendale style, this armchair has a Gothic-pattern back rail carved with tassels and a central coat of arms. The robust legs are connected by chamfered stretchers that do little to help the appearance overall: one of restrained 'movement' on curved surfaces.

5.   *Armchair, mahogany, c1760. H38, W28.*
The seat rail of this fine chair is restrained, in contrast to the boldly carved legs, which are designed with acanthus, triple cabochons and 'C'-scrolls. The design overall is related to that for a 'French Chair' in Chippendale's second edition of the *Director* (1755, Plate XIX).
Prov: Godmersham Park, Kent.

6.   *Armchair, mahogany, c1760.*
One of a pair, the armchair is a plain example of the type called 'French' by Chippendale and other makers. It is covered in damask and could have been used as a library chair.
Prov: The Earl of Sefton, Croxteth Hall, Liverpool.

7.   *Armchair, mahogany, c1755.*
The arm supports, seat rail and cabriole legs of the chair are carved in the rococo 'French' taste. The needlework on the back and seat was worked by Lady Barbara North, a daughter of the 8th Earl of Pembroke, who married Dudley North of Glemham in 1730 and died in 1755.
Prov: Glemham Hall, Suffolk.

1. *Armchair, mahogany, c1760.*
This is one of a pair with latticework back and arms and pierced stretcher. The arm rests and drop-in seat are upholstered, but it is the railing of the frame, suggesting close adherence to the Chinese style, which dominates the design.

British relations with China, established by commerce and strengthened by the importation of its manufactures, led to interest in copying the oriental originals. The adaptation of Chinese paling was a feature of the mid-eighteenth-century pattern-books, and was copied for the backs of chairs and garden seats. Equally it was an insatiable interest in collecting, encouraged by long travels in Europe on the Grand Tour, that led to the creation of collectors' cabinets. These housed a multiplicity of small objets. No one could check the passion for things Chinese or the mania of collecting, sanctioned as they were by people of wealth and fashion, who brooked no interference with their infatuations.

2.   *The Brand Cabinet, rosewood, c1750. H50, W38, D8.*
This hanging display cabinet in severe architectural, neo-classical style, is very similar to one now in the Victoria and Albert Museum that was made in 1743 for Horace Walpole, a close friend of Thomas Brand. Both cabinets were almost certainly made by the same hand, and for ardent collectors of 'curiosities'. We know that Walpole used his cabinet to 'contain my enamels and miniatures'. The doors are mounted with ivory plaques of classical subjects.
Prov: made for Thomas Brand; thence by descent to Viscount Hampden, The Hoo, Bedfordshire.

1. Chair, walnut, c1755.
One of a pair, the back of the chair is a simplified form of such designs found in the *Director*. The legs, with their claw-and-ball feet, and the deep apron are rather old fashioned, and the chair was probably made by a provincial craftsman for a patron a little out of touch with the current vogue.

2. Chair, mahogany, c1765.
One of a pair, the chair is in the style of chair-maker Robert Manwaring, with the characteristic back of interlaced loops he popularized in his books. The seat is upholstered and the chair bears the label of 'H. Carpenter, 17 & 18 Nassau St., Mortimer St., W'.

3. Chair, mahogany, c1760.
One from a set of six dining chairs in the style of Chippendale, this example has a fine back splat of pierced Gothic arches, and quatrefoils in the top rail. The seat is covered in Soho tapestry, which is fastened to the rails with two rows of brass nails.

4. Chair, mahogany, c1760.
One from a set of six, including two armchairs, this piece has a waved ladder back and a leather upholstered seat. This simple rendering of a popular design could have been made in the provinces, as the relationship between the heavy legs and the back is not well managed.

The splat of a chair—the central member of the back—was a small area which reacted well to the skill of the chair-maker. He had to incorporate elements which were strong enough to support the sitter resting against it, but could not resist embellishing the mahogany with Gothic or other patterns. Robert Manwaring's two books for chair-makers of 1765–66 popularized his particular form of interlaced loops. But Chippendale, Mayhew and Ince and others had been engaged for the previous ten years in providing endless designs for carved variations of the splat. They were even put together in matching pairs to form attractive settee backs.

Chair, mahogany, c1760.
The chair is one from a set of twelve dining chairs, including a pair of armchairs, and has Gothic-pattern back splats. It could be argued that an important architectural style like Gothic does not translate easily to a chair back, unless the maker has outstanding skills.

Settee, walnut, 1755. w55.
From a set including two settees and six chairs, the twin backs of this settee have vase-shaped splats with pierced fretwork. The drop-in seat is particularly well related in constructional terms to the slightly splayed and attractively panelled outer front legs. Nevertheless, the eye can still suppose that two chairs are joined together awkwardly.

It could be argued that the three most important categories of furniture are beds, chairs and tables. They allow some form of civilized existence to be pursued, attended as they are by countless variants and additions. The small portable tables at which one can write, read, play games, take tea, or use to serve from, were refined continuously through the eighteenth century. The frames could bear wooden or marble tops, be made to fold or rise at an angle, contain drawers and slides, as well as show the embellishments on edges and friezes of the carvers' skills. Little more could be expected.

1. Side table, mahogany, attributed to John Cobb, c1765. W72. The severe rectangular form of this table, with classical decoration of Vitruvian scrolls on the frieze, still shows evidence of the rococo style in its scrolled angle brackets. Cobb continued his business after the death of his partner William Vile in 1767.

2. Card table, mahogany, c1762. W36.
One of a pair of tables, this is similar to a design in William Ince and John Mayhew's *The Universal System of Household Furniture* (1762, Plate LII). The Gothic blind fretwork on the frieze and the small apron, carved with a wave pattern, are rococo elements which combine with the new, more formal, neo-classical style now being slowly introduced.

3. Reading table, mahogany, c1760. H30. W28.
The adjustable easel top of the table is covered in leather, and two drawers are fitted in the frieze. The richly-carved shaft and cabriole legs betoken an excellent craftsman. This table has similarities to a Plate (XXVI) in Ince and Mayhew's *Household Furniture* (1762).
Prov: Eleanor, Lady Abercromby.

. *Side table, mahogany, c1763.*
42.

he sinuous profile of this table
nd the crisply carved legs bear a
esemblance to the work of
William Vile. He set up in
ondon in partnership with John
.obb in 1751, and continued,
vith work for the Royal family,
ntil his death in 1767.

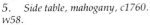

5.   *Side table, mahogany, c1760.*
w58.
Whilst the mania for things
Chinese — this table has finely-
carved blind frets on frieze and
legs — was declining somewhat
by 1760, it still enjoyed a strong
provincial following for a few
more years. The third edition of
Chippendale's *Director* (1762)
showed patterns which used
such motifs, and many provincial
makers copied the metropolitan
fashion. It was the gradual
domination of objects in the early
1760s by the new mood for
antiquity, and for classical
pattern, which eclipsed what
many critics saw, unthinkingly,
as the barbarity of the Chinese
style.

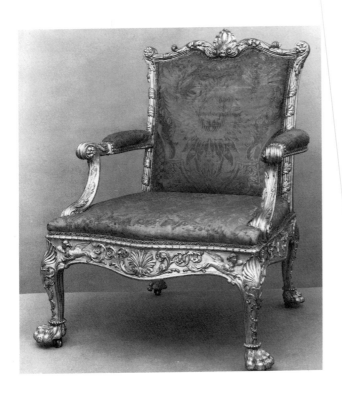

In his pattern-book the **Director** (1754), Thomas Chippendale gave some recommendations about upholstery. Of some chairs he wrote: 'these seats look best when stuffed over the Rails, but are most commonly done with brass Nails in one or two Rows . . . they are usually covered with the same stuff as the window curtains'. For the French elbow chairs he said that 'both the backs and seats must be covered with Tapestry or other sort of needlework'. Some additional attention was drawn to both nailing patterns and the fabrics used by the rococo forms of seat rail and leg. The sinuous lines of carved mahogany acted as a frame to hold the stuffing, linen undercovers and webbing firmly in place. There was also the chance for an occasional collaboration of pre-eminent designer and furnituremaker. Robert Adam and Thomas Chippendale realized the armchair (1) for Sir Lawrence Dundas (see page 166).

1.   *Armchair, gilt beechwood, made by Thomas Chippendale to the design of Robert Adam, 1765.*
The armchair is from an important suite of furniture, consisting of eight armchairs and four sofas, which was designed by Robert Adam in 1764 for Sir Lawrence Dundas's London house. The bill, amounting to £160, from Thomas Chippendale was for '8 large Arm Chairs exceeding richly carved in the Antick manner and Gilt in oil Gold stuffed and cover'd with your own Damask . . .' The commission is the only documented example of Adam and Chippendale's direct collaboration.
Prov: The Marquess of Zetland, 19 Arlington Street, London. One now in the Victoria and Albert Museum; others at Aske Hall, Richmond, Yorkshire.

2.   *Armchair, mahogany, c1760.*
The back, arms and seat of the chair are covered in *gros point* needlework. The rococo style is still apparent in the curvilinear outlines, scrolled arm rests and cabriole legs, although it was soon to be ousted by the onrush of neo-classical forms.

3.   *Armchair, giltwood, c1755.*
One of a pair in the 'French' manner, this armchair has similarities with Plate xx in the *Director* (1755). It is realized with great verve: wonderfully scrolled rear legs and arm supports are joined to the serpentine seat rails amid carved scallop shells, bulrushes and cabochons.
Prov: The Earl of Harrington, Elvaston Castle, Derbyshire.

Armchair, giltwood, attributed to John Cobb, c1765. H41, W28.
his is one from a suite consisting of six library armchairs and two
·ttees. One chair is inscribed in pencil 'Robt. France'. When William
·le died in 1767, his partner John Cobb continued as a furniture-
·aker. William France had trained under them and took on some of
·eir royal work from 1763. Robert France, obviously a relative, is
·nrecorded other than by this inscription.

5.   *Settee, giltwood, attributed to John Cobb, 1768. H40, W101.*
The settee is part of the suite described above. The suite is
traditionally thought to have come from Croome Court, where there
was another set of six chairs and two sofas in mahogany of precisely
the same design, and probably made in 1761 by William Vile and John
Cobb. Bills survive, dated 1768, from John Cobb 'For 8 french pattern
arm'd Chairs Carv'd and gilt in burnish'd gold, with hollow backs,
stuffed & quilted in Linnen . . . gilt nails . . . & Covering do Comp
with your Crimson silk damask' and 'for two french sofas, stuff'd and
quilted in Linnen . . . and the frame Carv'd and gilt in burnish'd
gold', which could have applied to this suite. If so, it is interesting
that Lord Coventry should have ordered a set of old-fashioned
rococo-style chairs in 1768, identical to those he had purchased seven
years earlier.

6.   Inscription, in pencil, 'Robt. France', on one of the chairs, above.

1.   *Chairs, mahogany, 1765. H37, W (armchair) 27.*
These two dining chairs are from a set of eight, which
includes a pair of armchairs. The arrangement of the
backs derives from a design in the 2nd edition of
Chippendale's *Director* (1755, Plate XII). This was
copied by many provincial cabinet-makers, a
testimony to Chippendale's competence and the
popularity of his book on many a work-bench.
Prov: 1st Viscount Clive, Walcot Hall, Shropshire.

2.   *Chair, giltwood, c1765. W (seat) 24.*
This is one of a set of six, of which two bear
inscriptions: 'DC/SC/AI' and 'R.O. Fayle Sept 23 1765'.
The seat rails are particularly attractive, being carved
with 'C'-scrolls centred by shells, with moulded
cabochons and acanthus at the heads of the legs. The
padded backs and upholstered seats of all six chairs
are covered in Chinese cream silk embroidered with
flower-sprays.

3. Settee, giltwood, c1760. w72.

This settee poses all the hazards of attribution: it is competent and similar to documented work by Chippendale, with its undulating rococo framework carved with neo-classical motifs of a central anthemion, paterae and husk chains. However, no relevant bills have been found for its documentation.

The graduations of seating furniture are many and subtle, but in basic form comprise the stool, chair and settee. Either the seat was covered in leather, fabric, or some other related material such as wool needlework on canvas, or, as usual in stools, fashioned from a solid piece of wood. Competent furniture-makers had to maintain a stock of all the component parts to make up into the finished article. They had also to be able to upholster to specific requirements, to have coats-of-arms painted when necessary and finally to set up the furniture— and all the accompanying curtains and bed hangings, carpets and even wallpaper—at the house itself. Morbidly, many of them also specialized in arranging funerals—of those who had sat sedately on the stools, chairs and settees, which had been provided but paid for tardily, if at all.

4. Stool, painted to simulate oak, c1765. w23.
The seat of this hall stool is painted with the Radnor armorial achievement, and the central cartouche on the curved support bears the family crest and coronet. The design is similar to stools Chippendale made for Christ Church, Oxford.
Prov: Miss M. E. Pleydell-Bouverie.

5. Stool, mahogany, c1764. w23.
The design of this piece conforms to the large set of stools for the library at Christ Church, Oxford, supplied by Thomas Chippendale in 1764. In The Life and Work of Thomas Chippendale (1978), Christopher Gilbert suggests that other local makers probably copied Chippendale's design, as there are several similar sets in other Oxford buildings.

1. *Coffer, mahogany, c1755. w49.*
The front and sides of the coffer are panelled with Gothic arcading and trefoils, with corners of cluster columns. For forty years, Horace Walpole's enthusiasm for Gothic never wavered: he was at the head of a prevailing taste, and his home, 'Strawberry Hill', was the outstanding exemplar.

2. *Cabinet, black and gold lacquer, c1765. w58.*
Few pieces of furniture are visually as splendid as those which incorporate black and gold lacquer panels. With the depiction in gold of Chinese buildings, mountains and trees, the cabinet is arresting as a single piece. However it is *en suite* to another, and the pair were in the collections at Harewood House, Yorkshire, and are attributed to Thomas Chippendale. The bills relating to Chippendale's activity at Harewood are incomplete, and start only when a considerable amount of furniture had already been supplied.

3. *Chest, mahogany, c1760. H32, W42, D24.*
The serpentine chest exhibits careful craftsmanship in the choice of woods, with alternating rosewood and fruitwood stripes framed by ebonized and boxwood lines. It was also made to be useful, having at the top a fitted dressing drawer with divided interior. The dust was excluded from this by a baize-lined slide. Finally, it was given rococo gilt-bronze handles.

4. *Commode, mahogany, c1760. w42.*
One of a pair, this commode is decorated with fretwork of various designs. The dominant style is Chinese, which runs over the two doors and even on the bracket feet. The fact that the doors hide sliding shelves seems almost incidental beneath the riot of carving.
Prov: The Earl of Chichester, Stanmer, Sussex.

The large areas of the fronts and sides of chests and commodes (the latter is merely the French name for a chest of drawers) allowed the furniture-maker to display his skills in a variety of ways. He could fashion the carcase in serpentine form and then cleverly cover over the shape with thin veneers, chosen carefully to show the grain and figuring, and often edged with contrasting woods for a heightened effect. Lacquered panels, either from the orient or copied in England, could also form part of the decoration. Furthermore, a few pieces of furniture could be more attractively fitted with gilded mounts, to draw attention to the subtle lines of the shape, its doors and drawers, and the feet, corners and key-holes.

5.   *Chest, mahogany, c1760.* W44.
This chest has a restrained elegance, which comes from its satisfying proportions, the curved shape of the carcase and the large, rococo, ormolu handles. A slide is carefully inserted above the top drawer: neat, unobtrusive, eminently practical.

6.   *Chest, mahogany, c1762.* H44, W55, D25.
Ince and Mayhew publish a design in *The Universal System of Household Furniture* (1762) for a 'Comode Chest of Drawers' (Plate XLIII) which, except for the handles, exactly conforms to this piece in every detail. That detail shows unerring attention to choice of wood, its figuring, applied decoration, and, above all, carefully balanced proportions.

7.   *Commode, mahogany, c1755–60.* W51.
In stylistic terms, this commode is part of a group in the French taste, which includes one made in the late 1750s for the 9th Duke of Norfolk for Norfolk House, London. It has a cross-banded serpentine rising top, fitted with two false drawers and two long drawers. The ormolu mounts are cast with shells, 'C'-scrolls and masks, and the carrying handles on the sides are centred with masks and scrolled plates cast with rocaille cover, hoof feet. The veneers of quartered panels at the centre and sides of each drawer front, and on the side panels, are a particularly attractive feature, applied by a skilled craftsman.
Prov: Wateringbury House, Kent.

1. *Library writing table, mahogany and pine, c1758. L32, W80, D68.*
The table can be dated to about 1758, when the Countess of Pomfret's Gothic Revival London house, Pomfret Castle in Arlington Street, was completed. Following her death, the table obviously stayed at the house, and Horace Walpole refers in 1779 to W. G. 'Single Speech' Hamilton residing there. He gave it to his nephew, and by descent it came finally to the saleroom. It bears an engraved brass tablet recording W. G. Hamilton's ownership. The cluster columns and carved tracery on the cupboard doors are indicative of the motifs of the Gothic style, which was thought suitable for library furniture. The table is now at Temple Newsam House, Leeds (No. 426).

2. *Commode, mahogany, pine and oak, c1760–65. H35, W53, D31.*
This commode is one of a pair, the companion of which is now at the Temple Newsam House, Leeds. According to family tradition, it was owned by William-Wyndham Grenville, Bt., Prime Minister to George III. No relevant documentation has been traced, but it can be tentatively ascribed to Vile and Cobb, who favoured this ambitious yet restrained form. The door frames have pierced and engraved gilt-brass grilles, centring on circular fronded whorls. All corners are set with elaborate fronded mounts. The commode is now at the Victoria and Albert Museum (No: W.32–1977).

We know all too little about the various specialists who assisted the creation of fine furniture. Here are three pieces which show skills additional to those of the maker—in carving and the working of brass. The Gothic style motifs on the library table (1), the engraved gilt-brass grilles in the doors of the commode (2) and the carved mahogany foliate ovals on that attributed to William Vile (3), are all evidence of sub-divisions of skilled attention overall. Many of the specialists—as indeed the furniture-makers—remain anonymous: whilst some 50,000 or more names of makers were published in 1986, it is tantalizingly evident that they are but a significant talented portion of a much greater whole.

3.   *Commode, mahogany, c1760–65. H36, W41, D21.*
When such carved, foliated ovals are applied to the doors or sides of furniture of this period, the piece is inevitably attributed to William Vile (d. 1767). This is because he supplied a bookcase to Queen Charlotte, in 1762, which has such ovals (now in the Royal Collection). However, other makers, such as William Hallett and Benjamin Goodison, did use similar ovals, which may have been supplied by a specialist carver such as Sefferin Alken (*fl*.1744–83). Whatever the correct attribution, the curved forms of the serpentine front and overall attention to detail of this commode are consistent with the output of a quality London shop.

1. *Commode, lacquer, c1760, H37, W58, D26.*
The commode is one of a pair, with doors and sides veneered with panels of Chinese lacquer, cut from screens showing scenes in gold and vermilion on a black ground. Another similar pair of commodes remain at Uppark, Sussex. All four were probably ordered (from an unknown maker) by Sir Matthew Fetherstonhaugh, Bt. He returned from the Continent in 1751, and with his wife Sarah Lethieullier, daughter of a rich merchant, set about the decoration and furnishing of Uppark.

2. The commode open, showing the drawers which are concealed behind the two doors containing panels of lacquer.

*Commode, mahogany, slate top,
760–65. H36, W72, D26.*

his commode, one of a pair,
ay be attributed to William Vile
. 1767), on the basis of a very
milar one attributed to his
stwhile apprentice, John
adburn. The shaped drawer
onts flanking the oval are false,
it both commodes have four
ak drawers sliding on channels,
idden behind the two panelled
oors.

rov: Earls of Leven and Melville.

B. Sprague Allen's *Tides in
nglish Taste (1958) it is noted:
When it is realized that lacquer
as imported from the Orient
id France and was also being
anufactured on a large scale in
igland itself, one can surmise
what an extent japanned furn-
ure was a rival of porcelain as a
edium by which an element of
coticism was introduced into
e corniced and pilastered apart-
ents of English mansions . . .'
ere Chinese lacquer panels have
en cut up and mounted to form
1 attractive commode (1). In
ntrast, the French ébéniste
ierre Langlois has used veneer-
ig and good mounts to achieve a
imparable effect: furniture
hich assailed the eye with its
iape, beauty and evident
uality.*

*Commode, mahogany, c1765.
'59.*

Whilst another commode from
ie Arundel Castle collection
ttributed to Pierre Langlois was
old at the same time, there is no
eason also to attribute this one
› him. Whilst it has some similar
rench characteristics, of slight
ombé form, with a serpentine-
haped front with panelled doors
nd good ormolu mounts, the
iece could have been supplied
y any of the numerous makers
vorking for the 9th Duke of
Norfolk. These probably
ncluded both Thomas
Chippendale and Paul Saunders.
his commode was made for
Norfolk House, St James's
square, which was completed in
756 and demolished in 1938.
Prov: The Duke of Norfolk,
Arundel Castle, Sussex.

The use of mahogany for furniture-making became popular in the 1720s. It had come into England from the late seventeenth century as a veneer for marquetry, and from about 1715 was imported regularly, being abundant in Jamaica and the British-owned islands in the Caribbean. These sources, because of differences in climate and soil, each produced different varieties. That from Santa Domingo, heavy, strong and close-textured, when old was, as in this cabinet, nearly black.

John Evelyn, the diarist, applauded the use of walnut by the French. English sources of walnut were limited, and had been depleted throughout Europe by a severe frost killing many trees in 1709. It was imported from various places including North America: its use in the mid-1750s for the clothes press is, however, unusual.

1. *Cabinet, mahogany, c1755–60. H90, W53, D24.*
The history of this cabinet is complex, in that it is signed on the carcase of the base, 'William Hallett, 1763 Long Acre'. The cabinet is likely to have been made in the 1750s, with the inscription added for some reason in later years. Recent research has confirmed that Hallett Senior had retired by 1755, and his son carried on the business casually, until his own death in 1767. The doors enclose shelves, and the base has four drawers flanked by almost freestanding columns.
Prov: Lt. Col. Norman Colville.

2.   *Clothes press, walnut, c1755. H65, W54, D26.*
The design of this 'commode clothes press' is based upon that in the 1st edition of Chippendale's *Director* (1754, Plate CXXXI). The upper part has lively decoration on the doors in the form of foliate 'C'-scrolls. The *bombé* lower part contains two short over a long drawer, inlaid with light and dark line borders. The angles are carved with lions' head masks and suspending acanthus and bell-flowers, terminating on carved, ogee, bracket feet.

In matters of thought, the early eighteenth century was one of great and sometimes brilliant activity. It digested the scientific revolution of the preceding hundred years and produced literate groups eager to buy and read books, and to form libraries, however modest. So active a trend led to the creation of many fine library and writing desks, well served with drawers and pigeon-holes, as well as handsome many-shelved bookcases. The fine mahogany library bookcase follows a Chippendale design, but its contemporary owner was concerned as much with what it contained—arrays of books in gold-tooled morocco bindings, the latest theological treatise, Pope's and Swift's satiric jibes, Fielding's novels, even his groaning account-books.

1.   Library table, mahogany, c1755. H31, W49, D27.
Tables for libraries or for writing are often now regarded as 'kneehole desks'. However, the former terms are consistent with mentions in eighteenth-century bills. The cabriole legs are carved vigorously with acanthus foliage, and terminate in hairy paw feet. A cupboard door is fitted both at the back and at the left side, with two drawers at the right side. The top is leather covered.

2.   Library table, mahogany, c1755. H33, W54, D26.
The curved forms of serpentine top, console corner brackets and arched kneehole of the table are consistent with the desire of cabinet-makers to provide practical furniture. There is ample drawer space, but there are false drawer fronts where necessary. This, however, encourages a fussy appearance, with too many handles—at least twenty-four are used overall.

3.   Bureau, mahogany, c1760. W46.
The practical, plain exterior of the bureau contrasts with the more ornate interior, where curved drawers, fluted pilasters and waved friezes attract the eye. The writing flap is supported by lopers, and the ogee-shaped bracket feet reflect the curves of the fitted interior.
Prov: Earl of Sefton, Croxteth Hall, Liverpool.

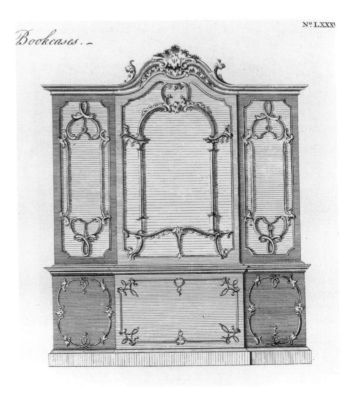

Library bookcase, mahogany, c1762. H93, W74.

he design of the upper part of the bookcase is based on a plate in the
rd edition of Thomas Chippendale's *Director* (1762). The rococo
rolled foliage of the glazing bars and pediment is continued in the
pplied decoration on the lower side cupboards. This is similar to that
f the lower central cupboard in Chippendale's design. However, it is
lutary to remember that following a Chippendale design is no
uarantee that the piece was actually made by him.
ov: Cuffnells, near Lyndhurst, Hampshire.

5. Detail of the library bookcase.

6. *Design for a library bookcase in the 3rd edition of Thomas Chippendale's Director (1762, Plate LXXXVIII).*

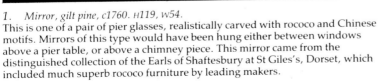

2.   Girandole, giltwood, c1755–60. H59, W24.
This formed part of the elaborate chinoiserie
decoration of the Tapestry Room at Ditchley,
Oxfordshire. The scheme incorporated picture
frames, appliqués, pendants and swags—all in
the fullest rococo-chinoiserie idiom. The girandole
is of a very unusual design, with painted
blackamoor figures seated on rockwork shelves at
the bases. It owes something to the rococo designs
of both Matthias Lock and Thomas Johnson, but
the verve of this girandole exceeds even those.
Prov: The Viscounts Dillon, Ditchley, Oxfordshire.

1.   Mirror, gilt pine, c1760. H119, W54.
This is one of a pair of pier glasses, realistically carved with rococo and Chinese
motifs. Mirrors of this type would have been hung either between windows
above a pier table, or above a chimney piece. This mirror came from the
distinguished collection of the Earls of Shaftesbury at St Giles's, Dorset, which
included much superb rococo furniture by leading makers.

hilst the frothful verve of good rococo carving is always attractive
the eye, some of it had the practical purpose of hiding divisions in
rror plates. It had always been difficult to obtain large plates of
en thickness, and the growing practice of re-using old plates
couraged the careful hiding of the joints. In mid-eighteenth-
tury patternbooks the fantasies of carved ornament were popula-
ed, and agitated birds and figures crowded the gilded wood rococo
mes themselves. Amid the amazing variety of these mirrors, it is
ely possible to identify the work of individuals, but a look at the
terns of Chippendale, Mayhew and Ince, Lock and Johnson show
sources for the fertile ideas.

. Chimney glass, giltwood, c1760. H58, W66.
his fine overmantel mirror is somewhat in the manner of Thomas
hippendale: he provided an elaborate one to the Earl of Dumfries in
759. However, where he used a velvet tapestry picture, this chimney
lass incorporates Chinese mirror paintings, centred by one
urmounted by a mirrored pagoda cresting.
Prov: H.R.H. The late Duke of Kent; Wateringbury House, Kent.

Clothes lying neatly in the drawers of the tall-boy, books in the bookcase, oriental china on the china cabinet with its suitable pagoda cresting, the firescreen shielding eyes from the fire, the candlesticks flickering on the torchères—furniture is obviously concerned with a function, but equally can be fashioned with a keen concern for its appearance. Everything here is not made in mahogany; the cheaper beech intervenes, together with black lacquer. But whatever the material or intended use we have to recognize the growing rivalry between Chinese modes and classical patterns. Finally, as the writer William Whitehead (1715-85) had it: the struggle was resolved by 'that simplicity which distinguished the Greek and Roman arts as eternally superior to those of every other nation'.

2. *Secretaire cabinet, mahogany, c1760. H105, W52.*
The Gothic-arcaded, broken triangular pediment surmounts a cabinet which has splendid geometrical glazed cupboard doors. The lower part has a drawer with a baize-lined writing surface, an alphabetically-enumerated, divided, lidded drawer on the left, and four drawers on the right. Finally, there is a cupboard at the base, with contrasting veneers in ovals.

1. *Tallboy, mahogany, c1760–65. H79.*
This handsome tallboy was made by someone concerned to choose finely-figured veneers. They provide a lively surface, which is held in check by the broken scrolled cresting in neo-classical style, and the chamfered angles carved with rams' heads, pendant bell-flowers and acanthus scrolls. The lower drawer of the upper stage is fitted as a secretaire.

3.   Library bookcase, mahogany, 1764. H85, W131.

This important, documented bookcase was provided by the firm of Chippendale and Rannie (his business partner at the time) to Sir Lawrence Dundas in January 1764. The account reads: 'To a very large Mahogany Bookcase of fine wood with a Scrol pediment top & Rich folding doors glaz'd with plate Glass on the upper part & Cupboards with folding doors of very fine wood in the under part. £80.' Another was supplied in the same year to Sir Lawrence at a cost of £73. Both were based on Plate XCII in the 3rd edition of Chippendale's *Director* (1762).

4.   Torchères, japanned pine, c1760. H41.

These torchères should be compared with designs for a 'Tea Kettle Stand', a 'firescreen' and a 'candle stand' in Mayhew and Ince's *Universal System of Household Furniture* (1759–63), Plates XIV, L, and LXVIII). The torchère has an octagonal top, and the whole is decorated in gilt on a black ground. *Prov:* Lord Swaything.

5.   Cheval firescreen, beechwood, needlework panel, c1753. W26.

A plaque on the needlework is inscribed: 'This screen was worked before her marriage by Jane Jesup, afterwards Peckover . . . her estates . . . are now in the possession of her great grandson Alexander Peckover of Wisbech.' Jane Jesup married Richard Peckover in April 1753, and the house depicted may be Wisbech Castle, Cambridgeshire.

6.   China cabinet, black lacquer, c1755. H55, W20.

This cabinet is almost identical to two pairs from the Chinese Bedroom at Badminton, Gloucestershire, which were sold at Christie's on 20 June 1921, Lots 50–1 (from the collection of the Duke of Beaufort). They were made, together with a bed, by the firm of William and John Linnell, and this cabinet may be attributed to them on that documented evidence. *Prov:* Wateringbury House, Kent.

Cabinet on stand, satinwood and marquetry, c1775. H84, W40, D20.

The cabinet was designed in the neo-classical style, largely as a vehicle for the display of marquetry. Views of English abbeys and castles, taken from Samuel and Nathaniel Buck's *Antiquities* (1774), are worked in engraved, stained and shaded woods on the interior drawers and central cupboard. Each building is named, although licence has been used in the spellings, as follows: *left*, Beaumaris Castle, Comb Abby, Wenlock Abby, Dunstable Priory, Butley Priory; *centre*, Malmsbury Abby, Salisbury Cathedral, Netley Abby; *right*, Leicester abby, Caldecot Castle, Kennelworth Castle, Durham Castle, Tinmoth Monastery. The views of classical ruins on the inside of the doors are after Charles-Louis Clérisseau, who had been a draughtsman in Robert Adam's London Office.

This splendid cabinet was almost certainly made for William, 6th Baron Craven (1738–1791), who inherited the extensive Craven properties in Berkshire and Warwickshire in 1769. It has been attributed as the work of Mayhew and Ince.

Prov: The Earls of Craven, Combe Abbey, Warwickshire.

CHAPTER 5

Classical Origins 1765–1790

The interiors of the great English Palladian houses of the early eighteenth century were based, in part, on the design of antique temples, but almost nothing was then known of the furniture of those early times. The archaeological excavations of Herculaneum and Pompeii, and the publication in Italy and France of many important manuals in the 1750s, widened knowledge of antiquity, and patrons were eager to purchase new designs. Architects such as William Chambers and Robert Adam trained for several years at this time in Italy, and returned to England ready to serve the active interest in the style of the ancients.

They were helped in 1763 when the Treaty of Paris brought to an end the Seven Years War with France, allowing a new period of prosperity and expansion to emerge and to coincide with their own ambitions. Each architect was his own able publicist, but Adam had little direct competition when he published his book on the ruins of the Roman Emperor Diocletian's palace at Spalato (now Split in Yugoslavia) in 1764, and followed it within ten years with his first parts of the *Works in Architecture of Robert and James Adam* (1773–9). Within the ten years he was able to claim, largely through his own efforts, 'a remarkable improvement in the form, convenience and arrangement and relief of apartments, a greater movement and variety in the outside composition and, in the decoration of the inside, an almost total change.' This change in scale, proportion and type of decorative scheme was so radical a departure from what was hitherto practised, that the architect Sir John Soane spoke in 1815 of Adam's achievements as 'a revolution of electric power'.

The early neo-classical forms of furniture used features of strings of husks or bell-flowers, acanthus leaf-tip mouldings, leaf-ornamented scrolls at the top of table legs, and supports shaped as human or mythical figures. To this was soon added a whole repertory of garlands and festoons, medallions and paterae, the trophies of weapons, vases, urns and tripods and sphinxes and gryphons all put together to enhance 'the beautiful spirit of antiquity'.

It should again be stressed that Robert Adam was a designer, and that he did not personally make furniture, fashion silver, weave carpets, or chisel the 'Adam fireplace' of many a saleroom description. It should also be emphasized that furniture makers such as Thomas Chippendale, John Linnell, John Cobb, and Ince and Mayhew were capable of realizing their own neo-classical ideas in superb furniture without any firm reference to Adam. There is only, to date, one recorded instance of Chippendale working directly to an Adam design: in the creation of the sofas and chairs for the Arlington Street house of Sir Lawrence Dundas. The same is true of John Cobb, whose early neo-classical chairs for Adam's patron, the 6th Earl of Coventry, show his complete acceptance of the new mood Adam was doing his utmost to promote, but show him capable of achieving it alone. In fact, whilst Adam was concerned that his interiors formed a unity of architecture, decoration and movables, he did not aim to design the entire contents. Permanent features such as pier tables, looking glasses and other important features of a room were his concern as a designer, and good furniture-makers could be found to carry them out precisely.

Adam furniture has been classified into four main chronological categories—Early (1762–4) in which neo-classical elements had not been developed with any assurance; Transitional (1765–8); Mature (1769–77); and Late (1778–92). The Transitional is a satisfying phase,

Commode, mahogany, c1765. w48.
The rococo form of this chest, with its serpentine shape, vigorously carved acanthus scrolls and tightly scrolled French feet, is continued in the gilt-metal carrying handles, which have back plates cast as chinoiserie pagodas. There are similarities between this commode and the one supplied by Chippendale's firm to Sir Rowland Winn, now in the private dining room of Nostell Priory, Yorkshire. The scrolled feet are almost the same, as are the moulded lower side mounts.

with robust vigorous designs and ornament on a bold scale. Classical decorative motifs in chair backs shaped as lyres or on the square legs of side tables are combined with acanthus foliage and fluting to excellent effect. In the Mature period the range of types of furniture is at its greatest, with articles of French character such as *confidantes* and sofas, and armchairs, stools and hall chairs of considerable variety. Colour assumes a greater importance with furniture in the Etruscan style, and is often particularly satisfying in pieces ornamented in terracotta on a black ground. Marquetry panels of classical scenes were also used to skilful and good effect on elliptical-shaped commodes; structural elements became thinner and more refined, with round tapering legs entwined by festoons a favourite device. The great pier glasses had compositions of a central urn or medallion flanked by sphinxes or gryphons and supported by delicately modelled female figures.

The last part of Adam's career, from 1778 until his death in 1792, found him much occupied with decorating London town houses. The furniture of the period was refined slightly from what had been provided in the previous years: there was no fresh invention—Thomas Chippendale had died in 1779 and John Cobb in 1778. They had produced superb marquetry furniture of a style approved by architect and patron, but in addition there were many other showrooms to choose from.

From about 1766 Chippendale had started to produce furniture of an advanced classical character, much of it for houses in which Adam was, or had been, in charge as architect. Whilst much was made in mahogany, increasing use was made of satinwood, gilt bronze ornaments and marquetry. The progress made can be established by comparing the Nostell library table (1767), carved with boldy-formed tapering term-shaped supports, lions' head capitals and paw feet, with the Harewood library table (1771) (see page 190; now at Temple Newsam House) which is of rosewood with marquetry and inlay of various woods. At this period there is no carved work and all the decoration is inlaid, except for the high-quality ormolu mounts with rams' heads and festoons which replaced carved mahogany lions' masks.

Similar changes can be seen by comparing a lyre-back chair (at Osterley Park House, Middlesex, or Nostell Priory, Yorkshire) of about 1767 in carved Cuban mahogany, leather-upholstered seat and a narrow brass moulding around the seat frame, with the highly-mannered oval-back chairs upholstered in Gobelins *petit point*, c 1770, in which the tapestry coverings atch suites of hangings on the walls (for example at sterley Park House, Middlesex, and Newby Hall, orkshire).

A more satisfactory way to examine the typical range f high-quality neo-classical furniture provided by rms such as Chippendale or Linnell is to examine vhat still survives in the rooms of a significant Adam ouse, such as Osterley Park. In the Great Hall (*c* 1767) re mahogany and pine hall seats, painted white. The orner legs still show Kentian influence with heavy aturalistic paw feet, but the two lighter intermediate egs show the use of the columnar neo-classical form, lthough tentatively and with paw feet retained. There re gilded wood lamps, brackets to support lamps, and ine pedestals (1774) also painted white. In the Eating oom the furniture did not include a dining table—one vas added to the furnishings in about 1800. According o a 1782 inventory, three mahogany dining tables tood in the North Passage outside and would have een brought into the Eating Room at mealtimes. At ther times the chairs would have been arranged in ormal patterns around the walls, leaving the centre of he room clear. Here the chairs were of the mahogany yre-back form with leather seats and splats made of hree-ply mahogany. At the end of the room was a ilded pine sideboard, two elegant mahogany, pine nd oak urns on pedestals, painted white and partly ilded, a pair of side tables of gilded pine with marble

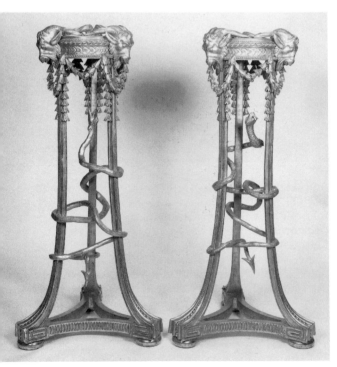

air of torchères, giltwood, c1770. H56.
he design of these candlestands is derived from the antique Roman ripod; such items of furniture were favoured by Robert Adam. The air, with beaded circular tops on splayed supports headed by rams' nasks, is stylistically analogous to a set of tochères at Osterley Park louse, Middlesex, but without the entwined snake.

mosaic tops (probably imported from Italy) and two large oval pier glasses in 'rich carved frames with ornaments gilt in burnish Gold'. Pier glasses were also used between four of the ten piers between the windows of the Gallery, hung so as to alternate with six girandoles of carved and gilded pine, with brass candle-branches. Comfort was ensured by the provision of twelve large mahogany 'French elbow chairs'. The seat rails have motifs of bound laurels and echo the moulding of the dado—the seats, backs and arms are upholstered and are *en suite* to four settees, and two larger settees. The seat rails of the settees are supported by eight tapered fluted legs and the upholstered arms are delicately scrolled and beaded.

Chippendale was adept at the provision of furniture for writing and reading. The Osterley library was furnished by his rival John Linnell and still contains very elegant seat furniture. The lyre-backs of the eight armchairs are surmounted by portrait medallions of classical female heads—different on each chair in the set—and the panel at the base of the lyre is of green stained wood with red painted decoration. A pair of library tables of oak and pine, veneered with rosewood, satinwood and other woods, are given ormolu mounts and are *en suite* to a library desk, which bears some resemblance to that Chippendale supplied to Harewood House. It is of oak and pine and is inlaid like the tables and given ormolu mounts, a green baize top and leather castors. The four doors of the pedestals are decorated with emblems of Architecture, Sculpture, Painting and Music. The pedestals have drawers and there are drawers in the frieze extending through the full width of the desk.

The highest-quality furniture—commodes veneered with several woods, standing under pier mirrors with pine frames, and gilded oak and beech armchairs—was put in the Drawing Room. The chairs are covered in damask, the legs are delicately carved and curved with the arm rests entering the seat rail in pillars of wreathing foliage. Other armchairs upholstered in Gobelins tapestry were put in the Tapestry Room, and the State Bedroom contained a State Bed with eight painted and japanned columns supporting a carved and gilt cornice and dome tester with a carved and gilt headboard.

The availability of fine fabrics to the upholsterer was a considerable advantage to fashioning fine furniture, and had grown steadily in importance from the late seventeenth century. Admittedly there were years when its use was less popular, but when costly fabrics were used it was customary to protect them with serge case-covers.

Changes as advanced as those introduced by Adam and his contemporaries, and carried into effect by what Adam called his 'regiment of artificers', were bound to attract both admiration and criticism. In particular, Horace Walpole was ready to note the 'harlequinades of Adam, which never let the eye repose a moment' and 'Mr Adam's gingerbread and snippets of embroidery', but many designers, cabinet-makers and tradesmen profited from popularizing the Adam style. One

Side table, painted and gilded, c1770. W35.
The semi-elliptical top is painted with 'The Triumph of Amphitrite' in cameo, which follows an engraving of Raphael's *Amphitrite* in the Farnesina, Rome. The table, stamped 'G IV 55', was probably made for King George III for Buckingham House, London. It was possibly designed by Sir William Chambers (1723–96), Surveyor-General and comptroller of the Royal Works, who rivalled Robert Adam as a creator of the neo-classical style. A well-known pair of larger companion tables from this set are also stamped: one is now in the Victoria and Albert Museum, the other in the Metropolitan Museum, New York.
Prov: King George IV; Henry Ford II.

who showed that it was a style which could be adapted for general consumption as opposed to high fashion was George Hepplewhite. Although he died in 1786, his wife produced in 1788 his influential *The Cabinet-Maker and Upholsterer's Guide.*

The *Guide* had over 300 designs and was the largest of its kind to appear since Chippendale's *Director.* The work was almost immediately successful, and was followed quickly by a second edition (1789) and a third (1794). The first two editions perpetuated the Adam manner at a time when reaction was setting in to the over-ornamentation of the Late Adam style. However, many of the oval-back, wheel-back and shield-back chairs, bookcases with vase-shaped door-glazing and urn-decked pediments, beds with painted posts and cornices, and bow-fronted commodes (some by Thomas Chippendale the younger) are among the most beautiful productions of English makers.

George Hepplewhite's life is shadowy—he is not known to have made any furniture himself, but a notice in October 1786 (*Public Ledger*) announced the sale of 'the valuable stock in trade and household furniture of Mr Hepplewhite, cabinet manufacturer deceased'. His designs, therefore may have been the result of practical experience, and they certainly conformed in overall elegance and refinement to Adam's late drawings, although never actually corresponding to them. In the

Card table, sabicu, c1780. H29, W42, D20.
The top, which encloses a baize-lined playing surface, is decorated
with marquetry flowerheads, leaves and tulipwood cross-banding.
The practical design of the table is enhanced by its clear forms, good
proportions and by the use of an unusual wood: sabicu is a hard,
durable wood, native to Cuba.

designs of chairs, of which few by Adam survive,
Hepplewhite displayed limitless invention, especially
in the forms of the backs. The legs were usually of
tapered square section, outswept in a singular manner.

The Prince of Wales's feathers used as a decorative
device in chair backs are synonymous with Hepplewhite's name, but the motif had been used as early as
the 1720s, and in about 1730 Benjamin Goodison used it
when designing a fine looking glass for Frederick,
Prince of Wales. It was, moreover, a motif used widely
by adherents of the Whig party, with which the Prince
had associated himself in opposition to his father,
George II. The displayed plumes are, however, also a
decorative device of elegance and distinction and they
were used widely in the 1780s to embellish furniture
and glass candelabra.

The *Guide* had suggested that shield-back chairs
should be upholstered, as they were considered most
suitable for drawing rooms. They were referred to as
'Cabriole' chairs, as they bore some similarity to the
chair-like seat of a light two-wheeled carriage, the
cabriolet, which was invented in 1755 and was all the
rage in Paris during the Hepplewhite period. By the
time the third edition of the *Guide* appeared in 1794,
oval-back chairs which were well represented in the
first 1788 edition had largely disappeared, and those
with heart-shaped backs and splats of stylized wheatsheaf form, whilst very common, only appeared in one
design in 1788 and none in 1794. Wheel-back chairs
were also ignored, although they were highly prized
and demanded skill in manufacture.

For the friezes of his tables Hepplewhite suggested
the use of simple vertical fluting, as compared to
Adam's highly-mannered designs, using linked wreaths,
rosettes and palmette or anthemion motifs. He took in
ideas from Chippendale's patterns, especially in his
depiction of sideboard tables with urns and pedestals
en suite. In his decorated table tops the ornament was
usually placed in the centre with loops of festoons
around a motif of a small rosette, star, or shell-pattern
ornament. In Adam's designs a central motif was
supported by secondary ones in the form of medallions

Armchair, giltwood, c1765–70.
Cabinet-makers such as Chippendale and Linnell were adept at blending neo-classical details with sprightly rococo elements. Both mention 'French chairs' in their bills of the late 1760s, and Chippendale included ten designs for them in the 3rd edition of the *Director* (1762,

Plates XIX-XXIII). He stated that, as in this example, 'both the Backs and Seats must be covered with Tapestry, or other sort of Needlework'. Chippendale also visited France in 1769, and the following year was apprehended for attempting to import illegally sixty French chair frames.

Armchair, giltwood, c1765–70.
The curvilinear frame of this chair, in the French style, is carved with neo-classical ornament of husk chains and swags. The central back splat is boldly carved with laurel leaves, and the serpentine upholstered seat is supported on fluted cabriole legs. The frame is a splendid achievement by the chair-maker—strong but sinuous, elegant yet practical.

or tablets suspending from festoons. Another interesting variation from Adam was that Hepplewhite did not suggest in his furniture designs any use of human or animal figures, or panels or medallions painted with classical landscapes or figures. There are also no military trophies, swords or weapons of conflict and no Venus, Diana or Mars supporting the thin attenuations of the pier glasses. Hepplewhite's *Guide* was concerned with the realms of intimate domesticity, and he stated in the Preface that he had purposely omitted those articles 'whose recommendation was mere novelty'.

In 1772 Mrs Delaney noted that when she was visited by the Princess Amelia, relaxation in the French taste being still frowned upon, 'all the comfortable sophas and great chairs were banished for that day and the blew damask chairs set in prim from around the room'. There is often confusion over the use of the terms sofas and settees, and Hepplewhite referred to sofas as settees. Sofas were held to be completely upholstered whilst settees consisted of an open frame with cushions. Adam favoured the French '*confidante* sofa', which had two end sections divided from the main seat by upholstered partitions, and had as many as ten legs, front and back. Hepplewhite admired them but also went in for sofas that corresponded closely with the chairs with which they were associated, in terms of the frame and its fabric covering. One of the most beautiful of his designs is for a settee in which the back is made up of three, four or even five shield-pattern chair backs, joined together. Another form, adapted from the French and intended for the boudoir, was the *Duchesse*, which consisted of two bergère chairs and a rectangular stool placed together to form a sofa or *chaise-longue* for reclining upon.

Almost as frequently made as chairs or sofas were various forms of pier, side, card, Pembroke and dressing tables. Console tables (those which have to be supported by the wall on console brackets) was a term used widely from the time of George II (1730–60) for almost any kind of pier table or side table. In the Hepplewhite period, of the late 1780s, pier tables were, however, given even more distinction than Robert Adam had endowed them with by their recognition as a class distinct from side tables. They were, said Hepplewhite, tables which admitted 'with great propriety, of much elegance and ornament'. He only gave general designs for two in the *Guide*, but included representations of eight pier and card tables, which could be inlaid, or painted and varnished. Their proportions were those of the pier walls between the windows, but the usual height of twenty-eight inches could be exceeded if it was thought proper to rise level with the dado rail in the room.

It is casually thought that the Pembroke table was a late eighteenth-century innovation, but Chippendale included one as 'a Breakfast Table' in the 1754 *Director*. Expressing well the delicacy of both the Adam and Hepplewhite styles, the table is characterized by being oval-shaped or rectangular with two flaps. The top and flaps provided excellent spaces for the display of marquetry or painted decoration. Adam designed a painted one for the Etruscan Room at Osterley. Smaller tables, those for shaving or dressing, are amongst the most satisfying and ingenious. The shaving table was cubical in shape on four tapered legs, and a tilting mirror could be lifted upwards from a slot at the back. The top itself opened into two trays for toilet articles and a basin, tumbler and other requisites were contained inside. The Hepplewhite *Guide* illustrated a variant as 'Rudd's Table, or reflecting Dressing-Table'. Two side drawers opened outwards: one contained a looking glass, and from the other a flap was hinged on a quadrant. It was said 'to possess every convenience which can be wanted'. One wonders if the possessors of these tables still found time to explore or use all their mechanical functions before descending from the bedroom to the dining room.

In the active years of Chippendale's rococo period, sideboards were merely tables without drawers. Adam developed the theme by unifying elements, and adding pedestals with urns, and a wine cooler below the table. Hepplewhite developed a design for a large sideboard which was self-contained, consisting of a centre section containing a drawer supported on each side by two deep pedestals with cupboards and drawers. One of the cupboards was fitted for bottles, whilst the other had a lead lining to hold water in which to rinse glasses and cutlery. All editions of the *Guide* also featured veneered knife boxes to stand on the top of the sideboard, fashioned with sloping tops and serpentine, bowed or concave and convex shapes.

The consumption of wine had given pleasure for centuries and the furniture makers gave serious attention to the ritual. Cellarets and wine-coolers have the same outside form, but the cellaret was divided to store bottles, and wine-coolers were lined with lead so that bottles could be surrounded by ice to cool them for a meal. They were adapted by Adam to the sarcophagi form of the ancients and the lids were often fluted like a shell and surmounted by handsome pineapple finials. Others were japanned in 'Adam green'.

When a gentleman retired from the table after dining alone he might well have gone to his library. Library tables, bookcases and bureaux (in which a sloping desk-front opens flat and is supported upon slides) had assumed growing significance from the early eighteenth century. The firm of Gillow, among others, produced some splendid ones in what might be called Hepplewhite style. The *Guide* only has three designs for library tables of plain appearance and modest size. His most elaborate design showed the traditional kneehole type with a central drawer, supported by two pedestals on plinths, with delicate husk carving on the pilasters at each corner, and the sides of the kneehole. The sides of the top are recessed at the centre to allow the user to draw up nearer to the reading area. Hepplewhite also illustrated four designs for bookcases, ranging from six to thirteen feet in height, having cupboards and drawers in the lower part, and glass doors, four to eight, depending on length. These bookcases sometimes included a secretaire in the centre portion.

Adam had designed several libraries, at Newby and Kenwood, for example, but he is not known to have designed any free-standing bookcases, or any bureau bookcases. Hepplewhite said that if the bookcase top was to be ornamented, a vase, bust or other ornament of mahogany, gilt, or light-coloured wood should be placed between a scroll or foliage. Although the Gothic style was also popular, neo-classical patterns still persisted.

Secretaire-cabinet, painted and gilded, c1790. H89,
W48, D19.

One of a pair, this arch-crested cabinet, with
Gothic-pattern glazed doors and brass bars, has a
lower cupboard door centred by a ribbon-tied oval
of a Cupid and Venus in the manner of the painter
Angelica Kauffmann (1740–1807). At each side, a
narrow cupboard is headed by oval vignettes of
the houses at Whitton Park and Shardeloes, taken
from engraved plates issued around 1788. The
fresh colours of the ribbon-tied summer flowers
and roundels with mythological scenes, painted
in an airy, light style, invest this secretaire-cabinet
with a classical distinction.

1. *Sideboard table, mahogany, c1770–5. w84.*
The table is made in the Adam style, with a fluted frieze, legs headed by paterae and an apron carved with scrolled acanthus foliage, rams' and eagles' heads. It is in the style of a sideboard table depicted by Robert and James Adam in their *Works in Architecture* (1773), and is intended as part of a dining room suite.

2. *Side table, giltwood and marquetry, by Thomas Chippendale after a design by Robert Adam, 1775. H38, w94.*
The table was made to stand under a pier glass in the Yellow Damask Sitting Room at Harewood House, and was invoiced by Chippendale in 1775 for £60. The top is finely veneered with satinwood, rosewood and various stained and shaded woods in a radiating design, with drapery festoons, anthemions, musical trophies and inset ivory heads.

As the neo-classical style gained hold in the mid-1760s, the ornament became more precise than the creations of the rococo years, with an overriding concern for symmetry and proportion. This could be sustained by a whole array of classically-inspired ornament—rams' and eagles' heads, the small fans and medallions, precise swags, bell-husk relief carving, fluted friezes or scrolled acanthus foliage. It could be well realized in carved and gilded wood or gesso, various light compositions using gypsum and size as a base, and was matched by carefully arranged floral marquetry of high quality. Satinwood, rosewood and various stained woods helped along the mannered displays of the marquetry workers' dexterity.

3. *Side table, giltwood, c1770. w57.*
The straight, French-style tapering legs and husk festoons draped over paterae bear a close resemblance to a table design by Matthias Lock, dated 1769. The green marble top is of later date. As the neo-classical style gained hold, the ornament became more precise and restrained, albeit with the same concerns for symmetry shown here.

4. *Side table, marquetry, c1765. w42.*
One of a pair, this table, with its curvilinear form, marquetry decoration and high-quality ormolu mounts, is in the manner of Pierre Langlois.

Sir Lawrence Dundas (c 1710– 81), one of the most outstanding and judicious patrons of neoclassical architects and craftsmen, had become very rich through his activities as Commissary-General and Paymaster to the Army from 1748 to 1759. He spent lavishly but employed great taste and discernment and patronized the most fashionable architects and furniture-makers. These included, as architect, Robert Adam, and as furniture-makers both Chippendale and Vile and Cobb, and the latter's former workmen, William France and John Bradburn. They provided furniture which had to satisfy Dundas. He was 'the Nabob of the North', and as one who left at his death an estate worth £16,000 per annum and a fortune of £900,000, could not be trifled with, or provided with less than the best.

1.   Side table, marquetry, attributed to John Cobb, c1770. w55.
When John Cobb's partner William Vile died in 1767, Cobb continued the business until his own death in 1778. He turned increasingly to the production of fine marquetry furniture, and rivalled the successful firms of Thomas Chippendale and Mayhew and Ince. The marquetry of all his pieces incorporates floral motifs, the standard being set by a commode and two stands supplied by him to Paul Methuen of Corsham Court, Wiltshire (where they survive) in 1772. One mount on this side table is stamped on the underside with a four-leaf clover mark and a single leaf above.
Prov: A. F. Clarke-Jervoise Esq.

2.   Console table, carved and gilt gesso, by William France and John Bradburn, from a design by Robert Adam, 1765. w66.
Adam's design, for Sir Lawrence Dundas at 19 Arlington Street, was inscribed: 'A Table Frame for Long Room next the Eating Parlour'. On 12 January 1765, the partners France and Bradburn invoiced a table: 'For a Circular Frame, for a

Marble Table, richly carv'd with ramsheads at top, & Husks falling down the 3 Shaped Legs & gilt in burnished gold and putting up the above . . . L.37s.10 d.0'. France and Bradburn succeeded to some of the successful patronage formerly bestowed on their masters William Vile and John Cobb.

3.   Detail of top of the side table (4).

4.   *Side table, satinwood, mahogany, purpleheart, marquetry and parquetry, c1770.* H33, W43, D23.
Side tables similar to this example have generally been ascribed to John Cobb's workshop. Their characteristics include decoration with either bouquets of flowers or fruit in basketwork, cube or trellis borders and pendant husks on the legs.

1. Dining table, mahogany, c1775. L (including 3 extra leaves, two of later date) 172, W52.
This type of table, made up from two 'D'-shaped end sections and a hinged central part, was convenient for many houses. A dining table would be brought into the eating room at mealtimes from the passage outside, and returned there after use.

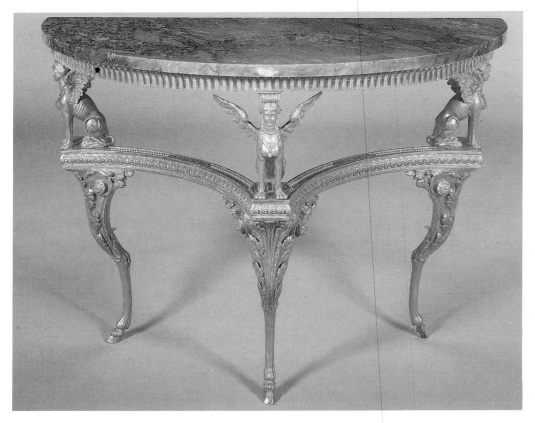

2. Console table, giltwood, c1770-5. H32, W45, D21.
Elements of the design of this table, one of a pair, probably derive from Piranesi's engravings in his *Diversi Maniere D'adornare i Cammini* of 1769—particularly the upright foliate goats' legs. In this example, three crisply carved, displayed chimeras sit on their haunches above a double in-curved tier. The architect James Wyatt designed a table in this mannered style as late an 1788 for the Earl of Chichester.

the high years of neo-classical taste, the late 1770s
d early 1780s, furniture-makers had developed
erring instincts for providing furniture for specific
rposes that was good to look at. Dining tables were
oved into position, but small side tables stood in
most any convenient spot and were decorated on
and sides almost to the lavish point where any
ject placed on them disturbed the pattern. There
s still an overriding concern to follow engraved
ecedent, whether from the works of Robert Adam's
end, Piranesi, or by the architect himself. The
servation produced much of consummate quality.

Side table, carved giltwood, top painted satinwood,
780. H33, W41, D17.
e refined neo-classical mood of this table, which is
e of a pair, reflects the influence of the French
aftsmen, particularly carvers, working in England
the 1780s for architects such as Henry Holland. The
tter's clients numbered many of the Francophile
hig circle around the Prince of Wales, including the
dfords, Devonshires and Spencers.

Table, painted and gilt, c1780. H28, Diam 14.
his small table, or torchère, in the Adam style, has a papier mâché
ray top and is fitted with a small frieze drawer. Both the top and
rieze are painted with mythological motifs in the style of the
wiss-born artist, Angelica Kauffmann (1740-1807). She settled in
ondon around 1766, and came into contact with one of Adam's
avourite painters, Antonio Zucchi, whom she married in 1781. Most
f the painted medallions on contemporary furniture were inspired
y her many canvases.
rov: Algernon Heber Percy Esq.

5.   Side table, painted white and gilded, c1790. W23.
Delicate classical decoration is painted on the top and shelf of this
table, with grisaille panels and purple and white borders. The swags,
paterae and central urn on the frieze are carved. The top of the table,
one of a pair, is of a later date. These tables may have been created to
copy the successful productions of the French ébénistes, who
incorporated floral Sèvres panels into their pieces in the late
eighteenth century.

1.   *Armchair, mahogany, attributed to Thomas Chippendale, c1770-75.*
This chair is part of an important suite of furniture originally comprising two sofas, two card tables and at least twelve armchairs. The suite was supplied to Dingley Hall, owned by the Hungerford family for a century from 1770. The central tablet on the seat rail bears the Hungerford crest, and the crimson silk brocade cover is contemporary. The chair corresponds with Chippendale and Haig's standard design types of around 1770-75.
Prov: The Hungerford family; 8th Viscount Downe, Wykeham Abbey, Yorkshire.

Here we have the dominant observance by the furniture-maker of the pattern-book. In the workshop there would be at varying times perhaps half a dozen manuals, ranging from Chippendale (1754, 1755, 1762) to Sheraton (1793). They gave proportions to ideas, they showed how the talented had tackled the problem, and they were up-to-date in respect of the indefinable element of taste. It is therefore natural to allude to 'in the style of', although all recognize that what is always preferable is firm documentation. It does not alter the appearance of good furniture, but gives posthumous credit to its careful maker.

2. *Writing table, satinwood and purpleheart, c1790. w41.*
The kidney shape was used by Chippendale for a commode table in his 1762 *Director*, and was developed later by Thomas Sheraton in his *Drawing Book* of 1793. The terms 'kidney' or 'horse-shoe' table are contemporary with the introduction of the style in the mid-eighteenth century, and were also used to describe ladies' work tables.

Perhaps more than any other category of furniture, tables have reflected changes in social behaviour. They came into being for many reasons: as a result of dining together (refectory tables), playing games (cards, backgammon), taking tea or wine, serving in the dining room, or eating meals alone. They stood beneath pier mirrors, held countless objets d'art, helped when writing or drawing, and in humbler circumstances served as places to prepare food, scrub linen, and support piles of dishes, pewter and silver after washing or cleaning.

Whilst most tables are supported by four legs, many ingenious arrangements were made to increase the area of the top (fold up or over panels and inserted panels) and to support it when so extended (gate, stay, extra leg, concertina or pull-out action, as in the architect's table [2–3]). The use of strong mahogany allowed the satisfactory manufacture of small tables, supported on a central pillar and tripod foot, and for even smaller versions for specific purposes, such as supporting a silver kettle on stand when serving tea. By their construction of frequently having large tops, friezes, drawers and many legs they were excellent places to disport the latest stylistic fad—a centred urn, an oval fan of marquetry—and to incorporate examples of the turner's art in spiral fluted pedestals and legs. Finally, they were invariably carved with crisp motifs which furthered the overall satisfying appearance of something so essentially useful.

1. Games table, mahogany, c1780. w29.
This piece was designed as a Pembroke table, with the central section of the oval top fitted with a sliding inlaid panel, with a chess board on the reverse, and concealing a leather backgammon field. The fan medallion, veneered on both flaps, betokens the precise symmetry which became such a feature of neo-classical furniture.

3. The architect's table open.

2. Architect's table, mahogany, c1770. w35.
Also termed an artist's or writing and reading table, this is an example of a thoughtful design, with the rising top held on a double ratchet. The writing flap is lined in leather, and a slide at each side is provided to accomodate candles. The craftsman has completed the table with false drawers at either end, which enhance its compact symmetry when closed.

Pembroke table, mahogany, c1780.

5.

[Thi]s is a practical piece, easily moved,
[for] use as a breakfast or tea table, with a
[dra]wer in the frieze. This type of table
[wa]s also invoiced as a 'Fly Table' by
[cab]inet-makers like Mayhew and Ince,
[wh]o charged between £2. 6s. and £13s.
[6d.] for one in the early 1780s.

. *Tripod table, mahogany, c1765–70. Diam 29.*
[T]he lobed tip-up top is finished with radiating veneers; the curved
[d]esign continues through the cabriole legs and scrolled feet. Such
[t]ables, able to take tea equipage, were eminently practical, being
[e]asily stored with the top in its vertical position.
Prov:: Elveden Hall, West Suffolk.

6. *Kettle stand, mahogany, c1765–70. w11.*
Attention is focused on the crisply-carved acanthus leaves and fluting
on the baluster stem, but the widely-splayed tripod supports ensure
that the silver kettle which would have rested on the tray top
remained steady.

What concerned furniture-makers in the early 1760s was how easily and effectively they could react to the rapidly growing interest in neo-classical forms. The excavations at Pompeii and Herculaneum in the mid1750s had stimulated an interest in the antique, which was already present in the many British aristocrats journeying over Italy on their Grand Tours. Both William Chambers and Robert Adam, the two most inflential architects in the new movement, had returned to England in the late 1750s from several years of training in Italy. The concern the makers had was to break away from rococo forms, and even Thomas Chippendale's important third edition of his pattern-book, the **Director**, issued in 1762, makes few overtures to what he was whole-heartedly to commit himself and his workshop to within a matter of a year or two—neo-classical patterns. The transition can be noticed by comparing the two armchairs (1 and 2) dated to about 1765, with that (3) attributed to Chippendale, of some ten years later, about 1775. The sinuous seat rails and legs are supplanted by lines bearing applied classical ornament. The refined elements of neo-classicism are more evident in the wheel-back chair (4) and that with the attractive looped splat (5). They may not be incorporated with any degree of success, but the ovals, circles, arms and legs are effective in portraying classical lines in a proportioned harmony.

1. Armchair, mahogany, c1765. H41, W28.
The curved forms of this chair, with its carved shellwork and scrolled acanthus, are well reflected in the border of the cover, which is worked overall in *gros* and *petit point*. They are forms, however, which developed from the 'C'- and 'S'-shapes of the rococo style, and during the 1760s were overlaid with the motifs of neo-classical ornament. Such chairs were often termed 'library armchairs', although they were also used in many other rooms.

2. Armchair, mahogany, c1765. H41.
This is one of a pair, which are nearly identical to a set of fourteen armchairs supplied *en suite* with a pair of sofas and card tables by Thomas Chippendale to the 5th Earl of Dumfries, Dumfries House, Ayrshire, in 1759. This was Chippendale's most important commission of his rococo years, and set the standard for his work in the early 1760s. This example, intended for library use, is upholstered in suede, brass nailed and supported on cabriole legs headed by 'C'-scrolls.

3. Armchair, giltwood, attributed to Thomas Chippendale, c1775.
An armchair of nearly identical design was supplied, with a suite of furniture, by Thomas Chippendale for the salon at Brocket Hall, Lincolnshire, around 1773. This example was probably from a set of eight or twelve, and would have been *en suite* with one, a pair or even four sofas.

Armchair, gilded beech, c1790.
⠇is chair would probably originally have been painted and gilded, ⠇ its design is similar to that of a chair at Ham House, Surrey. These ⠇themion-back chairs epitomize the refined elements of neo-⠇ssicism, but surprisingly were not illustrated in Hepplewhite's ⠇*ide* of 1788. One does, however, feature in the Gillow firm's ⠇cords for 1785.

4. Armchair, mahogany, c1780-85.
One of a pair, the sinuous curved members of this armchair are firmly held in place by the circular wheel-back, with its radiating palm leaves and festooned laurel. Whilst it can be argued that the elements of this chair do not blend harmoniously with each other, the wheel-back chair became increasingly popular and more refined by the late 1780s.

1.   Armchair, giltwood, c1770.
This chair, one of a set of eight, was originally at Saltram House, Devon, and was sold from there in 1920 by the 4th Lord Morley. The firm of Thomas Chippendale supplied furniture to Saltram between 1770 and 1772, and there is an opulent salon suite of eighteen gilt armchairs and two sofas in the house which is confidently attributed to him. They all correspond to one of Chippendale's standard 1770s drawing room patterns. The chair bears signs of green and cream paint under gilding.
Prov: Lord Morley; Ian Farquhar Esq.

2.   Armchair, giltwood, c1770-75.
This chair, one of a set of eleven *en suite* with a sofa, is similar to several from the successful London workshop of John Linnell. One in the Victoria and Albert Museum (Design no: E78-1929) is close to this example, and to a design by Linnell of 1768-70.
Prov: The Dodge Collection, listed originally as 'Franco-Flemish'.

3.   Armchair, giltwood, c1775.
This is one of a set of six armchairs in the Adam style, which have close affinities with contemporary French models. Most of the leading neo-classical makers produced chairs of this form: for example, Thomas Chippendale provided them in 1773 for the salon at Brocket Hall, Lincolnshire. The frame of this chair is well defined, with crisp carving; it has been re-upholstered with floral brocade.

4.   Armchair, mahogany, c1775. H *(back) 35,* W *(seat) 24:*
The armchair is one from a set of four in the manner of John Cobb (d. 1778). The very delicate, sinuous frame is characteristic of the period when Cobb carried on the business after the death of his partner William Vile in 1767. There are a number of variants of what was undoubtedly a successful model, in which the cabriole legs are headed by acanthus clasps, sweeping through to a gadroon-bordered seat frame.

This array of eight armchairs conveys effectively some of the problems of furniture history research, as well as demonstrating the varied skills of the chairmakers and upholsterers. A chair (2) may be similar to a pattern by Chippendale's rival John Linnell, but may never be proved to be by him. Similarly three more (1, 3 and 4) are in the established styles associated with Chippendale and John Cobb. Again the matter has to rest there.

Then there are the workshop stages of passing the frame over to the upholsterer who would prepare stuffing, webbing, under covers, tacks and the expensive cover fabric and shape, and sew and fasten it all in place. It is frequently this overall camber of seat and back which is disturbed by any casual re-upholstery, but there is growing knowledge and concern to do it as well as or better than the original maker, whoever he was.

5.   *Armchair, beechwood, c1770-75.*
The chair is one of a pair, with upholstered bowed seat and shield-shaped back. It is inscribed in ink: '3071 Hubberd'. The crisp decoration was worked with tools on thick gesso paste, which had been laid onto the beech frame, and was gilded to provide the final appearance.

6.   *Armchair, mahogany, c1775-80.* H *(back) 37,* W *(seat) 24.*
This is one from a set of six armchairs. Although the front legs are of straight neo-classical form, rococo curves still dominate the chair: it has cartouche-shaped back, splats opened to receive paterae and sharply-splayed back legs. It is an early example of what Hepplewhite was to refine so successfully for his *Guide*, which his wife published two years after his death, in 1788.

7.   *Armchair, mahogany, c1765-70.*
This design of generous but good proportions, with wings to exclude draughts, emphasizes comfort. It would have been a suitable chair for a library. The regular nailing pattern perhaps implies re-nailing when re-upholstery took place. The robust square legs are connected by stretchers, which have been partly renewed.
Prov: Wateringbury House, Kent.

8.   *Bergère, beechwood, c1765.*
The chair is in the French taste, with arched back and serpentine seat in leather, and with slender cabriole legs headed by shells. The French term *bergère* denotes a winged armchair of a type introduced in the 1720s. The name was anglicized and applied to couches by Mayhew and Ince in their *Universal System of Household Furniture* (1759-63).

1.   Settee, giltwood, designed by Robert Adam, 1780. w51.
The settee is from a suite, which included its pair, a larger sofa and a *confidante*, made for Sir Abraham Hume of 17 Hill Street, London. Adam's design for these, dated 9 March 1780, is among his drawings in Sir John Soane's Museum, London, and differs only by showing four rather than three front legs, The maker is unfortunately not known, but would be drawn from a small circle whom Adam could recommend to supply furniture of a high quality.

The liaison which existed between Robert Adam as architect and the craftsmen he used for various tasks—his 'regiment of artificers' as Mrs Elizabeth Montagu referred to them—is an interesting one. There were those he directed precisely, and others who were exceptionally competent and able to do work which satisfied both Adam and their joint patrons with little or no interference from either. The settee (1) was part of a suite designed by Adam for Sir Abraham Hume. The unknown maker has matched strength and elegance in the giltwood frame, taking proportions from the architect's drawing, but deciding that the weight of any sitter could be borne on three, rather than the four, front legs the design shows.

At the end of the 1780s, makers were more concerned with delicate shapes, caned seats, and mannered simulated feather-plumed backs— a far cry from the solid mahogany and circular fan-back of the neo-classical hall chair (3) produced a few years prior to the settee.

2.	*Armchair, mahogany and marquetry, c1790.* H *(of back) 36,* W *(of seat) 24.*
The arched, curved, shield-shaped backs appear with regularity in Hepplewhite's *Guide* of 1788 and Sheraton's *Drawing Book* of 1793. The splats are cleverly tapered to join in foliate lunettes, and the slender arm supports flow down into the square tapered legs, ending in block feet. Made in the last years of Robert Adam's 'reign' — he died in 1792 — they demonstrate very refined and delicate late neo-classical elements.

3.	*Hall chair, mahogany, c1775.*
This chair is similar to hall chairs suplied by Thomas Chippendale for Nostell Priory, Yorkshire, around 1775. It is stamped 'G.W.': such stamps are usually the initials of the journeyman who made the piece. It is interesting to note that a 'George West, cabinet-maker' subscribed to Chippendale's 1754 *Director*, although the association may be mere coincidence.
Prov: Wateringbury House, Kent.

4.	*Armchair, painted, c1790.*
The armchair is one from a set of six, with a shield back filled with Prince of Wales feathers. This motif became synonymous with Hepplewhite's name, and chairs bearing it appeared in his *Guide*. At this late date for neo-classical forms, the decoration is painted rather than carved, thus hiding a cheaper carcase wood.

*Here is the counterbalance common to furniture research: the documented settee by Thomas Chippendale for one of the Lascelles family, and the **confidante** (2) attributed to a French emigré worker in England, François Hervè. The one has the security of firm tenure, the other may never move beyond that, albeit near-certain, state of attribution to be firmly by Hervè. The latter presumably trained in France under a system which required its ébénistes to mark their furniture, and when first in England he worked with John Meschain, and took an apprentice Gabriel Laurent La Porte, presumably also of French origin. In his years in England, Hervè had to work against those versed in providing neo-classical stools and windowseats or mesmerized by the nuances of revived Gothic: much of it he may well have found strange and unfamiliar.*

1.   *Settee, mahogany, by Thomas Chippendale, c 1772. w47.*
The settee is one of a pair, supplied with a set of chairs by Thomas Chippendale to Daniel Lascelles for the dining room at Goldsborough Hall, Yorkshire. Originally covered in nailed red morocco leather, *en suite* to the chairs, it has been re-upholstered in recent years. The *guilloche* carving and husks, with the oval medallions at the head of the legs, is crisply executed.
Prov: Harewood House, Yorkshire.

2.   *Confidante, giltwood, attributed to François Hervè, c1785. w121.*
This piece has been attributed to François Hervè due to its similarity to that Hervè supplied in 1783 for the State Bedroom at Chatsworth.

The *confidante* was a type more favoured by French makers, and the distinctive stepped panels heading the legs have been noted as characteristic of Hervè's work.

3. *Hall seat, painted blue and gilded, c1785. W55.*
The Gothic taste was fashionable in the 1750s, and became so again in the 1780s. This hall seat, one of a pair, has a pierced Gothic tracery back and an upholstered seat. Such chairs were favoured for libraries, but are less usual designed for halls, which were places where wet and muddy clothes were discarded.

4. *Window seat, mahogany, attributed to John Cobb after a design by Robert Adam, c 1765. W48.*
The seat is one of the smaller of two pairs made for the Gallery at Croome Court, Worcesterhire. Adam's provision of a design, dated February 1765, for 'a Sopha or Scrol Chair', appears among his bills to the 6th Earl of Coventry. Adam was fond of the classical form of the 'Scroll Stool', and designed a similar one for Sir Lawrence Dundas for Moor Park, Hertfordshire, in 1766.

5. *Stool, mahogany, by Thomas Chippendale, 1772. H18, W26, D18.*
This is one of a set of four stools, supplied for the dining room at Mersham Le Hatch, Kent — probably for the window recesses. It is docmented by a bill. The distinctive foliate feet are also found on the set of green-japanned stools supplied by Chippendale for the State Bedchamber at Nostell Priory, Yorkshire, in 1771.

1. Commode, fustic and marquetry, c1775. H36, W58, D28.
The *bombé* form and decoration of this commode are in the manner of
John Cobb (d. 1778), although the decorative motifs are much simpler
than his normal style: for example, there are no gilt-brass corner
mounts. The top is cross-banded in kingwood and satinwood with a
central oval fustic panel of entwined ribbon and bell-flower pattern in
engraved purpleheart on a harewood ground. The cupboard doors
conceal two short and two long drawers.

It says much for the skill of competent furniture-makers of the calibre
of Thomas Chippendale and John Cobb that they could amend both
their style and workshop output to suit changing taste. Both were
capable mahogany furniture-makers, and Cobb had also trained as an
upholsterer in the early 1730s. And yet both were able to produce
marquetry furniture of superb quality. Admittedly they had large
workshops, and the degree of specialization therein and the use of
skilled out-workers has not yet been fully ascertained. Nevertheless,
the overall quality control had to come from the master of the shop. It
is present in these two commodes, one of which is confidently
attributed to Chippendale (2).

Commode, marquetry, attributed to Thomas Chippendale, c1778. W52.
The commode was made for Sir James Ibbetson, who hired a number of cabinet-makers to furnish his new home at Denton Hall, Yorkshire. According to a surviving account of money spent on furniture, Chippendale received the largest remuneration. The high standards of technical finish, and the character of the neo-classical decoration of this commode, very close to Chippendale's work at this period, justify confident attribution to the master.

The advances in the decoration of furniture referred to on the previous page are here further demonstrated. A mahogany chest (1) of good figured veneers is overshadowed by three superb pieces of marquetry furniture—one (2) showing in rare inscriptions both the identity of the artist of the engraving, the woman Royal Academician, Angelica Kauffmann, and that of the emigré marqueteur working for the Linnell workshop, the Swede Christopher Furhlohg. And then, supremely, the elliptical commode (4) in the context of the documented one for the Earl of Derby by Mayhew and Ince—precisely ornamented, decked with high-quality ormolu mounts, and paying the usual observance to matters of classical mythology, 'Diana surprising the sleeping Endymion'.

1. Chest, mahogany, c1765. w56.
This is a generous-sized serpentine chest of drawers, with chamfered corners and a veneered oval set in the top. The fronts of the drawers have a fine figure, a normal consideration of a good cabinet-maker using his mahogany veneers to best advantage.

2. Cabinet, marquetry on a sycamore ground, signed 'C. FURHLOHG, FECIT, MDCCLXXII' (1772). w66.
This cabinet, one of a pair, is signed by the émigré Swedish cabinet-maker, Christopher Fuhrlohg, who came to London about 1766-67. He is of particular interest in the context of the neo-classical movement, as he seems to have introduced into England a type of French commode of more or less rococo profile with neo-classical details of ornament. He worked in London for John Linnell. Furhlohg's signature is engraved in the marquetry panel, while on the lefthand side of the same panel is inscribed the source of the design, the Muse of Erato: 'Angelica Kauffmann'. The pair to this important cabinet is in the Lady Lever Art Gallery, Port Sunlight, Cheshire.
Prov: M. Knapp Esq.

3. Commode, sycamore, harewood, satinwood and marquetry, c1775. H34, W43, D18.
The coffer form of this commode is most unusual. The lid is hinged, and six drawers at the front are suitable for storage of cutlery, and the space beneath the lid for table linen. The bold neo-classical motifs are designed to conceal rather than emphasize functional aspects, and the horizontal mouldings and feet are gilt.
Prov: W. D. Clarke Esq.

4. Commode, satinwood and marquetry, c1775. H36, W72, D29.
This important elliptical commode, having a top with three applied ovals and a front one showing 'Diana surprising the sleeping Endymion' in the centre, is attributed to the London firm of Mayhew and Ince. A number of similar, highly-decorated commodes of this form survive, and fortunately the documentation for that supplied by the firm to Robert Adam's patron, the Earl of Derby, was discovered in 1984. This has allowed those which are similar to the Derby commode to be attributed to Mayhew and Ince. The firm excelled in creating a distinctive group of neo-classical marquetry commodes, making full use of exotic veneers flanked by ormolu mounts.

1. *Commode, harewood, fustic and marquetry, attributed to John Cobb, c1770-75. H36, W46, D22.*
The commode is one of a pair of *bombé* form, with the serpentine top edged with brass moulding, cross-banded in kingwood, and veneered with an oval fustic panel of ribbon-tied flowers in engraved and stained woods on a harewood ground. Certain features, like the brass banding, the apron that forms an integral part of the doors and the doors hinged on the side faces, are characteristic of John Cobb's workshop.

2. *Commode, kingwood and marquetry, attributed to Pierre Langlois, c1765-70. H35, W54, D21.*
In general shape, and in the use of crisp foliate ormolu mounts, this commode, one of a pair, corresponds to those identified as the work of Langlois by Peter Thornton and William Rieder. The sinuous foliage borders, the urns on the sides and the chevron banding are of a high order, with good use of cross-banded rosewood and natural green-stained woods.

When the French ébéniste *Pierre Langlois was resident in London in the 1760s, he advertized on his trade-card that he made 'all Sorts of Fine Cabinets and Commodes made & inlaid in the Politest manner with Brass & Tortoishell'. His first known commission was for the 4th Duke of Bedford (1759), which suggests that by this time his reputation was established in London, and the marquetry-decked commode (2) is attributed to him. His eventual competitors were to be Chippendale, John Linnell, Mayhew and Ince and John Cobb. But by the time they had changed their style he had perhaps changed his too. He paid rates on his Tottenham Court Road premises until 1781, but surprisingly few bills and references to his furniture are known, and what there is does not get further than 1764, when he worked for Robert Adam's patron, the 6th Earl of Coventry.*

3.   *Corner commode, tulipwood and satinwood, possibly by Thomas Chippendale, c1770. W29.*
The commode is in the Louis XV style, with a shaped front which opens to reveal shelves. The marquetry top is veneered with bouquets of flowers tied by ribands on a satinwood ground. One of the pair has ormolu foliage mounts to the legs.
Prov: Harewood House, Yorkshire.

4.   *Commode, sycamore and marquetry, c1780. H34, W59, D24.*
The rich neo-classical marquetry decoration of this commode, which is one of a pair, is offset by the horizontal ormolu borders; the feet are also fitted with cast ormolu mounts of acanthus leaves. Three drawers are concealed in the frieze, two at either side being spring operated, and the curved sides contain cupboards. An unidentified coat of arms, veneered on the semi-elliptical top, points to the piece being made as a special commission. It was obviously still regarded as important in the nineteenth century, when two copies, differing only in minor details, were made (sold Christie's, 5 October 1972, Lot 156).

The work William Vile and his partner John Cobb did at Croome Court, Worcestershire, for the 6th Earl of Coventry was their most prestigious contract (apart from work in the Royal palaces), and brought them into contact with Robert Adam. Their account opened in May 1757 and continued beyond Vile's death (1767) in Cobb's name. It contained well over 1300 items, and concluded about July 1772. They worked the mahogany well, with applied carving in robust forms, all betokening the new interest in the antique. Lord Coventry hardly patronized Chippendale at all, but many others did. The assured library table (4 and 5) was supplied to a London banker, and his pre-eminent marquetry one (on page 190) to a Yorkshire aristocrat. The mahogany clothes press (6) is of very fine colour, and also bears a label denoting its former ownership.

1. Cupboard, mahogany, 1765. H105, W72, D29.

The 6th Earl of Coventry, of Croome Court, Worcestershire, was one of Robert Adam's earliest patrons. Adam started work for him in 1761 and continued to supply designs over the following twenty years. In addition, he assembled a talented 'regiment of artificers' (as he later called them) to carry out the varied work, including a large team of cabinet-makers. This cupboard and its companion show the robust forms of early neo-classicism which William Vile and John Cobb used as decoration. They had been working for Lord Coventry as early as 1757, and therefore preceded Adam's own introduction to the Earl. The cupboards, called 'Cloaths Press' in Adam's design of 2 October 1764 (Sir John Soane's Museum), are similar to two formerly at Combe Abbey, Warwickshire, whilst the design for the plinths occurs in an Adam design of an organ case for Lord Bute in 1763. These cupboards are now in the Victoria and Albert Museum.

2. Detail of one of the four female heads on the mahogany cupboard.

3. Detail of the carved urn and foliated ornament on the door panels of the mahogany cupboard.

4. Library table, mahogany, c 1772. H30, W85, D47.
This library table was probably made around 1772 for John Martin, a banker. The timber has been carefully selected and the mouldings are well cut. The table descended in the Martin family until 1924 (Christie's, 27 March 1924, Lot 81); then by purchase to the Lords St. Just. The discovery of a definite connection between Chippendale's firm and the Martin family extends the maker's select group of commissions.

5. The Library table, detail. The locks have s-shaped brass keys (a favourite Chippendale mannerism) operated by one key.

6. Clothes press, mahogany, c1760. H59, W50.
It is always satisfying to encounter an item of furniture in which extra care has been taken in the selection of the mahogany. Whether in solid or veneer, the elements in door panels, drawer fronts and sides are carefully matched, flanked by beading where relevant and surmounted by good gilt-brass handles. The clothes press bears a label inscribed 'This wardrobe belonged to Radick Fowler (née Barnard of Coalbrookdale) . . .'

The contrast here, unfair as it may be, is between Thomas Chippendale's superb library writing table for Edward Lascelles of Harewood House, and a competent mahogany bookcase by an unknown maker. All makers needed, ideally, the balance of both kinds of commission in their output, but few achieved it. At least nine woods are used in the Harewood desk, predominantly rosewood, with the exterior having faded during two centuries' exposure to light. Reference to that on the interior shows the rosewood once provided a much stronger contrast to the inlay and mounts.

1.   *Library writing table, rosewood, oak , pine, mahogany and various other woods, by Thomas Chippendale, c1771. L207, H84, W120.*
Although Thomas Chippendale's existing account for furnishing Harewood House does not refer to this table, there is evidence that it was entered in an earlier bill which has not survived. It is known that between 18 and 25 April 1772, Chippendale's foreman-in-charge, William Reid, was partly occupied making covers for the completed library table supplied to Harewood. The dark chocolate-coloured rosewood on the inside door and drawer surfaces indicates how the exterior has bleached over two centuries' exposure to light. The cabinet wood is lavishly mounted with ormolu rams' mask pilasters and mouldings. Whilst it is fashionable always to assume these ormolu mounts were provided by Matthew Boulton, there is no evidence to support the idea, and Chippendale is known to have used various suppliers, including the King's founder, James Palmer.
Prov: Lascelles family at Harewood House, Yorkshire; Christie's, 1 July 1965, Lot 57; by purchase to Temple Newsam House, Leeds (No. 427).

2.   Detail of the 'Harewood library writing table' by Thomas Chippendale, c1771, showing the rams' mask pilasters, the linked rosette medallions in the frieze and the festooned vase surmounted by anthemion motifs. All four cupboard doors are so decorated. The end panels are inset with large rosette medallions, bordered by husk wreaths and foliate sprays.

3.   *Bookcase, mahogany, c1780. H99, W67.*
The carved foliate scrolls applied to the two lower cupboard doors (which flank four long drawers) are the only relief in an otherwise austere, but functional, design of this bookcase. Nevertheless, the geometric pattern of the glazing mullions, the broken pediment and the use of fine quality mahogany make this a handsome piece.

1.   Sideboard, mahogany, c1785. H35, W71, D29.
The bow front and neo-classical detail of pendant husks framing the deep cellarette drawers of this sideboard, the gilt-metal handles cast with urns and the shaped fluted frieze centred by a patera, result in an example of some quality.
Prov: Frederick Behrens Esq.

2.   Dining room suite, painted, c1775-80. Sideboard: H33, W58. Pedestals with knife urns: H67, W18. Wine cooler: W26.
A sideboard table, with a wine cooler below and a pair of pedestal urns on either side, was often used by Robert Adam to form a decorative unit in a dining room. He illustrated those he provided to the Earl of Mansfield in his *Works in Architecture* (1773). The painted furniture, with neo-classical motifs, matched similar painted and stucco decoration employed by Adam on the ceilings and walls of his patrons' houses.

To furnish an eighteenth-century house satisfactorily with the best achievements of the furniture-makers was an expensive and time-consuming affair. There was need to consider the dining room and seating furniture, to assess how grand they should be compared to their function, and to consider much more. Trays, knife-boxes, peat-buckets, jardinières were all easily available—but should they be mahogany, painted, brass-edged, having armorials thereon, or merely show that in every small item the patron was exercizing his superior judgement and taste? Pieces might also be acquired with delayed payment. Sir Edward Knatchbull wrote testily to Chippendale in January 1771: 'as I receive my rents once a year, so I pay my Tradesmens Bills once a year wch is not reckoned very bad pay as ye world goes . . .' It is surprising much was made at all in such circumstances.

3. Cutlery box, satinwood and marquetry, c1790. H15, W12, D6.
Decorated with neo-classical ornament in marquetry, and with the crest of the Bullock family of Norton and Darley, Derbyshire, this box is fitted with a spring-operated lock. Originally, the interior would have been divided into slots in which knives could be stored, blade downwards.

4. Peat bucket, mahogany, c1780. W15.
This is a functional, but carefully made, piece, with a fluted tapering body and spirally-turned handle. The top is mounted with a brass ring for added strength, as well as decorative value, and the liner is detachable.

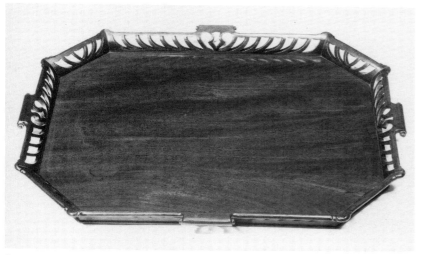

5. Tray, mahogany, c1765–70. W25.
The octagonal shape and curved pierced gallery with paper-scroll handles transforms a utilitarian product into one suitable to bear silver and porcelain into the drawing room.

6. Jardinière, mahogany, lead lined, c1775–80. H24. Diam 27.
A massive urn, boldly carved with gadrooning, stands on a spreading fluted base. The plinth is of a later date. It is surprising that the comparatively slender base is able to support the lead-lined urn when it is full of plants.

1. Bureau, mahogany, c1765. H44, W25.
When closed, the baize-lined writing flap of this bureau appears as two simulated drawers. The top, of good figured mahogany, has a gilt-metal gallery. There are identical handles on a commode now in the Metropolitan Museum, New York. Whilst such pieces of furniture have been regarded as in the manner of William Vile (d. 1767), any competent furniture-maker could have supplied them.

2. *Bed, beech and pine, painted, c1775. H96.*
This bedstead was made for David Garrick's riverside villa at Hampton, Middlesex. The painted hangings were produced at Masulipatam, Madras, to the order of the East India Company. Garrick reported that his wife had trouble with the customs authorities when bringing them into the country. Mrs Garrick objected to Thomas Chippendale's high charges for the work he did for her and her husband, The height of this bed has been slightly reduced by a former owner, and the hangings altered accordingly. It is now in the Victoria and Albert Musuem (No: W70-1916).

1.   *Mirror, giltwood, c1770. H60, W36.*
The precise form of this mirror corresponds to Robert Adam's design for a pier glass for 'the Parlour' at Kenwood House, Hampstead, London, included in *Works in Architecture of Robert and James Adam,* 1774 (Vol I, No. 2, Plate VIII). A number of mirrors of this evidently popular model are known.
Prov: Dame Rebecca West.

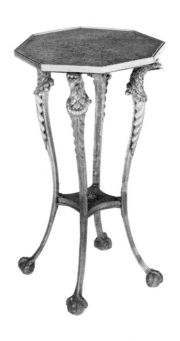

2.   *Lamp table, amboyna and giltwood, c1780. H29, Diam 16.*
The amboyna top edged with ormolu is supported on handsomely-carved eagle monopodia, providing a firm base for a candelabra.
Prov: Godmersham Park, Kent.

3.   *Torchère, giltwood, c1780. H49, Diam 11.*
One of a pair, the slender reeded shaft of this torchère is carved with acanthus leaves, and rests on a base raised by three splayed legs with paw feet. It is salutary to remember that in the eighteenth century candle-light was an important method of illuminating a room, necessitating the provision of strong, tall, yet elegant stands to bear the candelabra.

4.   *Torchère, simulated amboyna and giltwood, c1775. H58.*
This is one from a set of four torchères, which are related in style to a number designed by Robert Adam. With their trellis-pattern splats, rams' mask heads and concave-sided triangular bases resting on paw feet, great sophistication is encompassed in a small, if linear, area.
Prov: Hinchingbrooke House, Huntingdon, Cambridgeshire; Wateringbury House, Kent.

5.   *Library staircase, mahogany, c1770. H122, W49, D67.*
This example is on an imposing scale, with a return flight of
steps. The risers and base are pierced with similar curved
forms, while a mildly Gothic flavour is produced by the
cluster column supports with applied and pierced quatrefoil
patterns. The growing importance of the gentleman's library
in the late eighteenth century produced the need for strong,
practical steps, a combination of the arts of the turner and
the cabinet-maker.
Prov: Belton House, Lincolnshire

Secretaire cabinet, satinwood, c1790. W33.
The upper section has two rectangular cupboard doors, glazed with
oval panels. A long secretary drawer opens to a fitted interior. A
deep, drop-front drawer is decorated with two panels in the manner
developed by G. B. Cipriani, a painter who came into England in 1758
and who worked on the panels of George III's Coronation coach. The
whole is supported on square tapering legs. There are some
similarities in the lower stage to Thomas Sheraton's 'A New Design of
a Ladys Secretary & Cabinet' (*Drawing Book*, Appendix, dated
21 April 1794).

CHAPTER 6

Sheraton and
and Elegant Taste
1790–1805

Hepplewhite's *Guide* was followed by another important publication in 1788—*The Cabinet-Makers' London Book of Prices*. Sponsored by the London Society of Cabinet-Makers, it appeared again in 1793, 1803, and at various dates in the nineteenth century; a facsimile edition for furniture historians was published in 1982. The Society consisted of journeymen who had banded together as a collective organization to protect and improve wages and conditions—an early form of trade union activity. The *Book of Prices* was drawn up to present to the masters for approval. It set out piece-work rates for cabinet work—articles such as beds, chairs and settees were excluded—and contained twenty engraved plates, seventeen of which were contributed by Thomas Shearer. Despite the fact that the rates for work in the first edition had not been agreed with the masters prior to publication, and were therefore only suggestions, the price books gained in popularity. The second edition of the London one ran to 1000 copies, and at least twelve other price books were issued in provincial towns in the nineteenth century.

Thomas Sheraton praised Shearer's sound and workman-like designs—and, indeed, used them to advantage in his own work. He was not impressed by Hepplewhite's *Guide*—a serious challenge to his own work—and noted in respect of the *Book of Prices* that: 'it may be observed, with justice, that their designs are more fashionable and useful than his, in proportion to their number . . . I doubt not but they were capable of doing more than Hepplewhite has done, without the advantage of seeing his book: and it may be, for any thing I know, that the advantage was given on their side.'

Sheraton was born at Stockton-on-Tees, Durham, in 1751. He came of poor stock and described himself at thirty-one as 'a mechanic, and one who never received

the advantages of a *collegial* or *academical* education'. He progressed as a very competent draughtsman, undoubtedly trained in a furniture-making capacity but, like Hepplewhite, is not known to have made a single piece of furniture. His books of design and instruction ensured his lasting reputation, and like 'Hepplewhite' the name 'Sheraton' denotes a type of elegant furniture, usually in satinwood, made after the dimensions in his engraved plates. About 1790 Sheraton left the north of England, and was said after 1793 to have 'supported himself, a wife and two children, by his exertions as an author'. His trade-card advertises that he taught 'Perspective, Architecture and Ornaments' and made 'Designs for Cabinet-makers' and sold 'all kinds of Drawing Books'. On the title page of his *Drawing Book* he did, however, describe himself as 'Thomas Sheraton, Cabinet-Maker'.

Sheraton's *The Cabinet-Maker and Upholsterer's Drawing Book* came out in parts between 1791 and 1794. Parts I and II concern themselves with geometry and perspective and parade Sheraton's fascination with both subjects; Part III, much the most valuable, states his intention 'to exhibit the present taste of furniture, and at the same time to give the workman some assistance'. The intention was very successfully realized, and the work displayed its author's technical knowledge of the cabinet trades. The *Appendix*, which gave 'a variety of original designs for household furniture', was issued in 1793 and an *Accompaniment* containing 'ornaments useful for learners to copy from, but particularly adapted to the cabinet and chair branches: exhibiting original and new designs of chair legs, bed pillars, window cornices, chair splats and other ornaments' in 1794.

The extent to which Sheraton was responsible for inventing his designs is uncertain: he seems to have taken what was good and current in the London

Pembroke table, sycamore, c1795. H29, W39, D30.
The top of the table, with twin flaps supported on hinged brackets, is cross-banded in satinwood with ebonized border, and the elegant square tapering legs are outlined in boxwood. George Simson, whose label this table bears, also provided tables with neo-classical painted (as opposed to veneered) decoration.

Trade label on Pembroke table. 'George Simson, Upholder, Cabinet Maker & Undertaker, No 19, South side of St. Paul's Church Yard, London'. George Simson was established at this address between 1790 and 1827.

workshops, and he acknowledged his indebtedness to others. For example, in the note to Plate LVI for a 'Harlequin Pembroke Table', Sheraton writes: 'I assume very little originality and merit to myself, except what is due to the manner of shewing and describing the mechanism of it: the rest is due to a friend, from whom I received my first ideas.'

Sheraton's designs differed from those of Hepplewhite and Shearer, and had a greater affinity with furniture being produced in the later years of the reign of Louis XVI in France. Much furniture of this type had been brought into England by the first *émigrés*, as many craftsmen took refuge in England when the French Revolution began to impose its intolerable policies. Sheraton, like Hepplewhite, made use in his designs of a slender tapered leg of square section, and a turned cylindrical leg, but relied more on the latter form, particularly for pier tables, ornamental cabinets and drawing room chairs. He preferred reeding to fluting, circular brass handles, ornamental or plain, and freely adapted many ornamental motifs made popular by Robert Adam, such as the vase, urn, swags, paterae, garlands and ribbons and plumes. He also advocated extensive use of ornament of inlaid stringing lines of a contrasting wood to the carcase. His sense of propor-

Sofa table, satinwood, c1800. w (open) 60.
The top of the table is cross-banded in rosewood and tulipwood.
Stringing is used to emphasize the drawers, and to outline the arched
splayed legs, which are united by a strong cross stretcher. Such tables
became popular towards the end of the eighteenth century.

tion and balance was that of an aesthete, but some of
the designs reflect over-elaboration and an effeminate
use of drapery and upholstery. He remarked on his use
of brass, a new feature of furniture design, in *The
Cabinet Dictionary*, issued in 1803: were it not for the
excellence of French brass mounts 'by which they set
off cabinet work' it would not 'bear comparison with
ours, neither in design, nor neatness of execution'. He
used brass to enrich small galleries or for stringing, and
brass rods were provided at the back of sideboards,
focusing on a central two-branch candelabrum. Sheraton
also showed a willingness to experiment, supportng a
Pembroke table on a 'pillar and claws', and his designs
for writing tables and work tables incorporated lyre-
shaped end supports on splayed feet, a feature which
was to appear subsequently with great regularity.
Stretchers were united with shelves or low platforms,
and it might be said that Sheraton was at his best when
proposing new forms.

Since 1783 Henry Holland, as architect to the Prince

of Wales, had been engaged in supervising the re-
decorating and refurnishing of Carlton House. Furniture to his designs or made under his direction came
from the leading makers. These included the considerable firms of Seddon's, founded by George Seddon
about 1750; Gillow of Lancaster and London, who had
set up in the late 1720s; John Mclean, who was included
by Sheraton in his 'List of most of the Master Cabinet-
Makers, Upholsterers and Chair-Makers in and about
London, for 1803' (appended to *The Cabinet Dictionary*);
Oakleys, referred to in 1801 as 'the most tasteful of the
London cabinet-makers'; Charles Elliott, 'upholsterer to
his Majesty, and Cabinet-maker to the Duke of York';
Thomas Chippendale the Younger (1749–1822), who
had contined his father's business after 1779; and Ince
and Mayhew, established in the late 1750s, and still
active into the early nineteenth century.

The London cabinet-makers still used mahogany
extensively, both in solid and veneered form, but it was
being challenged by their interest in satinwood. This
was imported from the West and East Indies and
ranged in colour from a pale yellow to a deep orange.
Sheraton liked it for its 'cool, light, and pleasing effect
in furniture', and it provided an admirable ground for
inlaid decoration, often banded against a dark wood

Chair, painted and gilt, c1795. H38, W20.
There is a school of thought which argues that the Gothic style never really died away: that its revival was merely a 'survival', albeit unheeded. The neo-classical architect, Robert Adam, had an abiding interest in Gothic matters, as did his younger contemporary, James Wyatt. Those patrons who had an interest in the Gothic took their lead from Horace Walpole, whose concern for its stylistic nuances occupied most of his adult life. Whilst Gothic is perhaps a style best suited to stone, the motifs of tracery and rosettes are faithfully rendered in this piece of furniture. The chair has a caned seat.

In the last years of the eighteenth century marquetry, which had supplanted carving, was itself superseded by painting or japanning: two ways of decorating in colour at little expense of time or money. Sheraton had noted that 'inlaying, in cabinet-making' had been 'much in use between twenty and thirty years back' but 'laid aside, as a very expensive mode of ornamenting furniture, as well as being subject to a speedy decay'. Veneering—'the art of laying down and gluing very thin cut wood, of a fine quality and valuable, upon common wood' as Sheraton described the process— continued in popularity, as it gave excellent decorative effects when contrasted by banding. The banding was done in exotic woods by either cutting along the length of the grain (straight-banding) or across the grain (cross-banding). A variant was feather-banding, in which the wood was cut at an angle between 'straight' and 'cross'. The bands were often edged with strings of box, sycamore, holly, or other light-coloured woods. Inlaying with brass was, however, more durable, and looked well let into a dark wood such as rosewood. Sheraton had recommended its use in his *Drawing Book* for 'A Library Table', dated 1791 (Plate XXX): 'the strength, solidity, and effect of brass mouldings are very suitable to such a design, when expense is no object . . . the astragal which separates the upper and lower parts might be of brass, and likewise the edge of the top together with the patera in the upper panel . . .'

A pleasing effect could be obtained by the use of common or of inlaid fluting. The common form, applied to the frieze or legs of a table, consisted of grooves cut in the solid wood. The inlaid form used stringing to point the edges of the grooves in, say, satinwood or mahogany, and when done diagonally on the apron of a bow-fronted sideboard looked very effective. The reverse of fluting was reeding, and when done spirally (Sheraton showed three patterns of chair legs in the *Accompaniment* to the *Drawing Book*, 1793) gave a great richness to the chair. The reeding, often on the lower tapering sections of the legs, was often surmounted by a round collar of rich acanthus carving, and above a square section head with applied carved motifs of feathers or plumes. Finally, the structured parts of furniture could be given emphasis by adding mouldings of various profiles. These were made by the use of moulding planes and, as in banding, could be 'long-way' (with the grain) or 'cross-way'. If the moulding was shaped to apply to a serpentine surface, the *Book of Prices* showed a charge of four times more than 'long-way' for such work across the grain. Many of these techniques were indicated in the pages of Sheraton's *Drawing Book* and used to enhance the furniture itself.

As in Hepplewhite's *Guide*, the most numerous designs in Sheraton's *Drawing Book* were for chairs and chair backs. Sheraton could not resist another dig at the *Guide*—after all there was only Mrs Hepplewhite to answer since the death of her husband in 1786: 'notwithstanding the late date of Hepplewhite's book if we compare some of the designs, particularly the chairs, with the newest taste we shall find that this work has

and inlaid with panels of other woods. It could also be painted, but beech was in extensive use for painted furniture as well as for the seat rails of chairs, settees, bed frames, and all forms of carcase work. It was, said Sheraton, 'the cheapest wood in use', but he had also to reckon with pine or fir (deal) boards brought in from Scandinavia and the Baltic. Since yellow deal was soft and free from knots, it made an excellent base for veneers.

Amongst types of decoration, carving had fallen into disuse about 1765. Robert Adam and his craftsmen could achieve many of its effects by the use of gesso, which was light, easily turned from moulds and readily carved and decorated with scrapers, punches and other tools. It made an excellent base for subsequent gilding.

already caught the decline, and perhaps in a little time, will suddenly die in the disorder.'

Chairs of this 'newest taste' were rectilinear in form, a near rectangle back composed of four or more carved bars arranged vertically, with a curved top rail carved with a trail of husks, and the uprights of the back reeded. Sheraton favoured this form to the oval heart or shield types beloved by Hepplewhite, and which despite his strictures continued to be made throughout the 1790s and on into the early nineteenth century. It was a marked change to a design of greater elegance and proportion, with a restrained use of ornament.

Sheraton distinguished between chairs for the parlour and chairs for the drawing room. The 'Dining Parlour' chairs were to be 'substantial, useful things avoiding trifling ornaments and unnecessary ornamentation'. Mahogany was the wood specified, with a straight grain. He observed that the Spanish or Cuba mahogany 'will rub bright, and keep clearer than any Honduras wood'. The drawing room chairs, in contrast, were to be painted and gilt or japanned. The 'legs and stumps' were in one example he engraved (*Appendix*, Plate VI) to 'have twisted flutes and fillets, done in the turning, which produce a good effect in the gold'. The drawing room chairs had rounded seats, turned, fluted or reeded legs tapering to the foot, and turning was also applied to the back uprights and arm supports. The parlour chairs had straight-fronted seats, square taper legs, and flat moulded uprights.

The fashion for painting furniture was now widespread, and Sheraton included several 'Backs for Painted Chairs' in the *Drawing Book*, reflecting taste of the 1790s. The chairs were made, usually, of beech, with caned seats, and the floral ornament was painted on to the uprights and top rail. About 1795 small figure subjects in small oval or rectangular panels were introduced, particularly for 'Tea Room' chairs. When he was writing later in *The Cabinet Dictionary* in 1803, Sheraton implied some change of mind: 'The tea-room or breakfast-room may abound with beaufets, painted chairs, flower-pot stands, hanging book shelves . . . and all the little things which are engaging to the juvenile mind.'

Sheraton had favoured filling the backs of rectangular chairs with vertical bars, but many makers improved, or so they thought, on his recommendation. The diagonal lattice was popular, as were fillings which consisted of either a horizontal lattice between horizontal bars, or one in which an oblong or oval panel was put into the back of a larger cane-work oblong or oval. The seat rails, legs and uprights would be japanned black with gold lining and painted floral motifs. The interest in the orient persisted, particularly in work for the Prince Regent at Brighton Pavilion. Elward, Marsh and Tatham supplied in 1802 chairs of imitation bamboo, with cane seats, and cane oblongs in backs with top rails of pierced quatrefoils. They were to be finished with 'canvas hair cushions for the back and seats covered with red morocco leather'. In his *Drawing Book* (Plate XXXII) design for two 'Drawing Room Chairs',

dated 1792, Sheraton noted: 'The figures in the tablets above the front rails are on French pleated silk or satin, sewed on to the stuffing, as is the ornamented tablet at the top of the left-hand chair. The top rail is pannelled out, and a small gold bead mitred round, and the printed silk is pasted on.'

There was no mention in the *Drawing Book* of hall chairs (which had been at their most handsome in designs by Kent, Chippendale and Adam), although they were widely produced. As they were not made for comfort and had no upholstery, being in mahogany or painted, they escaped Sheraton's attention, as did stools. No development in the design occurred before 1800, but in the early nineteenth century a revival of archaeological interests encouraged production of the 'X'-pattern chairs of antiquity. At the same time Sheraton did favour a 'conversation chair' which had a wide, deep seat narrowing at the back. The conversationalist, although there was no need for him to say anything, sat with his legs across the seat, facing the back with his arms on a padded top rail. It had a similarity to the earlier library chairs, in the arms of which candlestands or ink wells on brass slides were mounted. Settees of chair-back form, upholstered or caned, were handsome creations, severe in outline with usually a straight back centring on long oblong panels in the top rail. A variation was the *chaise-longue*, which Sheraton said was 'to rest or loll upon after dinner'.

The *Drawing Book* had no design for a dining table: as with Chippendale and Hepplewhite before, it held little scope for Sheraton's inventiveness. Dining tables were also cheap to produce—the 1793 *Book of Prices* showing them at a basic price of 1s. 2d. a foot, and they could be produced with many flaps for extending, joined together by 'tongues and mortices' or 'hinge and button fastenings'. A popular form was made in three parts: a rectangular centre with two extensions, a pair of semicircular ends, with a single flap. When not in use the ends stood against a wall or were used as side tables. Jane Austen refers to them in a letter of 1800: 'The two ends put together form one constant table for everything, and the centre piece stands exceedingly well under the glass, and holds a great deal most commodiously without looking awkwardly.' Many dining tables were supported on central pillars only—the 'pillar and claw tables'. A handsome turned pillar would have four short legs or 'claws' ending in brass caps and castors. They could be made to any size (Sheraton indicated a measured allowance of '2 feet to each person sitting at table') by having a sufficient quantity of pillar and claw parts with loose flaps joined together by iron or brass fork straps. It was not a wholly satisfactory system and many patents were filed in the early nineteenth century for tables with flaps 'which are made to draw out, and loose flaps inserted'. Richard Gillow patented one in 1800 and Richard Brown and George Remington followed in 1805 and 1807 respectively. Thomas Shearer even gave a design for a 'Horseshoe Dining Table' (1788) in the *Book of Prices* which extended to form half a circle, 2 ft. 6 in. in width of flap. Some were adapted as

Invalid's chair, mahogany, c1795-1800.
The back and seat of the chair are comfortably padded, and hand controls are fitted to the arm rests. The chair moves on turned brass wheels. This is an imposing exemplar of an early wheelchair, refined in later years as a (covered) Bath chair, and now made in tubular steel. The provision of patented furniture suitable for invalids was a remunerative trade, practised by many London cabinet-makers from the late years of the eighteenth century onwards.
*Prov:*Wateringbury House, Kent.

wine or social tables, fitted with movable coasters attached to a brass rail.

Breakfast tables—the meal as a substantial event is perhaps a British phenomenon—were introduced a little before 1800. The poet Robert Southey had one large enough 'for eight or nine persons, yet supported upon one claw in the centre'. He wrote of a visit of 1802–03 in his *Letters from England* (1807) that 'this is the newest fashion, and fashions change so often in these things, as well as in everything else, that it is easy to know how long it is since a house has been fitted up, by the shape of the furniture.'

As only five years separated the publication of Hepplewhite's *Guide* (1788) and Sheraton's *Drawing Book* (1793) there are some similarities. Sideboards in both were indicated 'without drawers of any sort, having simply a rail a little ornamented, and pedestals with vases at each end, which produce a grand effect'. Hepplewhite had given two designs for sideboards without drawers to fit into a recess and noted that 'a dining room [is] incomplete without a sideboard'. The sideboard table and cellaret sideboard types were given in the *Book of Prices*, variously shaped, so as to seem

almost confusing: made with 'Eliptic Middle, and Eliptic Hollow on each side'. Sheraton, however, concentrated only on sideboards with drawers, having the candle or lamp-branches at the back, 'which, when lighted, give a very brilliant effect to the silverware'. Bottles or plates were kept in the fitted drawers, that for bottles being divided and lead-lined, that for plates lined as a baize division. His sideboard measured overall about 7 ft. 6 in. in length for, as the percipient Sheraton observed: 'If a sideboard be required nine or ten feet long, as in some noblemen's houses, and if the breadth of it be in proportion to the length, it will not be easy for a butler to reach across it'. He therefore proposed a hollow front which 'would obviate the difficulty . . . [and] sometimes secure the butler from the jostles of the other servants.' Such a long sideboard needed at least six legs, turned in their whole length, or rounded as far as the frame and turned below it, with carved leaves and flutes.

Other tables which came into general use were kidney-shaped library writing tables and ladies' writing tables. A kidney-shaped one in the *Book of Prices*, dated 1792, was 'Four feet long, two feet wide, and veneer'd front and ends, four drawers in each wing, and one ditto above the knee hole, cock beaded, an astragal round the bottom of the carcase; on eight taper stump feet, £5. 2s.' Modifications, at extra charge, allowed for lining and veneering the top, making the table in three carcases, veneering partition edges 'askew and cross

Bergère, brown painted, c1800.
Sheraton, in *The Cabinet Dictionary* (1803), describes a bergère as 'having a caned back and arms. Sometimes the seats are caned, having loose cushions'. Bergères were often *en suite* to a matching sofa with a triple cushion back and a cushion seat.
Prov: Wateringbury House, Kent.

...mmode chair, beechwood, c1800.
...he lifting circular cane seat of the chair is fitted with a massive blue
...d white Chinese porcelain jardinière decorated with a lake scene.
...his chair exemplifies the odd but sturdy proportions of such
...esigns. The jardinière was surely incorporated later, rather than as
...e maker's original intention.
...ov: Wateringbury House, Kent.

Cylinder writing desk, mahogany, c1800-03. w (closed) 34, w (open) 52.
The piece was made after a design which appeared in Thomas
Sheraton's The Cabinet Dictionary of 1803 (Plate 38). The centre section
of the leather-lined writing slide lifts to reveal a cedar interior, and
the two semi-circular side flaps fold down when not in use, The
designs in Sheraton's books are characterized by great mechanical
ingenuity, matched to excellent proportions, and by the suggested
use of fine woods and veneers.

...ay' with 'king, tulip or any other hard wood', provid-
...ng decorative pilasters at the front, or cupboards in the
...wings.

Cabinets, or ladies' writing tables were made small
...ike the work and writing tables, fire screens and trio
...nd quartetto tables of the pattern-books) to be moved
...rom room to room. They often served a double func-
...ion, occasionally assisted by ingenious mechanisms to
...nove flaps and other parts, and the *Drawing Book* gave
...nany designs for them. The table was supported on
...lender taper legs with one long drawer in the frame,
...itted to contain ink, pens and sand. A detachable low
...uperstructure of drawers and pigeon-holes could be
...obtained, secured by a beading and provided with a
...nandle for lifting. It was made no more than twenty
...nches wide and was decorated, frequently, with a vase
...notif introduced in the back of the upper shelf. Such
...ables were usually made in satinwood and had painted
...lecoration.

A distinct form of writing or library table which came
...nto use about 1790 was the 'Carlton House Table'.
...Whilst the architect Henry Holland had been working
...or the Prince of Wales at Carlton House, and using
...nany French craftsmen, since the early 1780s, the
...origin of the term for the table has not been established.
...t remained in fashionable use until about 1810, and
...consisted usually of a mahogany writing table sup-
...ported on plain taper, square-section legs. The table

was fitted with a rising desk; there were three drawers
in the frame and various small drawers and compartments in the superstructure, which had curved ramps
at each end. One was illustrated in a 1792 engraving 'by
Hepplewhite' in the *Book of Prices*, 1793 (Plate XXI).

The term 'bureau', wrote Sheraton in *The Cabinet
Dictionary*, 'has generally been applied to common
desks with drawers beneath them, such as are made
very frequently in country towns.' The place of this
common desk had, however, been taken by the bureau
with a roll top or cylinder front and by many small
writing tables and cabinets. The bureau, which resembled contemporary bookcases, also gave way to the
'Secretary and Bookcase' and the 'Cylinder Desk and
Bookcase'. Sheraton's design for a 'Secretary and Bookcase' (*Drawing Book*, Plate XXVIII) was to be made in
mahogany, decorated in satinwood, and with japanned
ornaments. It was tall with applied pilasters, had a
straight cornice, lunette-shaped pediment 'cut in the
form of a fan' and in its lower stage had a secretary
drawer letting down on quadrants and clothes-press
shelves behind two doors.

The 'Cylinder Desk and Bookcase' was lighter and
more elegant—examples have been noted in yew
wood—on taper legs, with a desk of drawers and
pigeon-holes behind a tambour front. The upper section of a pair of glazed doors with shelves in grooves
behind was surmounted by a pierced scrolled pediment

with a central plinth to support a small plaster bust, urn or vase. Sheraton was fascinated by the tracery of glazing bars and gave many patterns for bookcase doors, and several for bookcase pediments (*Drawing Book*, Plate LVII). Segmented, lunette-shaped or fan-shaped pediments often centring on a veneered or japanned tablet, were in general use at the end of the eighteenth century. They were occasionally set atop wardrobes as well as bookcases, but on balance the proportions of both wardrobes, chests of drawers and clothes presses called for a straight cornice.

No drawing or dressing room was complete without a mirror. The circular convex ones, thought of primarily as Regency, were in fact introduced about 1795, having been used in France since the 1750s. It was the only form Sheraton noted in the *Cabinet Dictionary*—'a mirror is a circular convex glass in a gilt frame'—but chimney glasses or overmantel mirrors in carved frames, made to rest on the length of the chimney shelf, were popular. They were made in three horizontal divisions, with a larger central section flanked by two smaller ones, all with bevelled plates, and all surmounted by a broad frieze containing low-relief decoration—frequently a casual version of Guido Reni's *Aurora going before the Sun*.

Two types of dressing glass were in use: the full-length cheval glass, known as a 'horse dressing glass' which reflected the whole person, and the small toilet mirror on a stand. The latter declined a little in favour as fitted dressing tables containing a 'rising glass' became available. Mahogany or rosewood was used to make them, and small oval feet were fashioned from ivory or bone with handles and diamond keyhole surrounds in the same materials.

It is important to remember that candles were still in general use for lighting, and Sheraton preferred their light in drawing rooms. They needed to be set upon candle stands, and it was simple to adapt such delicate tripod stands for flowers. They were invariably gilded, or furnished in white and gold: only in 'inferior drawing rooms' were they 'japanned answerable to the furniture'. Light and heat from a fire encouraged the introduction of pole screens to protect eyes and complexions. Sheraton recommended mahogany for their construction. They were tall, slender and on convex or concave curving claws or standards, with taper feet. The screen itself, in oval or shield shape, was fastened by a ring and screw to the pole, and contained fine prints, worked in satin, gathered silk or even 'filigree' rolled paper work. A more sophisticated variant had a pulley and weight arrangement to allow the screen to be balanced at any desired height.

Many of Sheraton's designs in *The Cabinet Dictionary* reflect the changes in taste in England and Europe. Whilst we might regard them as 'Regency', that eclectic style had little to do with the personal taste of the

Pembroke table, harewood and marquetry, c1790. W (open) 43.
This is a versatile table: it has an easel top to facilitate the polite accomplishment of drawing, and its twin flaps give a wider surface when the easel is lowered to form the centre. The piece is made even more precise and desirable by the central roundel of a classical scene and the ribbon-tied swags centred by ovals. It is set on slender, square, tapering legs with castors to aid movement.

Prince Regent. There was a new interest in the archaeological remains of Egypt, Greece and Rome, in fashioning work in bronze and marble and in the French Empire style. Sheraton had little to offer to this academic mood and he was failing in health and disordered in mind. *The Cabinet Dictionary* did include a few patterns for 'Grecian' chairs (based on the *klismos* which had a curved back and sabre-shaped legs), and for couches and 'X'-framed chairs.

Sheraton died on 22 October 1806 'after a few days illness of a phrenitis, aged 55', and for one so talented 'left his family in distressed circumstances'. His widow Margaret Sheraton inherited but £200, and her husband's final work, *The Cabinet Maker, Upholsterer, and General Artist's Encyclopaedia*, of which only a single volume, 'A–C', had appeared in 1805.

Secretaire cabinet, mahogany and satinwood, 1795. H97, W49.
The cabinet's geometric patterns and borders in satinwood stand out against the mahogany background, producing an austere design only partly relieved by the curved cornice, vase finials and waved apron. A baize-lined secretaire drawer is fitted above the cupboards in the lower section. The growing importance of furniture for the display of books and china, and as a place to write and store papers, is shown by the large number of good late eighteenth-century cabinets which survive, all neatly veneered and of good proportions.

1.　*Dining table, mahogany, c1795. L (extended) 112, w54.*
Here is an example of strong, practical furniture, intended by the maker for a busy dining room. The centre section of the table, with twin flaps supported on gate-legs, serves to extend an otherwise octagonal-shaped table. Boxwood stringing outlines the plain, deep frieze.

2.　*Dining table, mahogany, c1800. L (including two extra leaves) 112, w49.*
Perhaps the most satisfying dining tables are those which are sturdily, yet elegantly, supported on two or more pedestals. The fluted, splayed feet, terminating in brass caps and castors, are pleasing yet practical, and the furniture-maker has been anxious to choose wide mahogany of good figure for the top.

3.　*Dining table, mahogany, c1800. L (including extra leaf) 131, w64.*
Fully extended, the table includes four pedestals (three are shown), one supporting each section. The fluted, splayed legs with brass castors contribute to a practical design, in which due consideration has been given to appearance overall.

In Thomas Sheraton's Cabinet Dictionary (1803), his comments on dining tables are of relevance '. . . there are various sorts now in use, and some under the protection of his Majesty's patent. The common useful dining-tables are upon pillar and claws, generally four claws to each pillar, with brass castors. A dining-table of this kind may be made to any size, by having a sufficient quantity of pillars and claw parts, for between each of them is a loose flap, fixed by means of iron straps and buttons, so that they are easily taken off and put aside'. The large central table was becoming a feature of dining rooms, and therefore serving the sitters necessitated the use of smaller tables; equally, a breakfast table (5) could merely seat two in comfort.

4.   Dining table, mahogany and rosewood, c1785. L (extended) 116, w40.
A 'D'-shaped leaf draws out at either end of the table from under the cross-banded top to increase the length. Consideration has also been given to the shaping of the points where it joins the square, tapering legs. It is a small modification calculated to improve the overall appearance of a practical piece of furniture.

5.   Breakfast table, mahogany, c 1790. w56.
A satinwood band decorates the oval top of the table, which is well supported on a turned, tapering shaft with a splayed quadripartite base, all in good proportion. Such tables could easily be moved to the centre of a room for use, and returned to a corner thereafter: the central fixed position of the dining room table was a nineteenth-century obsession, which has persisted.

6.   Serving table, mahoagny, c1795. w85.
As large families assembled for meals, greater provision than hitherto had to be made for the setting out of covered dishes, or to assist the household staff when serving at a centre table, This serving table, one of a pair, is in neo-classical style, and has a gilt metal border to the frieze and pendant foliage, swags and masks as decoration. The tapering, reeded legs provide effective support.

In his Letters from England *(1807),* Robert Southey *wrote: 'Our breakfast table is oval, large enough for eight or nine persons yet supported upon one claw in the centre. This is the newest fashion, and fashions change so often in these things, as well as in everything else, that it is easy to know how long it is since a house has been fitted up, by the shape of the furniture'. Obviously, between the large dining table, on as many as four pillar and claw supports, and the tip-up top breakfast table, there were many variations in size and consequent seating capacity. The newer forms of sideboard available from the early 1780s from firms such as Gillow were composite pieces which took the place of sideboard table, pedestals and urns (4).* Hepplewhite's *Guide (1788) observed that the conveniences afforded by sideboards with drawers rendered a dining room incomplete without them: for their part, Gillow said in 1779 they were made 'in a genteel style to hold bottles'.*

1. *Breakfast table, rosewood, c1795. W57.*
The oval top of the table, with its satinwood band, tips up for easy storage. A simple, functional piece, which has a splayed quadripartite base rather than a triple one, this form of table allowed the furniture-maker to lavish his attention on a fine figured top, which contrasted well with the silver and glass place settings.

2. *Dining table, mahogany, c1805. L174, H28, D60.*
This fine table has a top of good figured mahogany, and a reeded edge. The carved, quadruped bases are finished with brass lions' paws and castors to provide more than adequate support. During the later years of the nineteenth century, such tables were often covered completely in starched, white napery, with all view of their appearance lost.

3.   *Sideboard, mahogany, c1795. W84, D28.*
The furniture-maker has concentrated here on a clear form and on the practical aspects of providing good cupboards and drawer space, with just enough ornament to produce a pleasing result. The depth is but a third of the width, which enables it to sit back neatly against a long wall of the dining room, the shaped ends contributing to proportioned practicality.

4.   *Sideboard, mahogany, c1790. W103.*
This elaborately-shaped and ornamental sideboard demonstrates the strength of its structure — it is almost nine feet wide — as well as showing the contrasting use of satinwood and mahogany. The marquetry neo-classical decoration is carved out to great effect, with satinwood banding and *trompe-l'oeil* fluting to the raised back section.

Many small tables were 'universal', in the sense of Sheraton's design for a 'Universal Table', in that they were intended to serve as both breakfast and dining table. On a variety of slender legs and with many shapes in vogue—square, oval, round—they were also used for games (some have inlaid patterns for this), for serving tea or wine and as dressing, work and writing tables. Fanny Burney, writing to her father in 1801, noted that no room looked really comfortable, or even quite furnished, without two tables. One was to be kept near the wall and 'take upon itself the dignity of a little tidyness, the other to stand here, there, and everywhere . . .' and be used for a little work or to hold a few books. They suited a life-style with time for such pleasing activity.

1. *Card table, satinwood and marquetry, c1795. w40.*
This is one of a pair in the style of William Gates, a London maker who succeeded John Bradburn in service to the Crown in 1777. Gates was a competent craftsman. and seems to have specialized in inlaid furniture: he provided 'two very fine sattenwood inlaid commode tables to stand under peirs . . .' for the Prince of Wales's apartment at St James's Park in 1781, at a cost of £80. This table has a folding cirular top cross-banded with rosewood and inlaid with urns and flower festoons. The square tapering legs are headed by oval medallions.

2. *Side table, rosewood, c1795. w53.*
The shape of this table conforms to a design for a pier table by Thomas Sheraton (1793), with its curved stepped top, decorated with a broad satinwood band, slender turned legs and curved front stretcher. The frieze bears an ebonized painted and gilded central medallion and musical trophies.

3. *Side table, satinwood, rosewood and marquetry, c1795. w30.*
This elegant table shows French influence in its curved feminine forms and decoration. The trellis and rose pattern parquetry top bears a marquetry oval, and the shaped frieze is also ornamented with marquetry neo-classical motifs. The interest of the Prince of Wales in French decoration and in collecting French furniture was not lost on English cabinet-makers, who were anxious to be in the latest vogue.

4. *Side table, satinwood, c1790. w43.*
The table is in the 'French Hepplewhite style', the top embellished with marquetry anthemion, flower sprays and ribbon-tied swags, and cross-banded with rosewood. Carving is used to decorate the delicately curved legs. George Hepplewhite stated in the Preface of his *The Cabinet-Maker and Upholsterer's Guide*, published in 1788, two years after his death, by his widow, that 'English taste and workmanship have, of late years, been much sought for by surrounding nations . . .' Equally, he was concerned to show items 'derived from the French'

5.   *Pembroke table, satinwood and beechwood, c1790. w (open) 37.*
George Hepplewhite stated that 'Pembroke Tables are the most
useful of this species of furniture: they may be of various shapes. The
long square and oval are the most fashionable. These articles admit of
considerable elegance in the workmanship and ornaments.' The
waved, twin-flap top of this example is skilfully veneered, with the
wood grains laid in different directions, surrounding ovals of pollard
oak bordered with rosewood. The square, tapering legs are made of
beechwood.

6.   *Pembroke table, mahogany and painted, c1795. w35.*
En suite with a pair of card tables, this piece is in the Sheraton style
with a top veneered with curled maple and wide borders painted
with symmetrical peacock feathers and scrolls. In the
'Accompaniment' to his *Drawing Book* (1793), Thomas Sheraton
showed (Plate 7) that a cabinet-maker of ability could embellish such
a plain table top with a lavish symmetrical scrolled pattern centring
on a diamond lozenge of three cupids in musical mood — a riot of
veneers and stained woods.

7.   *Games table, satinwood, c1795. w39.*
This is a versatile table, one of a pair, made in the manner of Mayhew
and Ince. The central panel reverses to show chess squares, and
encloses a lift-out backgammon board. Makers in the late eighteenth
century rose above mere competence to near virtuosity in creating
and assembling increasingly lavish furniture — ingenious, fitted,
capable of several functions, yet still elegant and satisfying.

8.   The games table, partly open.

1.   Pier table, giltwood, c1785. H35, W35, D17.
This is one of a pair, with a marble top inlaid in the manner of
Giuseppe Bossi, an Italian craftsman who worked for Robert Adam.
Based in Dublin, he specialized in forms of scagliola, or imitation
marble decoration. A splendid example of his work is a side table at

Osterley Park House, Middlesex (Victoria and Albert Museum
No: OPH 57-1949). His patterns, as they appear in this table, can be
repeated on a ceiling or in a carpet pattern — the synthesis of
neo-classical ornament.

In 1788 there appeared, apart from Hepplewhite's Guide, a publication sponsored by the London Society of Cabinet-Makers, namely The Cabinet-Makers' London Book of Prices. It was reissued in 793, 1803 and at various later dates. A multiplicity of designs was included, and priced in detail—all the fashionable and novel forms of the day, including Pembroke, Chamber or work tables, those for dining, as well as pier tables and sideboards, a Carlton House table, dressing and basin stands and bookcases. Whilst the pier table, decorated by Bossi as one commissioned item, needs a pier mirror above to render it 'compleat', the Pembroke and Carlton House writing table were exactly what the Book of Prices was costing for manufacture in quantity. The balance of the unique item against the readily available one—each necessary to different kinds of business enterprise—makes for fascinating study.

2. *Carlton House writing table, mahogany, c1795.* H32, W49, D28. Such pieces were presumably named after the Prince Regent's Carlton House, and an example was first illustrated in *The Cabinet-Makers' London Book of Prices* (1792), and first named by the Lancaster and London firm of Gillow. In this example, the centre of the leather-lined writing surface rises to form an easel, and the drawers are lined with cedar.
Prov: Edward James Collection.

Cabinet-making was a traditional craft, and late eighteenth-century furniture represents its continuity of style. Much furniture was plain and serviceable with little regard to fashion. However, Thomas Sheraton's influence, through the publication of his Drawing Book (1794), was considerable, if indirect. Its subscribers were eager to copy his pattern for a 'Universal Table', and others experimented with various forms of revolving library tables, popularly called 'rent tables' and perhaps serving this function from time to time. The designs were the exemplars of what could be made, and among more than 100 subscribers to the first edition were many cabinet-makers, upholsterers, joiners, carvers, gilders, chair-makers and even musical instrument makers who profited from the compilation.

1. Carlton House writing table, mahogany, c1795. W59.
The elegantly curved superstructure of the desk is fitted with cupboards beside the drawers, and the hinged writing surface can be raised to form an easel. Sheraton illustrated a similar, but smaller, desk in his *Drawing Book* of 1793 (Plate LX), which he called 'A Lady's Drawing and Writing Table'. He asserted: 'the drawer in the middle of the front serves to put the drawings in . . . the small drawers below the coves at each end will be found convenient for colours . . .'

2. Library table, mahogany, c1800-05. Diam 45.
This type of table is also called a 'capstan' or 'rent table'. Some have ingenious mechanisms allowing them to revolve: all were made to withstand hard use. The leather-covered, circular top of this example is fitted with twelve alphabetically-marked drawers, divided by four numbered cupboard doors with false drawer fronts. The applied columns have brass capitals and bases.

3. Library table, mahogany, c1800. H30, Diam 44.
In this example, a hinged, locking, central well is slotted into the circular top, which is covered with gilt-tooled brown leather. Twelve segmental drawers, marked with inlaid ivory letters, are fitted in the frieze, and the heavy pedestal base contains a cupboard with shelves. This is an eminently practical piece of furniture.
Prov: Godmersham Park, Kent.

*Library desk, mahogany and leather
‌, c1795. L74, W50.
‌e important Lancaster and London
‌m of Gillow were pre-eminent
‌anufacturers of practical yet
‌ndsome mahogany furniture. They
‌ose the wood with great care, and
‌ecting finely-figured veneers and
‌atching them all together was an art
‌ey understood beyond most makers.
‌hilst we can only attribute this oval
‌sk with four concave kneeholes as 'in
‌e style of Robert Gillow', it is of a
‌ality worthy of him.*

*. Library table, mahogany, c1805. 42 square.
‌his unusual table was constructed to a design of Thomas Sheraton for 'A
‌Universal Table', published in his 1802 edition of the Drawing Book (Plate 25). It
‌as two extending leaves, which draw out from under the top, and a drawer
‌divided into lidded compartments.*

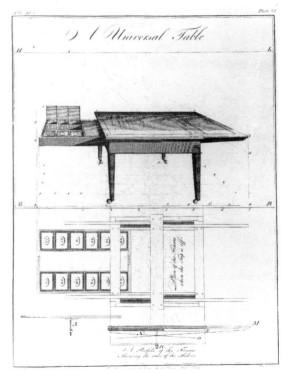

6.   Design for 'A Universal Table' from *The Cabinet-
Maker's and Upholsterer's Drawing Book* by Thomas
Sheraton (1802 edition, Plate 25).

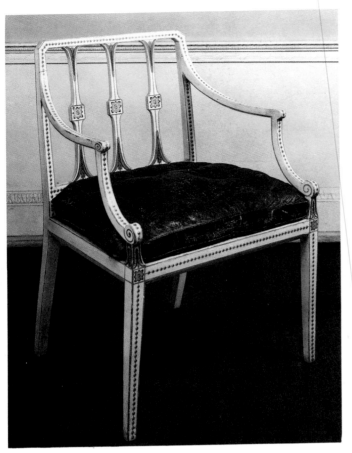

One of the distinctive ways in which late eighteenth-century chairs differed from those of earlier years was in the choice of wood. In earlier times oak was followed by walnut and that by mahogany. The period of Sheraton and Hepplewhite in the late 1780s saw much use of satinwood, painted beechwood and attempts at simulating rare woods such as ebony. Sheraton referred in 1803 to satinwood having been 'much in requisition among people of fashion for above 20 years past' due to its 'cool, light, and pleasing effect in furniture'. After about 1800 it was supplanted by dark woods such as rosewood, which contrasted well with brass inlay and mounts.

1. *Armchair, painted beechwood, c1790-1800. H47, W24.*
The chair is one of a set of six, which may have been made for one of the garden buildings at Osterley Park House, Middlesex. The frame overall is similar to those Robert Adam designed in 1776 for the Etruscan Room at Osterley, although the decoration is not as rich. Here the slats are decorated with wheatear motifs, and a leather squab cushion covers the caned seat. Rectilinear backs for chairs were illustrated by both Hepplewhite and Sheraton in their books of engravings of furniture. The chair is now at Osterley (Victoria and Albert Museum No: OPH 216-1949).

2. *Armchairs, ebonized and gilded, c1795-1800. H32, W21.*
These are two from a set of eight, which must have presented an attractive sight when ranged together, with their sprays of summer flowers painted in the panels of the top rails and the vigorous scrolling foliage painted on the seat rails, and down the baluster legs in long leaf form. The caned seats have been covered with squab cushions. The chairs are stamped with the journeyman's mark of 'G D': one is stamped 'I K' and two with cut 'S's.

3.   *Armchairs, satinwood and painted, c1795-1800.*
Chair-making reaches a high degree of perfection when the structure is so devised that its fluent construction is immediately apparent. Here the arms flow easily down into the front legs, and there is a satisfying relationship between the rails of the back, the U-shaped caned and painted insert and the shoulder of the back legs. The seats are caned, with loose squabs.

4.   *Armchairs, mahogany, c1800.*
These cane-seated chairs are attributed to Thomas Chippendale the younger and were made for Charles Hoare (1767–1851) of Luscombe Castle, Devon. The younger Chippendale was a maker of considerable ability, befitting his parentage. He carried on the business for some 25 years after his father's death. He was referred to by George Smith (*The Cabinet-Maker and Upholsterer's Guide*, 1826) as 'possessing a very great degree of taste'. The design of the Luscombe chairs is related to that of the satinwood armchairs he supplied to Sir Richard Colt Hoare in 1802 for the Stourhead, Wiltshire. Between 1796 and 1808 there are relevant payments to the firm in Charles Hoare's bank account, totalling £1,424.

There may well be many factors which one should consider in looking at chairs: the wood, whether plain or gilded, the carving, upholstery, the overall balance. It might, however, be argued that late eighteenth-century makers, following, in particular, the design books issued by Sheraton and Hepplewhite, were only interested in the backs of their chairs. Lyre-motifs, heart shapes, plumes of feathers, trellis patterns, pierced vase shapes—all were adapted in mahogany, satinwood, or were painted to simulate other woods such as ebony. Add to the ensemble touches of gilding or metal ornamentation, and the results were indisputably satisfying.

1. *Armchair, mahogany, c1800.*
From a set of eight, including two armchairs, this model is after a design illustrated in Thomas Sheraton's *Drawing Book*. The backs are pierced with lyre-motifs — a popular neo-classical ornament which the elder Chippendale had used with distinction in the Nostell Priory, Yorkshire, library chairs — here enclosed by vertical bars. The upholstered seats were covered in practical red horsehair.

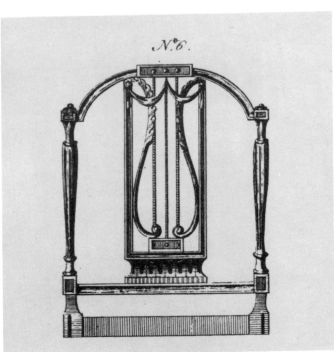

2. Design for a chair back from the third edition of Thomas Sheraton's *The Cabinet-Maker's and Upholsterer's Drawing Book* (1802, Plate VI).

3. *Armchair, painted and gilded, c1800.*
The trellis-pattern backs lighten the design of this chair which is one of a set of four. The squab cushion protects the cane seat. There was little practical necessity for the chair-maker to exaggerate the rake of the arm supports but he accomplished it with some verve and decorated their sweep with stringing.

. *Chair, mahogany, c1790-95.*
One from a set of seat furniture comprising a settee, two armchairs and six single chairs, this chair has a shield-back with pierced splat and carved wheatears. The serpentine seats are covered with leather, and are brass-nailed to the frame. These are chairs of typical Hepplewhite *Guide* form. His Plate 9, dated 1787, is very close in style, although the books merely gave ideas to competent craftsmen, who varied the details.

5.   *Chair, cream painted and parcel gilt, c1790.*
This is one from a set of six with broad, comfortable seats, suitable for the dining room. The backs are slightly curved, and the pierced vase-shaped splats well suited to the fluted legs. Hepplewhite favoured the painting of chairs, saying that it gave 'a rich and splendid appearance to the minuter parts of the ornament . . .'
Prov: Major-General Sir John Marriott, KCVO.

6.   *Chair, cream painted, c1790.*
This oval chair back has a refined form of the classical anthemion, made popular in decorative terms by Robert Adam and other important neo-classical architects. The chair is one of a set of six painted in red and black with lines and foliage. The tapering legs are strengthened for constant use by robust stretchers.

7.   *Chair, mahogany, c1805.*
Considerable sophistication has been applied to this chair, one of a set of four, in that the splat is formed of criss-crossing mahogany rails, terminating in relief carving on the ears of the seat rail in the form of a bird's head. It all seems too grand for the simple, reeded and collared, taper front legs, but they help to support it well enough. The French may have accomplished it better, but this is in an assured 'Louis XVI style'.

The neat rhythm of gilded brass nails pinning fabric or leather to a chair or settee frame is satisfying to the eye. However, the many occasions to re-upholster often disturb the overall appearance of a chair. When well done there is concern to preserve the camber of seat and back, to replace webbing in the same pattern and to think about all the varied aspects of the task. There is, of course, evidence of reupholstering on these chairs and the settee, but it is nevertheless of a competent nature. Hard decisions have to be taken when replacing an expensive fabric with a cheaper one, but this need not detract from the overall effect if care is taken.

1. Chair, mahogany, c1785. H37, w21.
This is from a set of fourteen, which included two armchairs. Whilst the union between the splat and the encircling frame of the chair is a little awkward — the top tier of fronds is somewhat tight to the top rail — they have been given elegant fluted legs and a neat seat rail. The seats are now covered with modern needlework.
Prov: J. S. Sykes Settlement.

2. Chairs, mahogany, c1800.
Fluting and reeding are the methods used to decorate these chairs, which are part of a set of eleven, including this one armchair. Some of the seat rails have been replaced during re-upholstery across the years, but they are typical and practical chairs, with a robust top rail and turned tapering front legs with ribbed collars.

3.   Sofa, giltwood, c1785. w69.
The waved upholstered back and carved frame of this sofa are in the late manner of John Linnell (d. 1796). There is a delicacy to the gilded frame: correct proportions are enhanced by the four fluted baluster legs at the front, and by the splayed ones at the rear. The arm supports are carved with acanthus, and the sofa has been re-upholstered.

Settee, painted and gilded, c1790. w78.
always surprises onlookers that something so seemingly delicate as this cream-painted and gilded settee can support weight on eight such slender legs. The maker would have given careful consideration to joining the rail and legs with mortice and tenon joints, and to using strong webbing and corner blocks to support the upholstered seat. The foliate arm supports are an upward continuation of the fluted, turned, tapering front legs, and flow through to continue as the sinuous top rail of the back.

The comparatively large areas of door panels and drawer fronts required extra care in selecting veneers to cover them. If the panel was not to have painted or marquetry ornamentation, there was the chance to choose the figure of the veneers to form matching patterns and to contrast them overall with crossbanding in different woods. Then in a chest or commode having, perhaps, seven drawers (4), there was need to provide handles which did not overpower by the dazzle of gilded brass or bronze (ormolu), and to match them to neat keyhole escutcheons in metal or inlaid ivory or mother-ofpearl.

1. Commode, satinwood and painted, c1795. W54.
The commode is of Sheraton type, with painted decoration, in the style of François Boucher, including neo-classical subjects of Muses, Cupids and medallion heads in panels. The piece is divided by turned columns inlaid with mahogany. It is a highly decorative piece of work, but the frieze hides useful drawers, and it also has three cupboards.

2. Commode, satinwood, c1790. H34, W43, D22.
This good quality commode has an unusual shape. The top and drawers are cross-banded with rosewood, and the shaped aprons continue the curved forms. Whilst the three long drawers are deep, and perhaps fit a little awkwardly between the turned, tapering legs, the function of storage was well observed by its unknown maker.

3. Commode, satinwood, c1795. H32, W58, D26.
The expanses of satinwood veneer show off the full figure and beauty of the wood of this commode, while the rosewood banding completes the design and outlines its function. The top drawer is fitted with a leather-lined easel and pen and ink trays. Late eighteenth-century cabinet-makers well understood the art of blending appearance and function. They chose veneers with care, and applied them with skill.
Prov: Godmersham Park, Kent.

4.   *Chest of drawers, mahogany and satinwood, c1795. H36, W42.*
The cabinet-maker's use of veneers in strongly contrasting woods
transforms this chest of simple, functional form into one of visual
interest. The mahogany banding may appear a little heavy to some
eyes, but it outlines a long drawer and seven various short drawers
below to some effect.

5.   *Chest of drawers, satinwood, c1795. W36.*
The top of the chest has a moulded mahogany border and is veneered
with an oval framed by mahogany stringing. The carved apron and
splayed feet, which give additional interest to the gently curved
front, are particularly attractive features.
Prov: The Countess Temple of Stowe.

6.   *Dressing chest, mahogany, c1795. W46.*
The cabinet-maker has selected strongly figured veneers to show the
gentle sinuous lines at the front and sides of the chest. The top is also
veneered with an oval panel of burr yew, and cross-banded in
satinwood, as are the drawers and sides. The top drawer is fitted as a
dressing drawer.

7.   *Chest of drawers, mahogany, c1795. L35, W44.*
The chest is in the 'Hepplewhite style', with serpentine front, straight
sides, splayed feet and cast and gilt drop handles on circular plates.
The third and last edition of Hepplewhite's *Guide* (1794) was very
widely used as a trade catalogue, especially by 'countrymen and
artisans', for whom it was particularly intended.
Prov: The Earl of Feversham.

1.   Chest of drawers, satinwood and mahogany, c1790. W41, H35, D22.
The moulded top of the chest is veneered with a batswing oval above
two short and two graduated long drawers, all with fan spandrels,
and stands on shaped feet. The contrast of the two woods, well-
finished mahogany and yellowish satinwood, shows up the
restrained use of neo-classical ornament. The proportions are well
managed, with the good serpentine lines accentuated by fluted,
canted corners.

In the years following Hepplewhite's Guide *(1786), and before
Sheraton's* Drawing Book *(1793), cabinet-makers were trying to
come to terms with creating fashionable furniture. They did not
always succeed, although they were able to provide attractive chests
of drawers in satinwood and mahogany, cross-banded with other
woods or by each other. These owed little allegiance to the pattern-
books, but more to competence bred by long years as apprentice,
journeyman and finally, in many cases, as master.*

2.   Commode, mahogany inlaid with satinwood, c1790. w48.
This mahogany commode is enhanced by a satinwood lunette inlaid
in the semi-elliptical top (which is also cross-banded with rosewood)
and by four satinwood ovals, two of which are set in the cupboard
doors. The commode's appearance on the square tapering legs is a
little heavy, but it provided ample storage space.

If one examines the bookcases and bureau bookcases which appear in Sheraton's Drawing Book *and the* Book of Prices, *it is apparent that changes have occurred from earlier years. In general, there is a reduction in width and an increase in the height of the lower stage. There is also a greater attention to the tracery of the glazing bars, and as Sheraton illustrates them they are invariably graceful, varied and incorporate the oval form (5.). A few years previously, Hepplewhite's* Guide *(1788) had not discriminated between bookcases and cabinets, but Sheraton pointed out that the latter were for 'the medals, manuscripts and drawings etc with places fitted up for some natural curiosities' gathered by gentlemen.*

1. *Cabinet, satinwood, c1785. H84, W49.*
The cabinet is one of a pair, each mounted with forty-two paintings on glass decorated with topographical subjects, including named views in Venice, Naples and Rome. Such cabinets were specially made for the display of eighteenth-century Italian Grand Tour souvenirs. To some eyes the effect is crowded, but a childish delight is found in placing the depicted views.
Prov: Northwick Park, Gloucestershire.

2. *Bureau cabinet, satinwood and mahogany, c1790. H100, W45, D28.*
The tambour shutter of this bureau cabinet is alternately inlaid with rosewood stripes, and conceals a leather-lined slide with a hinged easel and a fitted interior. The broken pediment, with classical urn at the centre, helps to give a balanced appearance to the outline. The Gothic style was appropriate for the design of the glazing bars.

3. *Secretaire cabinet, mahogany, c1790. H106, W49.*
This solid cabinet was intended to be used for books or for the display of porcelain. The pattern of the glazing bars is particularly attractive. The satinwood inlaid ovals on the shaped cornice reflect those decorating the secretaire drawer, which is fitted with pigeon-hole drawers, all faced with holly cross-banding and with tulipwood.

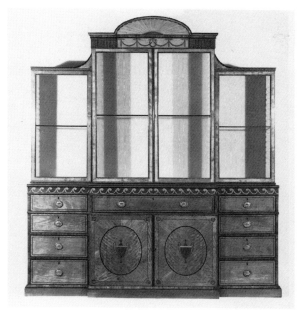

4. *Bookcase, satinwood, c1785. H100, W85, D21.*
A handsome breakfront bookcase, with pronounced neo-classical ornament. Certain features used here, such as the striking foliate swags and wreath inlay on the frieze, are found on pieces of furniture made by Chippendale and Haig, and suggest a possible link with that firm — although attribution is a hazardous business, and no documentation is known.

5. *Bookcase, satinwood and painted, c1795. H111, W84.*
The design of the upper section of the bookcase is unusual, with its central oval mirror held by carved drapery astragals, suspended from a festooned vase. The doors to the lower part are painted with allegorical figures of nymphs on cloud scrolls, and the pilasters are variously painted, contrasted by a lavish use of mahogany and kingwood bands.

6. *Bookcase, satinwood, c1795. W53.*
The bookcase's scalloped cornice, inlaid with rosettes, is a distinctive feature, complementing the wire trellis door fronts. The deep top drawer has a fitted interior. It could be argued that the wooden knobs on the centre of the canted base have replaced gilt brass handles at a later date. However, it is the canted urns, oval panel and painted sprays which attract the eye.

1. Secretaire cabinet, satinwood, c1800. H85, W38.

The cabinet is breakfront in structure, with glazed cupboard doors above a fall flap and base cupboard. A number of similar secretaire-cabinets are known. This is in the style of a Weeks cabinet, but is without fittings, having a convex mirror in the clock position. Most Weeks cabinets were fitted with 8-day clocks, often signed 'Weeks Museum, Titchborne Street', and contained an automatic barrel organ in the lower cupboard, connected to the striking movement of the clock. The Weeks' Museum of mechanical curiosities was established at 4 Titchborne Street in about 1797.

One of the places of amusement in London in the late eighteenth century was the museum which Thomas Weeks established in the Haymarket. Many of the 'mechanical cabinets' he produced are related to a design dated 1791 in Sheraton's Drawing Book *(Plate 48). The premises included a large exhibition gallery, and an adjoining shop. At least thirty Weeks' cabinets are known, and all bear a resemblance to the façade of his museum—tall, narrow, with a pediment and a gadrooned cresting featuring a clock. It is a sophisticated step ahead of the satinwood bookcase built for the sole purpose of holding books (2).*

2.   Bookcase, satinwood, c1790. H88, W56, D18
This breakfront bookcase is decorated with wide
rosewood bands and chequered borders. The
contrasting inlaid doors with rectangular panels
and ovals on the drawers may seem a little fussy on
such a relatively narrow piece.
Prov: Major General Sir John Marriott, KCVO.

1.   Cylinder bureau, mahogany, c1795. W42.
The bureau's tambour shutter encloses a satinwood-veneered interior with baize-lined easel, drawers and alphabetically-enumerated pigeon-holes. The bureau bears the trade label of 'Gwillim & Barnard Auctioneers, Appraisers and Undertakers at their Furniture Warehouses No 82 & 83 Fleet Market, London'.

2.   Cylinder bureau, mahogany and satinwood, c1795. W24.
The cylinder bureau was one of the most attractive pieces of late eighteenth-century furniture. Sheraton illustrated one in his *Drawing Book* of 1793. Pieces were usually well fitted, to suit even the most fastidious user. This example has a fitted interior, with baize-lined slide, drawers and pigeon-holes; the side drawer is divided, and the concave fronted basket is covered with pleated silk.

3.   Cylinder bureau, satinwood, c1795. H55, W37.
A development of the cylinder bureau was to give it a galleried superstructure with panelled doors, as in this example. These could be embellished with oval-framed representations of musical trophies, and the area was generous enough for the contrasting veneers to be well deployed. One rosewood band encloses a slide with a leather-lined easel, which contributes to the bureau's versatility.

4.   Bonheur-du-jour, satinwood, c1800. W28.
The *bonheur-du-jour* was a small writing table of French origin, and this example shows its main characteristic — a raised superstructure with pierced gallery and a pair of cupboard doors enclosing two drawers and pigeon-holes. The piece bears the partly obliterated trade label of 'J. Taylor, Colchester, cabinet maker and upholsterer'.

There are frequently 'Miscellaneous' categories in sale catalogues when the innocent hurry away and the knowledgeable often gain a bargain. The contents of these two pages are all desirable acquisitions. For the most part they are in satinwood, with some use of sycamore (painted) and of mahogany. A particularly neat feature of some of the items are the tambour shutters (1 and 7) in which narrow strips of wood are glued in the horizontal or vertical to a fabric backing, folding neatly away at a touch. Thomas Shearer gave a design for a 'Tambour or Cylinder-Fall Writing Table' in the first edition of the Book of Prices (1788), and they were clearly popular pieces, with the infinite variations, all carefully itemized, but costing in simple form £2 11s. 0d.

5.   Writing cabinet, painted and inlaid sycamore, c1795. w20.
The cabinet is inlaid with three ovals containing coloured prints in the style of Angelica Kauffmann (1741-1807). The fall-front reveals ten cedar drawers and a small cupboard with green-stained and holly borders. Such small cabinets were only of use in an age of polite accomplishments — the writing of a few letters by the lady of the household, in a refined and leisurely mood.

6.   Toilet mirror, satinwood and mahogany, c1800. H24, W19, D9.
The toilet mirror set on a chest was a functional object which occupied little space. It was therefore in most Georgian bedrooms, although its origin predates that period. Late eighteenth-century veneered examples are particularly attractive. The oval plate and plain frame of this example are set between foliate 'S'-scroll supports, carved with flowerheads and pendant foliage. The base is of serpentine shape, cross-banded, and fitted with three drawers.

7.   Bedside cupboard, satinwood, c1795. w21.
The bedside cupboard allowed small objects, medicine bottles, scissors, a water decanter and glasses, etc., to be concealed behind the tambour shutters. This example, one of a pair, has the shutters alternately inlaid with natural and green-stained stripes and has a commode-drawer mounted with ring and boss handles above strong, tapered feet.

8.   Polescreens, mahogany and giltwood, c1790. H53.
The polescreen came into use in the late eighteenth century to protect the eyes and complexion from direct firelight. A firescreen was mounted on a slender pole or shaft above a tripod or platform base. Here, the mahogany banners are of shield shape, and contain glazed, oval, coloured prints of rustic infants, bordered by rolled paper scrolls. The fluted baluster shafts are gilt.

Breakfront bookcase, burr yew, by Marsh and Tatham, 1806. H71, W73, D20.

This bookcase is one of four supplied in June 1806 by Marsh and Tatham to the Prince of Wales at Carlton House. The invoice provides an adequate description: 'Four elegant Yew Tree bookcases inlaid with ebony ornaments decorated with bronze antique heads, rich ormolu ornaments, open brass-work, and plate glass etc to complete the design £680 . . . Statuary marble tops and ledges for the same £140. 3s'. The firm of Marsh and Tatham of 13 Mount Street, London, was the principal supplier of furniture for Carlton House and the Brighton Pavilion.

CHAPTER 7

The Regency Style
1805–1840

In February 1811 the Prince of Wales, the most extreme of all the imperious and complicated sons of the aged and feeble-minded George III, became Regent. Whilst he waited for the position, without any of the training or strength of character to endure his long exclusion from affairs of state, he had pursued an extravagant life at Carlton House. Moving there when he came of age in 1783, he had employed Henry Holland to 'Frenchify' it. The Regent had many French friends, spoke the language fluently and collected art on an extensive scale. Many works of art were on the market as a result of the Revolutionary sales and the Napoleonic wars, and these were available to the Regent—he did not accede as George IV until January 1820—through friends and agents, or were sent on approval to him.

When peace came in 1814 there was every reason to brighten up the English Court. Classical taste was again in favour, and an interest in archaeology and ancient civilizations resulted in attempts to copy their artefacts. Events such as Nelson's victory at the Battle of the Nile encouraged interest in Egypt, and the preoccupation by many with the architectural wonders of Egypt and Greece was epitomized in the career of a wealthy newcomer, Thomas Hope (c.1770–1831).

The eldest of the three sons of a rich family of Dutch bankers and dealers who had fled from Holland at its occupation in 1794 by the French, Hope had not only spent several years studying and drawing in the Middle East and Greece, but in 1801 had acquired all of the second collection of vases, busts and bronzes assembled by Sir William Hamilton. The first collection had been denied to a private collector through its acquisition by the British Museum. In planning his Adam house in Portland Place as a setting for his collections, Hope designed 'ancient furniture' for the rooms, and

set these designs out in 1807 in an important book, *Household Furniture and Interior Decoration Executed from Designs by Thomas Hope*. In the meantime, he had bought Deepdene in Surrey and moved his collections there: his book, however, remained as the record of the Portland Place settings and the suite of apartments included his Egyptian or Black Room 'with ornaments from scrolls of papyrus and mummy-cases'—the furniture was pale yellow, blue-green, and black and gold. Surrounded by his two hundred Greek vases, tables, pedestals, and 'the mantlepiece of an Egyptian portico', people were admitted by 'application signed by some persons of known character and taste'.

Hope had informed his mind from a wide range of sources and impressions gained on his extensive travels. He was a friend of the French architect Charles Percier (whose seminal work with Fontaine in 1812 charted the French Empire style) and used French craftsmen to create furniture for him. He was also imbued with the true spirit of neo-classicism and read all the publications of its advocates—Piranesi, Winckelmann, Stuart and Revett's *Antiquities of Athens*—as well as those books on the great monuments of the known or newly excavated world sought out and described by his fellow members of the Society of Dilettanti. In the Preface to his own book Hope characterized what he looked for in contemporary furniture: 'breadth and response of surface, that distinction and contrast of outline, that opposition of plain and enriched parts, that harmony and significance of accessories . . . which are calculated to afford the eye and mind the most lively, most permanent, and most unfailing enjoyment.'

It could be argued that Hope was a detached aesthete out of touch with everyday reality and interested only

Sofa table, rosewood, c1810. w (open) 57.
This sofa games table is in the manner of John McLean, a London maker who flourished in the early nineteenth century. His pieces owe much to French influence, not only in the design, but in the lavish use of gilt brass mounts and dark rosewood. The rectangular two-flap top of this table is banded with satinwood and has a sliding centre inlaid with chess squares, and enclosing a backgammon board.
Prov: Godmersham Park, Kent.

in the literary exposition of fantasy interior design and furniture. The truth was that his furniture was made, enjoyed, and given the ultimate accolade of all successful designs of being copied, albeit with less attention to quality. The types of furniture associated with him were those which used monopodia, that is, supports in the shape of animals (lions or chimeras) which had the head and body formed with a single leg and foot. Tables had single pedestals of three-sided concave form, with lyre-shaped supports between baluster legs, or with monopodia legs; vase stands were fashioned as Roman or Grecian tripods; cross-framed chairs and stools had rams' head finials; and severe classical couches, either with lotus-shaped feet and arms or in the Egyptian taste, had couchant lions or sphinxes as terminal figures at the ends, or as arm-supports. The furniture was made with great attention to fine craftsmanship. The timber was solid, painted or veneered, straight rather than curved, and carefully formed. The metal ornaments were applied directly to the wood, and further decoration consisted only of reeding, which emphasized the purity of the line.

It cannot be said that Thomas Hope was the first to encourage interest in the Egyptian taste. Sheraton had illustrated sphinx heads and feet and simple forms of terminal figures in his last work, the uncompleted *Encyclopaedia* (1804–6), but it was Hope and others such as George Smith who developed the theme. In 1808 George Smith, a cabinet-maker and upholsterer then living off Cavendish Square, published *A Collection of Designs for Household Furniture and Interior Decoration*. He had seized upon much of what Hope had done (although the plates are dated 1804–7) and had presumably visited the former's London house which was opened on occasion to the general public. Smith was, however, less concerned with classical purity—he wanted to provide practical designs, many of them Gothic, for the wide range of articles needed to furnish an entire household. Hope's furniture, rather like the later grand pieces Burne-Jones painted for William Morris, was for an educated élite who knew of Hamilton's *Antiquities* (1766), Pierre François D'Hancarville's drawings of Hamilton's Greek vases (published 1766–67), or Vivant Denon's classic work *Voyages dans la Basse et la Haute Egypte* (1802).

Smith showed designs for tables with animal monopodia, and was even moved to use representations of the feet of blackamoors as well as lions' paws as supports. Like Hope he had taken careful note of the earlier designs of Charles Heathcote Tatham and modified some of them for his own use. Tatham had

Dwarf cabinet, satinwood, c1810. H48, W42, D18.
Only in the Regency and Victorian periods was pleated silk handled well in furniture decoration. It threw the gilt wire grille doors into relief and protected contents within from dust and light. In consequence, it deteriorated at a more rapid rate than the carcase, and has often been renewed. Some observance of prevailing style is given by the Egyptian pilasters. The whole is attractively cross-banded throughout with rosewood.
Prov: Godmersham Park, Kent.

worked in Henry Holland's office before going in 1796, at his master's expense, to study in Rome. Many of his drawings had been published in 1799 as *Etchings of Ancient Ornamental Architecture.*

We have noted the importance of the Chinese taste in the mid-eighteenth century, and of the Egyptian (which affected much less) in the early nineteenth century. The Chinese had enjoyed a new vogue in the work done for the Prince Regent both at Carlton House and his 'Marine Pavilion' at Brighton. Much of the furniture for the Pavilion was made to simulate bamboo, and was lacquered, usually in black and gold. George Smith put two Chinese designs for cornices and window drapery in his book of 1808. Almost twenty years later he announced that it was now 'wholly obsolete and inapplicable' in his last book, *Cabinet-Maker's and Upholsterer's Guide, Drawing Book and Repository* (1826). The Chinese style had passed its peak, but Smith retained Greek, Roman, Etruscan and Gothic as well as French taste, revived after the fall of Napoleon.

In 1812 Percier and Fontaine published their important *Recueil des Décorations Intérieures*, which showed the grandeur of the imperial palaces, and in the same year

Rudolf Ackermann also showed in colour French-style furniture in four numbers of his monthly magazine, *Repository of Arts.* It was an Empire style that matched the mood which came with the abdication of Napoleon and the restoration of Louis XVIII, and it caught on in England, owing partly to the Prince Regent's interest. In particular, an interest in the art of inlaying in tortoiseshell and brass, associated with the work of A. C. Boulle in the late seventeenth century, was encouraged by a Frenchman, Louis Le Gaigneur, who opened up a 'buhl manufactory' off Edgware Road, London. The Prince Regent patronized him, as he did the competent English maker George Oakley, who announced on his trade-card that he maintained a 'Magazine of General and superb upholstery and cabinet furniture'. Buhl was also available from Thomas Parker and from George Bullock, whose work had been admired by Maria Edgeworth, and who had been patronized by his friend Sir Walter Scott, who ordered furniture for Abbotsford.

Some found that the French style lacked substance; the decription of the Louis XIV style in the *Repository of Arts* for October 1828 summarized what many felt:

Card table, rosewood, carved and inlaid, c1805. H30, W36, D18.
With its precise gadrooned edges and light stringing lines, this
elegant table, one of a pair, has a swivel top which opens on
hinges to reveal a baize-lined playing surface. The trestle end
supports are on castors.

'heavy, cumbrous, and we may almost add, unmean-
ing decoration'.

One substitute the anonymous writer had advocated
a few months previously (March 1827) was Gothic,
which had appeared again, after its mid-eighteenth
century vogue, both in Sheraton's *The Cabinet Dictionary*
(1803) and in Smith's *Household Furniture* (1808). He
advised that no style could be better adapted than that
of the Middle Ages, particularly for libraries, because it
encouraged, by its 'sedate and grave character', study
and reflection. It suited not only the interiors of the
great mock-medieval castles built by Sir Robert Smirke
(Eastnor and Lowther) but could also be adapted in
scale to the smaller houses by J. B. Papworth and
P. F. Robinson. It was the style for the furniture designed by Augustus Charles Pugin for Nash's State
Apartments at Windsor Castle. It was what
J. C. Loudon also advocated in his important *Encyclopaedia of Cottage, Farm and Villa Architecture and Furniture*
in 1833, at the edge of Queen Victoria's reign:

The principal Styles of Design in Furniture, as at
present executed in Britain, may be reduced to four,
viz, the Grecian or Modern Style, which is by far the
most prevalent; the Gothic or perpendicular style,
which imitates the lines and angles of the Tudor
Gothic Architecture; the Elizabethan, which combines the Gothic with the Roman or Italian manner;
and the style of the age of Louis XIV, or the florid
Italian, which is characérised by curved lines and
excess of curvilinear ornaments . . . we have given
but few designs in the style of Louis XIV on account of
the great expense of carrying them into execution.

The Grecian style was Loudon's 'Modern Style'; he
considered it to be the one most appropriate for a
dining room, and it was the style which predominated
in the furniture provided for London clubs and livery
halls in the 1830s. Sir Walter Scott had commented in

the *Quarterly Review* (March 1828) 'that an ordinary chair, in the most ordinary parlour, had now something of an antique cast—something of Grecian massiveness, at once, and elegance in its forms . . .' It was a chair with a broad cresting rail or shoulder board, straight turned front legs, and rear ones splayed at a backward angle. It was a variation on what the Regency designers had done and, executed in mahogany with quilted seats, remained popular until 1850.

Some of the Grecian chairs which were designed by Hope and illustrated in his *Household Furniture* of 1807 had deep arc-backs, ebonized and gilt, some of which were also painted in the manner of Etruscan vases with a 'frieze' of classical figures, or with a shallow carved Greek fret on the seat rails. The legs were gently curved either to the sides or forwards and backwards: the curves at their most sinuous were cross-framed to form a stool, with lions' heads and feet and with lotus-leaf ornament. Other armchairs had lion monopodia front legs, and an upholstered back gently scrolled from half way up the back rails, or had arms carved with rams' heads and an outswept arc-back in shiny leather over a curved frame. The mahogany top rails could be inlaid with ebony, carved with volutes or be painted black and gilt.

The most characteristic of all Regency chairs were those which had deeply curved front legs. Of two basic sections, the legs were either square or oblong, with their narrower sides to the front. Much more dramatic was the latter form because the front legs were also curved in 'scimitar' or 'sabre' shapes. The side seat rails would then sweep up in shallow reverse curve, joined by a rope-moulded top rail and back supports. This rope-moulding was a reference to the victories of the British fleet, and as many of the chiars were made in the Trafalgar workshops at Catherine Street, Strand, of the distinguished firm of Morgan and Sanders (who had been 'honoured with the patronage of Their Majesties and several branches of the Royal family . . .' as well as of Lord Nelson), they carry the name 'Trafalgar' chairs. They remained in popular use in parlours long after 1815, made in beech, with caned seats and loose cushions, painted black, or in dark green in simulation of bronze.

Another preoccupation of the Regency chair-makers was to satisfy the near-insatiable demand for cheap, painted chairs. Ackermann's *Repository of Arts* for August 1814 says they were intended for use in 'best bed chambers, for secondary drawing rooms, and occasionally to serve for routs' at assembly rooms and other social venues. The best kind were the 'Trafalgar' mentioned above, but Elward, Marsh and Tatham made many in beech which were painted to simulate bamboo. The shaped rush seats seemed the only regular

Bergère and chaise longue, mahogany and caned, c1810.
Comfort is the main consideration here: to sit at ease on the thick leather upholstery. The seat extends with a hinged foot-rest to form the *chaise longue*. The square out-turned legs terminate in brass castors. The chair is upholstered in green suede.

Chair, mahogany, by Gillow of Lancaster, 1811.
The Lancaster and London firm of Gillow had an extensive trade — not least in the supply of chairs. This is one of a set of sixteen. The design, with curved top rail, shaped uprights and sabre legs, derives from the *klismos*. Originally covered in red leather, the chairs were supplied to the Rev. Mr Twemlow of Peats Wood, Market Drayton, Shropshire.

part of the chair, for the 'jointed' legs, spindle stretchers (as many as seven) and the back uprights were carved and painted with all the irregularities of bamboo. Some were made for the Brighton Pavilion in 1802 and, absurdly, given Gothic quatrefoil frets, or were painted 'drab and blue' to closely imitate bamboo shoots.

In 1800 the French painter Jacques-Louis David had painted Madame Récamier, the most famous beauty of the time, reclining on a classical sofa, and soon all the ambitious women of Europe wanted to rule their lavish households from so distinctive a throne. It was a piece of furniture that nevertheless also belonged to the gentleman's library, and the furniture-makers sought to fill the demand. Sheraton published designs in 1803 for Grecian sofas with one high end, and others with two ends of equal height. The back rail of a double-ended sofa usually had a central carved ornament on the top rail, and patterns of honeysuckle were common. Less so were the handsome gilded couches with lions' heads and feet, and with delicately fluted seat rails. The Lancaster and London firm of Gillow made some handsome gilded beech examples in the first few years of the nineteenth century.

After the successful publication of Thomas Hope's and George Smith's books on furniture and interior decoration (1807–8), tables with animal monopodia supports became more usual. Smith illustrated a design for a sofa table, one of the most popular forms of Regency furniture, with two end flaps. Good examples after the design survive, with gilt lion monopodia supports, and a rosewood top, dated *c*1808–10. Rosewood, a reddish-brown wood with black streaks imported from Brazil, was used frequently for making sofa tables. It looked effective set off by gilding, or inlaid with patterns in cut brass. The sofa table sometimes had a centre pedestal, and a reversible centre portion covered on one side with leather. This could be turned by sliding to form a writing surface, or if inlaid with light and dark squares to act as a chess or draughts board. The sofa table with end flaps (differing from a Pembroke table which had side flaps) continued until the 1830s in that form, but became then an 'occasional' table (Smith's term in his second book of 1826) with no flaps.

'Metamorphic' library armchair, mahogany, c1811.
Several firms specialized in making Patent Metamorphic Furniture, designed for more than one function — in this example a chair and library steps. It is attributed to one of the leading firms, Morgan and Sanders of Catherine Street, Strand, London. Their work was illustrated frequently in the influential Ackermann's *Repository of Arts* (cf. July 1811). The back, arms and seat swing forward on hinges to form four baize-lined treads. The piece is stamped '113'.

Another characteristic form of table was that to set
between the piers of windows. In rosewood, with two
gilded front columns and a mirror set in the full width
(above a platform and below the top) it looked even
more effective if fitted with a white marble top and with
carved and giltwood ornaments decorating the apron.

In September 1801, the writer Fanny Burney had said
in a letter to a friend that 'no room looked really
comfortable or even quite furnished, without two
tables—one to keep the wall and take upon itself the
dignity of a little tidyness, the other to stand here, there
and everywhere, and hold letters . . .' Many occasional
tables were to serve these needs, and to act as work
tables. These usually had a pleated bag of silk hanging
beneath a lifting or sliding top—a 'box' upon a pedestal.

The polite accomplishments of young men and ladies
extended beyond the singular pursuit of the latter,
needlework, to the common attainment of both—
music. They therefore needed pianofortes—the square
pianoforte of the Regency period (many by the Broad-
wood family) was mentioned by Thackeray in *Vanity
Fair*—and they also needed music-stands and music-
canterburies.

Those who preferred reading to needlework or music
were served by a wide variety of small occasional
bookcases, with lyre-shaped ends, or with two shelves
above a small cupboard which might have a brass fret
front, or one with pleated silk set neatly behind the
brasswork. Fitted libraries in the great houses were
common, and a number of handsome mahogany or
rosewood bookcases by Gillow and others, with heavily
scrolled pediments and lower panelled doors flanked
by animal forms or heavy scrolls, are known. Reaching
books on high top shelves was made easier by the use
of library steps. Some have newel-posts fashioned as
classical columns, others are formed as spirals, and yet
others were 'metamorphic', with two functions.

The best-known makers of 'Patent Metamorphic
Furniture' were Thomas Butler, William Pocock, Robert
Daws, Samuel Oxenham and Morgan and Sanders.
One of Morgan and Sanders' most sought-after pieces
was their library steps incorporated in an armchair.
Their showrooms were illustrated in Ackermann's
Repository of Arts in 1809, and their trade-sheet shows a
chair bed 'forming a handsome Easy Chair and is with
great ease transformed into a Tent Bed', 'a dozen of
which pack into the space of 2 Common Chairs', or
sofa-beds 'forming an Elegant Sofa, and may be transformed with great ease into a compleat Four Post Bed'.
Related to these metamorphic pieces was furniture for
those on campaigns and for invalids. Pocock, in particular, had the ingenuity and business acumen to
exploit public interest in furniture which involved
mechanical devices, such as chairs which helped pa-
tients get in and out of bed, and even Invalid Vibrating
Pendulum Beds—to give gentle exercise to the bed-
ridden or to lull insomniacs.

The more normal forms of Regency beds were either
four-posters, canopy-beds, sofa-beds or tent-beds. The
four-poster beds usually had front posts of mahogany
with back posts, canopy ribs and under-framing in
beech, and pine top rails, cornice boards and slats. The
bed-bolts to secure the frame were masked by sliding
panels.

Canopy-beds were usually painted so that cheaper
woods such as beech and deal were used. Both four-
posters and canopy-beds were dressed with valances
and curtains, which hid the metal supports holding up
the canopy, and many designs for them appear in
Sheraton's and George Smith's books, as well as in
Ackermann's *Repository of Arts*. The sofa-bed—French
ones are illustrated in Sheraton's *Encyclopaedia* (1804)
and Ackermann's *Repository of Arts* (November 1822)—
stood sideways to the wall. A fabric canopy hung from

*'Capstan' dining table, mahogany, by Robert
Jupe, c1835. Diam (closed) 55, (extended)
71.*
The table is stamped 'Johnstone Jupe &
Co. New Bond St. London'. This firm
patented an expanding circular table in
1835. The top of this table expands on
an iron frame to admit eight further
leaves.

Bonheur-du-jour, parcel-gilt and rosewood, 1800-10. H45, W32.
This piece is attributed to John McLean, whose designs for a
bonheur-du-jour were published by Thomas Sheraton in his *Cabinet*

Dictionary (1803, Plate 32a). The superstructure has an ormolu fret
gallery and there is a delicate edging to the in-curved shelf between
the ring-turned tapering legs.

Library armchair, mahogany, c1830. H41.
This chair makes an impressive statement: the blend of solid classical and other styles with fine wood and good carving. The curved top rail is carved with strapwork and bears a lion's mask of gilt metal (inscribed 'Celer et Audax') between two brass ring handles. The legs, held by an 'H'-shaped stretcher, terminate in lions' paws and bun feet. It is upholstered in leather.

a dome and was draped over two rods projecting from the wall, to fall at both ends of the bed. Tent-beds were small and light with a framework of curved rods acting as a support for the fabrics which were draped to form a small tent.

Bedroom furniture was completed by hanging presses or cupboards, small wardrobes, chests of drawers, dressing tables and various forms of *cheval* glasses and wallmirrors. The *Repository of Arts* noted (November 1818) that mirrors created 'those effects called the endless perspectives so much admired'. The discerning could note the quality of the fitted dressing-tables with many compartments for different toilet articles, and the houseproud could buff slightly the French-polished chest even if they could not make up the recipe for the polish themselves. French polishing was introduced to England about 1814, and Richard Brown in his valuable *The Rudiments of Drawing Cabinet and Upholstery Furniture* (1822) (after giving the various proportions of mastic, sandaric, shell lac, wax and rectified spirits of wine needed) encouraged all who dared to rub the furniture with the sticky concoction 'with a circular motion, until a gloss is produced'.

It was a surface which set the Regency furniture of a daughter apart from the wax-polished mahogany furniture owned by her grandmother. The observant needed no such fickle guide. In luxury furniture there was enough use of Egyptian sphinxes, rampant lions and lyre-shaped supports to point the difference. Whilst factors such as the Napoleonic wars had reduced the value of money, raised the cost of labour and materials and hastened the decline of expensive processes such as marquetry, help was at hand for easier solutions. Legs and chairs could be turned straight and cheaply on the lathe, and wood could be sawed, grooved, morticed, rebated and moulded by many machines. The transition of a craft into an industry had started, and was carried to a noisy, steam-hissing peak by the time Queen Victoria and Prince Albert opened the Great Exhibition in 1851.

1. *Dining table, oak, 1810-15.*
L (including three extra leaves and two
more pedestals) 229, W67.
This table is capable of considerable
expansion to meet varying needs. The
'D'-shaped ends and extra leaves are
cross-banded with pollard oak and
inlaid with ebony dot-and-line borders.
The turned supports are mounted with
gilt bronze laurel-leaf collars and stand
on quadripartite bases.

2. *Dining table, mahogany, by George*
Oakley, c1810. L147, W57.
This patent table has an expanding
action to admit three extra leaves.
Reeding is used to decorate the edge of
the table top, the trestle ends and
splayed legs. The brass handles at the
ends are inscribed: 'G. Oakley, Maker,
No 8 Old Bond Street, London'. Oakley
and his partners produced very stylish
furniture, particularly in the Grecian
taste, during the decades spanning the
turn of the nineteenth century.

3. *Wine table, mahogany, c1815. L102.*
Made in three sections, this table would
probably have been fitted, on its inner
edge, with movable coasters for bottles,
attached to a brass rail. It would be set
before the fire after dinner for a period
of convivial drinking.

One of the most distinctive forms of Regency furniture—copied in many veneered present-day reproductions—is the dining table supported by claws and pillars, and composed of a rectangular round-ended top with several leaves to extend it. It was made from the early 1790s, and many patented versions appeared, capable of being extended by 'telescopic action'. Circular or octagonal tables were also in use for dining, as well as narrow segmental wine tables (3). Two or more of these formed a greater arc for a convivial gathering. Other aids to dining well were a variety of serving tables and sideboards. They were made, often, in a classical style which added at least to appearance, if not to function.

4.   *Sideboard, mahogany and ebony, c1800. W69.*
The author, traveller and collector Thomas Hope (1769-1831) published *Household Furniture and Interior Decoration* in 1807, in which he showed his scholarly adaptations of Greek and Egyptian motifs to furniture. This sideboard, one of a pair in his style, has ebonized, winged chimera monopodia supports. The central cupboard has applied anthemion as decoration between a frieze containing a drawer and an inset grey marble top.

5.   *Sideboard, mahogany, by Blease, c1805. W95.*
This practical dining room piece bears the trade label 'Blease late Seddon/Upholstery, Cabinet & Carpet Manufacturer . . . No 24, Dover Street'. Inlaid key pattern lines are used to decorate the drawers. The pedestals with panelled doors are fitted, one with zinc lining, the other with three drawers.

6.   *Serving table, c1810. W69.*
The thin, attenuated Regency serving tables conjure visions of Jane Austenish dining rooms laden with covered silver breakfast dishes. But architectural form is also observed — the frieze is carved with reed ornament and fluted columns are used for supports, with panelled backs and plinth bases.

A quick tabulation of the main types of Regency table may be confusing, but is necessary—pier tables, console tables, side tables, sofa, card and games tables, Pembroke tables, occasional and quartetto tables. They had their origins in the late eighteenth-century pattern books of England and France, but following the publications of Thomas Hope and George Smith in 1807–8 tables supported by animal monopodia (1) became very popular. There was also a passionate concern with brass inlay, whose sharp, bright lines contrasted well with the dark or streaked woods like rosewood and calamander.

1. Table, rosewood, ormolu and bronze, c1810. H30, W25, D19.
No design for this table appears in Thomas Hope's *Household Furniture and Interior Decoration* of 1807, but in execution it is typical of furniture designed by him and produced under his supervision. It has ormolu Roman theatrical masks on the frieze and is supported by bronze lion monopodia, joined by an ormolu stretcher and raised on a rosewood plinth.

2. Dining table, mahogany, c1813. L (fully extended with five leaves) 142.
This dining table is attributed to the Lancaster and London firm of Gillow. It stands on turned, tapering, reeded legs with brass castors.
Prov: Belton House, Lincolnshire.

3. Sofa table, rosewood and brass inlay, c1815. L (extended) 59, H28, D30.
This table, with its mannered out-curved legs, which terminate in brass caps with lotus and acanthus leaf decoration, shows how sophisticated Regency makers could be. They used brass inlaid foliate scrolls to further decorate the top (which has twin flaps), while the frieze is also inlaid with anthemions and stylized flowers divided into panels edged with cast brass mouldings.

4. Centre table, rosewood, gilt mounts, c1815. W47.
Practical considerations weighed as heavily with Regency designers as the lavish use of decoration. This table has a tip-up top which is cross-banded with ormolu anthemions applied to the frieze. A spreading octagonal shaft is raised on a scrolled quadripartite base and applied with gilt-metal rosettes and foliage.

In his book on 'Household Furniture', published in 1808, George Smith wrote that the 'large projecting claws' of dining tables 'are a great inconvenience'. In place of claws he favoured plinths of various forms—square or triangular resting on paw or ball feet (2) or built up for use in drawing rooms with an elaborate infilled section above the base (3). The table was a favourite item for designers and makers to cover with stylistic motifs—the Gothic frieze, the richly-scrolled cabriole legs carved deep with acanthus foliage, the sphinxes and animal monopodia (which Smith favoured)—or even to emulate work like the ebony and buhl marquetry of the reign of Louis XIV, made relevant to the years of Napoleon Bonaparte.

1.   *Sideboard, mahogany, c1810. w50.*
This small sideboard would be able to stand unobtrusively in any small Regency dining room. It has a bow-fronted top, and the four drawers are inlaid in contrasted stringing with a key pattern.

2.   *Breakfast table, calamander wood, c1815. w54.*
The light brown, mottled and striped black wood calamander is used to particular effect in this table. The edge is cross-banded with burr maple. The tip-up top is on scrolled supports, which are ebonized and mounted with ormolu beading.

3.   *Centre table, rosewood, c1815. Diam 42.*
The lines of this handsome centre table are edged with ormolu beading. The top, rosewood with a tulipwood band, is over four frieze drawers, outlined with rope-twist borders, alternating with four false drawers. The triangular pedestal is supported by giltwood paw feet.

4.   *Side table, mahogany, c1805. w85.*
The flickerings of the medieval Gothic style never really died out, although it was superseded for long periods by other styles. Here the shaped top, cross-banded in rosewood, is accentuated by a Gothic arcaded frieze. The cluster legs are headed by carved acanthus leaves.

5.   *Side table, rosewood and buhl, in the manner of Louis Le Gaigneur, c1815. w42.*
The Frenchman Louis Le Gaigneur had a buhl manufactory in London in the early nineteenth century, and did a great deal of work at Windsor Castle. His work derived from the styles popularized by A. C. Boulle and others in the reign of Louis XIV. Here a central panel of ebony and buhl marquetry is set in the rectangular top. Panels inlaid with cut brass are used on the frieze drawers and scrolled legs.

6.   *Side table, carved giltwood, c1820. w59.*
The interest of Regency collectors in the multi-coloured patterns of various Italian marbles is here exemplified in a side table, one of a pair — the top is inlaid with various kinds of marble. It stands on an open platform base backed with mirror panels, surmounted by a richly-carved frieze and cabriole legs.

1.   *Sofa table, calamander, partridgewood and rosewood, c1815. w62.*
The rich blend of three woods in solid and veneered form is used to particular advantage in a small area, and continued on the frieze of applied ormolu. The table stands on a platform base with four turned column supports.

2.   *Sofa table, rosewood and amboyna, c1820. w45.*
The darkness of the rosewood and the burr patterns of amboyna throw into relief the rich ormolu mounts on the frieze, support and stretcher of this small sofa table.

Among the most attractive types of Regency furniture is the sofa table, with its flaps, placed at the ends, made more splendid when in rosewood, inlaid with brass, and even in streaked calamander or the rich burr veneers of amboyna. Whilst the brass lines and ormolu mounts were enough to 'gild the lily', makers were not content. They provided reversible panels for either working on or which were marked out for games such as chess. Silk upholstered baskets contained the needlework and stitched samplers of many a leisured afternoon's activity, and were set in beneath a deep frieze or drawer (4).

3.   Card table, rosewood, c1815. w36.
Card tables usually have a folding top which allows for easy storage and the use of the table for two purposes. This example is one of a pair, and the hinged top, inlaid with brass lines, encloses a baize-lined playing surface.

4.   Games and work table, rosewood, c1815. w30.
This table states its purpose openly, and all the various parts of its construction are enhanced with ormolu. The central sliding panel in the top is reversed to reveal the chess board, and encloses a backgammon board. The silk-upholstered basket slides out below the drawer. The double 'C'-scroll trestle ends, mounted with ormolu rosettes, are joined by a parcel-gilt stretcher.

Some pieces of furniture, such as console tables, are only meant to be viewed from the front and sides, not in the round. This last attribute was well understood by the makers of sofa and centre tables. From whichever side they were viewed they had to satisfy the eye. There is always splendid work in the two end-supports and central stretcher, varied by a single central support, which supplanted the earlier form from about 1812. And there were endless opportunities for delightful invention—the carefully formed ormolu anthemions and lotus leaves, the proud stance of monopodia supports, the display, on a top, of coloured marble squares.

1. *Sofa table, calamander, c1815.* w (open) 58.
The use of exotic woods, combined with the sharp contrast of gilt metal, was at its most successful in the Regency period. Here the rich, streaked calamander is flamboyantly edged with gilt scrolls, handles and reeded roundels on the stretcher.

2. *Centre table, rosewood, ebony and ivory inlay, c1820.* w (closed) 45, (extended) 75.
The solid, almost Gothic, design of the openwork ends, use of turning on the stretcher and inlay of this centre table recall the work of George Bullock and his designer, Richard Bridgens, who worked with him, 1810-18. The decoration of the top, sliding extensions and scrolled trestle ends is in ivory inlay.

3. *Centre table, giltwood and marble, c1825.* w40.
The use of exotic woods was always outdone by the use of various coloured marbles, here divided by white trellis with a black marble border, and edged by a gilt brass moulding. The frieze has applied anthemion and foliage clasps, and the tapered legs are carved with reeding and acanthus leaves.

Sofa table, rosewood, attributed to George Smith, c1810. W (closed) 36.
George Smith illustrates a design similar to this table in his *A Collection of Designs for Household Furniture* (1808, Plate 83). Brass lines and anthemions are inlaid in the top, and parcel-gilt anthemions are carved on the monopodia supports.

5. *Sofa table, rosewood, c1815. W (open) 59.*
This table is given enormous distinction by the elaborate central stem decked in parcel-gilt, above four richly-scrolled and ormolu-mounted feet. The rosewood square twin-flap top is inlaid with boxwood lines and anthemions. Two drawers are fitted in the frieze, which is panelled with ormolu beading and mounted at the corners with ormolu anthemion plaques.

6. *Harlequin sofa table, mahogany and rosewood, c1810. W (open) 65.*
Although the ingenious mechanism of this sofa table appears to be unique, the piece is of a type popular in the late eighteenth and early nineteenth centuries. The inlaid top is fitted with a pop-up section enclosing drawers and pigeon-holes, operated by a combination lock set on four alphabetically-enumerated dials on a sliding projection above the frieze drawer.
Prov: Wateringbury House, Kent.

7. *Sofa table, amboyna, c1815. W (open) 59.*
The lyre shape was a popular Regency motif for the supports of sofa tables. Here it stands over splayed legs ending in gilt metal mounts and brass castors to support a twin-flap top, cross-banded with mulberry and bordered with inlaid brass lines.

The small table was a popular item with Regency makers, but it did not enjoy universal acclaim. Admittedly, Lord Torrington may have had splenetic reason to write in his **Diary** in 1792 of 'little skuttling tables being brought before a hearth', but many others were ready to use them. Fanny Burney thought 'no room looks comfortable, or even furnished without two tables . . .' The tables which filled her need were made in an array of styles and forms. Some, like the 'quartetto tables', gave four almost for the price of one, whilst others allowed writing, sewing and games to be served by the same table. Given time, and there seemed no shortage of that in the past, a satisfactory toilet was possible when all the sections of the relevant table (4) were deployed. And in any case, its preparation and the provision of hot water was usually done by servants.

1. *Writing table, calamander, giltwood and ebony, c1810. L52, w26.*
In the mannered styles of Thomas Hope and George Smith, this writing table has attractive brass inlays (stars, gilt cabochon plaques), and dominant giltwood ornaments, volutes, rams' heads and anthemion motifs. With its black and yellow calamander veneers acting as the foil for the gilt, a rich appearance is created in a small area. Some of the details are taken from Plate 12 of Hope's influential *Household Furniture and Interior Decoration* of 1807.

2. *Writing table, yew and pollard yew, c1810. w46.*
The rarer use of yew in the Regency period for small tables is not to all tastes. It seems to contrast awkwardly with the cross-bandings. Here the leather-lined top is contrasted with rosewood, and the frieze drawers are surrounded with ebony beading. The table rests on spindle-filled splayed end supports.

3. *'Quartetto' tables, satinwood and rosewood, attributed to Gillow of Lancaster and London, c1810. w23-16.*
William Senhouse, member of a Lancashire family, appears to have ordered furniture from Gillow, which was delivered in 1772. His family continued to support the firm, and these tables are veneered with amboyna, rosewood and birds' eye maple, and cross-banded with a variety of the same woods in differing combinations.

4. *Toilet chest, mahogany, c1810-15. w28.*
Here the ingenuity of a Regency maker, bred on the designs in Sheraton's *Drawing Book* of 1793, comes into its own. The lifting top discloses an interior with compartments and a rising mirror. The front is fitted with a slide and drawers, some with false fronts and one with the original copper wash basin. It can all be moved, albeit with someone to help, by the use of two brass lifting handles.

Card table, calamander, c1810. W (closed) 36.
Wheeled forward on its brass castors, the card table could soon be put to use. This one has a baize-lined folding top inlaid with brass lines. Ormolu anthemions mounted on the frieze and platform base enhance the streaked calamander wood.

6.   *Dressing table, mahogany, by Gillow of Lancaster and London, c1811. W44.*
The Gillow firm had extensive trade in Lancashire and Yorkshire, as well as further afield. This dressing table was supplied to the Gascoigne family. Its three-quartered galleried top is edged with reeding and the table is supported by turned, reeded legs with brass castors.
Prov: Parlington Hall, Aberford, West Yorkshire; Lotherton Hall, Leeds, Yorkshire.

Writing, sewing and games table, mahogany, c1810. H29, W22, D20.
Writing, sewing and games: all could be catered for if one could remember which part of this table to activate. It is one of a pair, and has a top fitted with a rising screen. The frieze incorporates four small drawers, and a further one fitted with a backgammon board, with chess on the reverse. Another drawer at the front encloses a divided interior, and, below, the solid work-basket is also fitted with a drawer.
Prov: Wateringbury House, Kent.

8.   *Dressing table, birch and yew, c1810. W46.*
The Gothic piercing allied to the careful inlays give this table a dominant appearance. It was probably made *en suite* to bedroom furniture of bedheads, wardrobe, etc., for use at Lowther Castle, Sir Robert Smirke's great baronial pile in Cumberland.
Prov: The Trustees of the Earl of Lonsdale.

1. Armchair, ebonized and gilded, c1805.
The back of the armchair has an overlapping rosette border, and the arm supports are formed in the shape of cornucopiae. The reeded sabre legs are headed by grotesque masks, and the chair is upholstered.

2. Armchair, painted to simulate rosewood, c1810.
The architect Robert Adam did much to encourage interest in the 1770s in Etruscan forms of decoration. The Regency makers were no less concerned with the trappings of the antique race. This chair, one of a set of four, has its top rail painted with Etruscan figures, and is flanked by scrolled arm rests. The caned seat is above sabre legs.

3. Armchair, painted wood, c1810. w48.
This very distinctive chair epitomizes the important influence of the Regency publicists Thomas Hope and George Smith. It has winged sphinxes to support the arms, and carved lambrequins head the turned, tapering legs with paw feet. There are carved roundels and rosettes in the back border, and anthemions on the seat rail. The chair, painted white with an upholstered back, bears a plaque inscribed 'St George's Chapter no 410'.

4. Armchair, painted and gilt, c1810.
This flamboyant upholstered chair is in the manner of the Regency maker George Smith. It is dominated by the monopodia supports, which have gilt lions' heads, paw feet and anthemion decoration. The chair frame is given greater richness by being painted green, with a gilt pierced cresting of a shell and acanthus foliage at the top.

f one tries to set out the principal sources and characteristics of
lassical chair design, there are always exceptions: however, it is
ndeniable that many Regency chairs were based on ideas derived
rom Etruscan or late Greek vase-paintings and from French models,
s seen in the paintings of Jacques-Louis David. Straight front legs of
arying form and with monopodia arm supports are usually com-
ined with curved rear legs and there was much use of caning and of
imulated surfaces representing ebony or bronze. Side rails and back
upports could be in one sweeping curve, or be worked with rope or
able mouldings allusive of the victories at sea of the British fleet.

5. *Armchair, painted and gilt, c1810.*
The rich classical form of this armchair is emphasized by an
upholstered scrolled back, arms carved with acanthus leaves, and the
lions' masks. The seat rail is formed as fasces.

6. *Armchair, painted as rosewood, c1805.*
This chair shows the French influence which was being absorbed by
English craftsmen patronized by the architect Henry Holland. He
used French workers extensively at Carlton House, Woburn, Southill
and elsewhere. This chair is part of a suite of eight armchairs, two
settees and two window seats.
Prov: HRH The Princess Royal; The Earl of Harewood.

7. *Chair, mahogany, c1823.*
The design of this chair is similar to a set designed for Eaton Hall,
Cheshire, by William Porden, in the 1820s. It is one of a set of twelve,
with slightly arched backs mounted with gilt metal panels cast in high
relief, with vines set on gilt sheet metal grounds. The sloping sides
are filled with scrolls carved with paterae. The lower part of the backs
and bowed seats are upholstered in red leather.
Prov: Attingham Park, Shrewsbury, Shropshire.

1. Bergère, aburra wood and parcel-gilt, 1823.
This is one of a pair, supplied by Morel and Hughes for the Ante Room to the Crimson Drawing Room, Northumberland House, London, in 1823. The scrolled side rails are richly carved with acanthus and lotus leaves, and the seat rail is decorated with rosette mounts and rope-twist moulding. The cabinet-maker Nicholas Morel was joined by Robert Hughes soon after 1805, and the partnership ended in about 1827. The bergère is now in the Victoria and Albert Museum (No: W. 21–1975) and has been re-upholstered.

Although no firm evidence has been found that Nicholas Morel was of French extraction, he does seem to have been associated with the group of Anglo-French craftsmen who worked for Henry Holland at Carlton House and elsewhere. When he had already done significant work, he was joined soon after 1805 by Robert Hughes. The splendid throne armchair is attributed to them on the basis of similar ones in a watercolour of the Throne Room at Carlton House. The types of parlour chair with arc-backs, sometimes having the ends of the yoke curving strongly outwards or with carved volutes, were a popular form with many makers. Gillow charged 2½ guineas for each one supplied to Broughton Hall, Yorkshire, between 1811–13.

2. *Throne armchair, giltwood, c1825.*

Four armchairs of the same design as this example, except for the top rails, are shown in C. Wild's watercolour of the Ante Chamber in the Throne Room at Carlton House. The unwinking Egyptian winged caryatids support the arm rests, and the moulded foliate seat rail is raised on lion monopodia feet. It is a worthy 'throne', attributed to Morel and Hughes.

In 1822, Richard Brown— a London architect, and probably not the same Richard Brown who in 1805 had patented a method of expanding dining tables to a larger size—wrote of chairs in his The Rudiments of Drawing Cabinet and Upholstery Furniture (1822): 'this article has lately undergone a far greater improvement than any other branch of the cabinet art, inasmuch as it now baffles the most skilful artist to produce any new forms'. The variety on this page demonstrates how difficult innovation had become. Every variant of leg (sabre, monopodia, reeded, turned) and of back (arcshaped, 'U'-shaped, lyre supports, horizontal bars) is in evidence. There were also the ingenious efforts of the makers of 'patent metamorphic furniture' to reckon with, in which more than one function was catered for—sitting and reading in comfort at the same time being the simplest example of their work (1.).

1. *Library bergère, mahogany, c1830.*
A more comfortable chair for reading than this is hard to imagine. An ormolu baluster supports an adjustable reading stand. The scrolled arm supports are carved with acanthus foliage, and the gadrooned tapering legs are headed by rosettes. The chair is caned.
Prov: Ashburnham Place, Sussex.

2. *Chair, mahogany, by Gillow of Lancaster and London, c1815.*
This is one of a set of six dining chairs, with 'dropped' curved top rail. The upholstered seat has brass edges, and is supported on sabre legs. This design was called 'new French pattern', and the six were charged at £22 1s.

3. *Chair, rosewood, attributed to Gillow of Lancaster and London, c1825.*
A nearly identical chair to this is illustrated in a Gillow design for the dining room of Linton, for Earl Cornwallis, dated 1825. This is one of a set of nineteen dining chairs with balloon backs and bar splats, and the top rails are incised with anthemions. The seats are upholstered in leather.

4. *Chair, mahogany, leather upholstered, c1835.*
This is one of a set of eight dining chairs, with projecting, curved top rails and gilt brass handles. The front legs are turned and gadrooned.

5. *Chair, mahogany, c1820.* H35, W20.
George Smith illustrates similar types of leg to the ones on this chair (which is one of a set of twelve, including two armchairs). This example has a reeded frame, carved with lions' masks and 'U'-shaped back splats. The leather upholstered seats are supported on lion monopodia.

6. *Chair, simulated calamander and gilt, c1815.*
This is a very refined form of chair, one of a set of five in the manner of George Smith. The padded, scrolled top rail is framed by carved and gilt lions' masks, whilst the back rail is decorated with a gilt Greek key pattern. The upholstered seat rests on sabre legs.

7. *Chair, simulated rosewood, attributed to Thomas Chippendale the younger, c1820.*
This chair, of *klismos* design with gilt decoration, is one of a set of five. They were originally placed in the Entrance Hall at Harewood House, Yorkshire, which was fitted up in the Egyptian style around 1820. One chair is inscribed on the back rail 'F. M.'.

8. *Chair, ebonized and gilt, c1820.*
The gentle, lyrical art of music is personified in the back splat of this chair, with its gilded, lyre-shaped, laurel-leaf back. The curved top rail is unusually padded, and lotus leaves are ever-present to cap the turned front legs.

1. *Day-bed, rosewood, brass-inlaid, c1815. L76.*
The curved outlines of the day-bed are carefully considered in order to give support, but also to allow easy access to the upholstered seat. The seat frame has a tablet-centred frieze inlaid with geometric patterns, and the frame is carved with flowerheads and anthemions. The four sabre legs are on castors.

2. *Sofa, giltwood, c1820. L124, H48, D46.*
The sofa is one of a pair in Rococo Revival form, which are part of a large suite of furniture comprising armchairs, torchères, pole screens and tables. They were made to furnish the Whistle Jacket Room at Wentworth Woodhouse, Yorkshire. This room was recorded in 1801 as still 'not fitted up'.

Settees and sofas are two kinds of furniture with overlapping similarities and functions. The settee was an extension of the armchair, with two or more seating spaces side by side. The sofa was a development of the day-bed, but mounted on heavy supports (2). However, Thomas Sheraton consistently called the settee-type a sofa. Whatever the difficulties of nomenclature, there was much to interest and even 'deceive' in the furniture itself. Bamboo was simulated in paint, and the winged caryatids of the day-bed (4) so arrest the eye that the rest is almost un-noticed. The sabre legs of the stool (5) curve to the point of sharply decreasing confidence in their safety. But as George Smith noted in 1808, their principal purpose was to serve 'as ornamental and extra seats in elegant Drawing Rooms', and surely nothing untoward ever happened in such rich and luxurious settings?

3. Sofa, black and gilt japanned, c1810. L60. Whilst the casual eye might think that three Hepplewhite chairs have been placed side by side — such is the dominance of the pierced trellis-work splats — this upholstered sofa (over a cane seat) has delicate distinction. The top rails are painted with summer flowers, and the turned tapering legs are almost too slender to support three persons.

4. Day-bed, giltwood, c1810. L79. The fact that this is a day-bed is almost lost in the dominance of the scrolled head and seat rail, which is incised with Greek key pattern, and winged caryatids with lions' paw feet and a sphinx. It is in the flamboyant style popularized by the London maker, George Smith.

5. Stool, giltwood, c1810. w23. The massive sabre legs of this stool seem to defy the natural laws governing support. Deeply carved with guilloches, they support a reeded frame and upholstered seat. The stool bears an armorial label inscribed in ink: 'Sir Charles Stuart Kt'.

The appearence of some Regency cabinets is so lavish that one must have been taxed hard to fill them with appropiate objects. Could the handsome ormolu panelled or penwork decorated doors be opened, the caryatids ignored, to merely seek a chipped wine-glass or an ivory dice? They were created by makers capable of achieving all the intricate designs set out in the publications of Thomas Hope (1807) and George Smith (1808). The bills for them would be redolent of quality: 'Covered in fustic, set below inlaid brass anthemions, scrolls and stars, and between panels banded with ebony and brass . . .' With half-closed eyes it could be almost the furniture of antiquity, revered and impressive and never ignored or abused.

1. Side cabinet, rosewood, c1815. w47.
Small cabinets, of no great depth, were very useful for storing china and books, but provided considerable areas for decoration. This cabinet is inlaid with cut-brass stylized foliage, with a *verde antico* marble top mounted with an ormolu border, and two ormolu panelled cupboard doors. It stands on turned feet.

2. Cabinet, penwork on simulated ebony, c1810. w42.
This elaborate dwarf cabinet presumably came about by the impetus given to Chinese decoration by work for the Prince Regent at the Brighton Pavilion. It is entirely decorated in penwork, white on black, with chinoiserie designs, flowers, foliage and rockwork. A mirror is set in the centre of the raised back between two small doors, enclosing shelves.

. . *Cabinet, ebony and gilt, c1810. w50.*
This dwarf cabinet is firmly bounded by the giltwood eagle-headed
monopodia standing on either side. Further decoration is restrained,
but the top is inlaid with kingwood, and there is a mirror-backed
shelf, gilt metal anthemions and paterae to give life to the overall
shape.

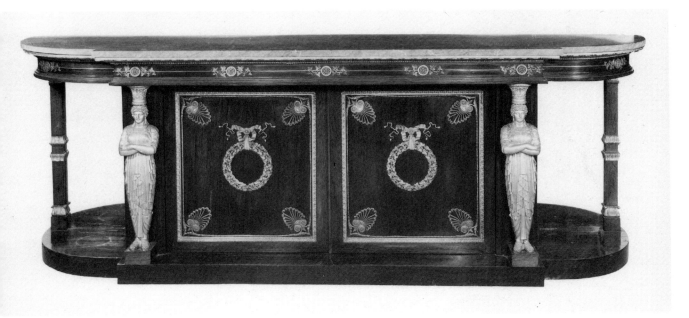

4.   *Side cabinet, rosewood and parcel-gilt, c1810. L100.*
The unwinking caryatids, with crossed arms and baskets on their
heads, support a grey marble top to this side cabinet. The rounded
ends are mirror-backed, and the sense of illusion — of architectural
forms in the dining room — is enhanced by the two columns and the
ormolu tied wreaths and anthemions on the two cupboard doors. The
figures are close to those on a table illustrated in Thomas Hope's
Household Furniture and Interior Decoration (1807, Plate 13, no. 3).

1. *Cabinet, rosewood, brass inlaid, c1810. H51, W34, D14.*
The dwarf cabinet has a superstructure with pierced brass gallery and
brass border. The cupboard doors, covered in fustic, are set below
inlaid brass anthemions, scrolls and stars, and between panels
banded with ebony and brass.

When Joseph Nash published his Views of the Royal Pavilion, Brighton *in 1826, showing rooms as they were about 1820, it provided a summation of interest in Chinese art. The Prince Regent had been fascinated by oriental-style interiors and by French art since Henry Holland had worked for him in the 1790s at Carlton House. His wide interests encouraged several makers to produce furniture both in the Chinese and in the French styles to go alongside that of Grecian and Egyptian outline, made fashionable by Thomas Hope and others. Perhaps it never blended happily with the rosewood and brass inlaid cabinets, for these owed little to any mannered movement and merely provided restrained and functional purchases.*

2. *Pedestal cabinet, ebony, black lacquer and buhl, 1820. H32, w25.*
The possession of a panel of Japanese lacquer needing to be suitably mounted resulted in this lavish cabinet, one of a pair in Louis XVI style. It has an inset marble top and a frieze drawer decorated with buhl marquetry. The corners bear ormolu scrolls, headed with satyr masks.

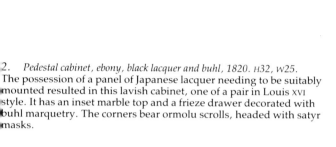

3. *Side cabinet, oak, lacquer panels, c1820. H36, w49, D22.*
The Chinese palaces, water gardens and obsequious courtiers fill the two cupboard doors of this cabinet, which are made from Chinese black and gold lacquer screens. Ormolu scrolled pilasters embellish the corners, and there is an elaborate veneered top.

The links between commodes and chiffoniers may not be at first apparent, as the latter has open shelves instead of cupboards, and a superstructure of shelves. George Smith illustrated a 'commode-chiffonier' in 1808 in which he added shelves above the normal cabinet area, and a further development was to fit out the cabinet as a secretaire. Deriving from Louis XVI patterns, it was natural that makers such as the Jamars should settle in London, and claim that their range of 'French furniture' was equal to any made in Paris, and cheaper, as no import fees were incurred and there was no risk of damage during the journey.

1.   *Chiffonier, rosewood, c1810. w31.*
The chiffonier was 'a piece of furniture with drawers in which women put away their needlework', but many served similar purposes of storage for small objects. This one is inlaid with brass stringing, rosettes, scrolled foliage and lozenges. It has a superstructure with a gilt brass gallery, and the lower part is fitted with an outward-folding, leather-lined flap.
Prov: Hinton Ampner House, Hampshire.

2.   *Cabinet on stand, yellow penwork on simulated ebony, c1810. H48, w25.*
Decoration may here be excessive to some eyes. The cabinet is decorated with Chinese garden scenes, foliage, flowers and geometrical design. The two doors enclose long drawers, and the stand is fitted with a drawer.
Prov: Lord Howard de Walden.

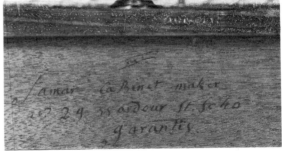

4.   *Trade label of the secretaire.*
The Furniture History Society's *Dictionary of English Furniture Makers, 1660-1840* records an S. Jamar working at this address from 1817 to 1826. William Jamar is shown at 29 Wardour Street, London, from 1817-20.

3.   *Secretaire, rosewood, by S. Jamar, c 1817. H55, w38.*
This fall-front secretaire is in the French Empire style. It is mounted with ormolu plaques of an eagle, between cornucopiae, and has an interior which comprises a colonnade of three bays with mirror backs, and drawers, veneered with yew, divided by ormolu caryatids. Egyptian terms are applied on each side. Many of the drawers are stamped 'S, Jamar'.
Prov: Sir Anthony Hornby.

5. *Chiffonier, satinwood and rosewood, c1810. H45, W36, D19.*
Character is given to this piece by the tambour shutter in the front, which is formed of alternating rosewood and satinwood splats, and the raised superstructure with its open centre. There is ample space for storage and ease of access, but practicality has been allied to good materials and concern for shape.

6. *Chiffonier, maple, c1810. W37.*
The narrow proportions of this chiffonier bely its ability to contain eight graduated shallow drawers. They are edged by rope-twist mouldings, and have gilt metal knob handles. The use of maple gives a fine figured surface overall.

7. *Secretaire cabinet, rosewood, c1815. W32, D14.*
A refined classical note is struck by the careful spacing of the painted oval and circular prints, on a background of satinwood veneer, of this cabinet. But within, the secretaire drawer also contains a well-fitted satinwood interior, with cedar-lined drawers, to serve the writer.

8. *Secretaire cabinet, rosewood, c1810. H58, W36, D16.*
John McLean was a very competent Regency maker, with a good clientèle, and this cabinet can be attributed to him. It has a mirror-backed superstructure, side latticework panels and shelves with turned ormolu supports. The secretaire drawer encloses a fitted interior of pigeon-holes and cedar-lined drawers.

1. *Bed, mahogany, beech and pine, c1825. H180, W112.*
The firm of Gillow supplied furniture to Clifton Castle, Yorkshire,
and this spectacular bed is attributed to them. However, it bears the
trade card of the obscure Benjamin Evans of Wheatsheaf Yard, Fleet
Market. He may have been involved in some way in supplying it.
The bed can be dated roughly from stylistic affinities with ornamental
designs in P. and M. A. Nicholson's *Practical Cabinet-Maker* (1826).
The bed was re-upholstered in a replica of the original material in
1985-86.
Prov: By descent from Timothy Hutton of Clifton Castle, Yorkshire;
gift to Temple Newsam House, Leeds, by Mrs J. H. Curzon-Herrick,
1963 (No: 23/63).

*It is easy to forget, due to their early eminence, that during the whole
of the nineteenth century the Lancaster and London firm of Gillow
continued to provide furniture of consistent quality. The important
bed (1.) has been attributed to them, despite the puzzling label
thereon of Benjamin Evans, who may have merely been one of their
agents. Gillow tried to keep well ahead of fashion, and one of the
important 'names' they would be aware of was Thomas Hope, a
traveller, archaeologist and writer. His interest in matters Egyptian,
purveyed through his seminal book on interiors and furniture (1807),
obviously inspired the unknown maker of the bookcase (2). It is
acocomplished, mannered and eminently desirable—an amalgam of
taste and quality.*

. *Bookcase-cabinet, mahogany, c1810. H110, W50.*
his magnificent and severely classical bookcase-cabinet follows in
most every detail a design by Thomas Sheraton given in his *Cabinet
ncyclopedia* (1806). The two portrait busts (Charles James Fox and

William Pitt) were supplied by the sculptor J. D. Gianelli of 33 Cock
Lane, Snow Hill, whose name is inscribed on the back of each, with
the date 'July 29, 1808'. The cabinet is now in the Victoria and Albert
Museum, London.

Many architectural styles were found acceptable to incorporate in library furniture, particularly the Egyptian and the Gothic. A good library in any case contained all the great architectural folios, from Palladio to Robert Adam, Stuart and Revett to Thomas Hope. The smaller pieces (5) seem to be overlaid with decoration, particularly the stylized lotus-leaf. All of them reflect the desire to incorporate as many books as possible, but not at the expense of inferior workmanship, timber, veneers and metal ornaments, and with due observance of the rules governing 'Taste', however indefinable they were.

1. Bookcase, mahogany, by George Oakley, 1810. W78.
This bookcase was made for a member of the Cheere family of Papworth Hall, Cambridgeshire, in 1810 by George Oakley. He invoiced it as a 'mahogany winged library case in the Grecian stile'. The cornice has a central pediment mounted with an ormolu plaque of mask and foliage ebonized background. The four cupboard doors, with borders inlaid with stylized ebonized foliage, are filled with brass trellis backed by pleated silk.

2. Secretaire cabinet, calamander, c1810. W31.
The rich streaks of calamander point up this small cabinet, which has Gothic-pattern glazed doors surmounted by a triangular cornice. The projecting lower section is fitted with a secretaire drawer and two cupboard doors, inlaid with satinwood stringing. A touch of the Regency interest in matters Egyptian is stressed in the term uprights.

3. Bookcase, mahogany, c1810-15. H94, W54.
This bookcase was reputedly made for Admiral Sir George Seabright, and he was obviously concerned to get maximum storage space. Three cupboards, three drawers and moveable open shelves are contained within the overall space. The bookcase seems to perch a little awkwardly on carved paw feet.

4. Bookcase, mahogany, c1830. H98, W100.
Possibly more than other pieces of furniture, the bookcase was capable of showing architectural forms to advantage — in the cornice and in the glazing, in the use of columns and pilasters and in the decoration simulating arches or wainscoted panels. This attractive William IV bookcase does just that: four free-standing column uprights with lotus-pattern capitals flank arched panelled doors, and the panelled uprights to the glazed upper section are headed by acanthus capitals. Like good architecture, it looks well and functions well.

5. Standing bookcase, rosewood, ormolu mounted, c1815. H48, W31, D16.
The heavy, scrolled, foliate sides give great distinction to this bookcase. It has throne-like proportions, the books swallowed on its three wide shelves, and lotus leaves dominant on the bronzed and giltwood columns.
Prov: Belton House, Lincolnshire.

6. Dwarf bookcase, walnut, brass gallery, c1825. W52.
The uprights of this attractive small bookcase are carved with strapwork and foliage on a pounced ground. When lined with books, it provides quiet storage, and its function is appreciated better than in the black voids of empty open shelves of this illustration.
Prov: The Lord Leigh, Stoneleigh Abbey, Warwickshire.

The Regency makers surpassed themselves in fashioning gilded and mounted furniture, and that which copied the best productions of earlier years. This was particularly true of Louis Le Gaigneur, a Frenchman who had transferred his workshop to London c 1815. He specialized in buhl, and had a manufactory at 19 Queen St, Edgware Road, specializing in furniture in the style of Louis XIV's cabinet-maker, A. C. Boulle. Whilst a carver of the 1750s might well have made a more satisfactory job of carving the trophies and dolphins on the girandole (2), it is the interest in reviving the rococo style which it is important to observe. The nineteenth century thrived on revivals, albeit robust versions of the originals, but they have their own place in the history of the decorative arts.

2.   *Girandole, giltwood, c1810. H49, W24.*
Great verve in a small area is demonstrated in this girandole — the twin dolphins with vertical tails are sporting under foliage and berried laurel wreaths. A satyr looks omnisciently from the upper stage, secure as always in an opulent setting.

1.   *Looking glass, gilded and ebonized wood, 1815. H36.*
The circular convex looking glass is a very typical piece of Regency furnishing, and was popular from about 1795 to the 1820s. George Smith described them in 1808 as 'an elegant and useful ornament, reflecting objects in beautiful perspective on their convex surfaces; the frames, at the same time they form an elegant decoration on the walls, are calculated to support lights'. This attractive glass is supported on a kneeling representation of Atlas, and is decorated with twined serpents. Two colza-oil lamps are suspended on chains and candle-holders are incorporated. A proud anthemion is on the top of the gilded 'world'.

3.   Bureau Mazarin, rosewood and buhl, c1815. H33, W48, D26.
This design is in the manner of Louis Le Gaigneur, the French
cabinet-maker resident in London 1815-16. Bureau Mazarin is a
nineteenth-century term for a desk with buhl-type marquetry
decoration. The decoration here shows scenes of dancers, monkeys,
cherubs and birds, all amid elaborate strapwork in the style of the
French designer and engraver, Jean Bérain I (1637-1711).

Among the miscellaneous furniture on these pages, the Englishman might turn constantly to the tea-poy (5.). They were described by George Smith in 1808 as 'used in Drawing-rooms, to prevent the company rising from their seats when taking refreshment'. Whilst it could be argued that the enormous range of small items of furniture prevented easy passage through a room filled with tables, desks, music canterburies, pole-screens, large settees and French chairs, makers were not inhibited. Even large pianofortes were 'an indispensable article for apartments', and we know that beds were large and high enough to warrant bed-steps (7.).

2.   Davenport, rosewood, c1825. H36, W19.
This small writing desk, with a sloping top, has a leather-lined slide on each side, a pen drawer and four graduated long drawers on the right. It is on columnar supports, and the concave-fronted base is on paw feet. It is stamped 'G & H Evans', but the address is unrecorded.

1.   Carlton House table, mahogany and rosewood, by Gillow of Lancaster and London, c1810-15. L63, H41, D35.
An estimate drawing for a Carlton House table of precisely this model, dated 1796, is in the Gillow archive. The estimated cost was £17 8s. 6d This example is stamped by the firm, and is typical of their important commission for the Egerton family of Tatton Park, Cheshire, pieces of which are so marked around 1811-12. There are abundant drawers and cupboards: one can write, draw (there is a hinged easel) and lock away all valuables in this table.

4.   Upright desk, mahogany, c1820. H46, W36.
Perhaps this desk was intended for a rather grand clerk to an even grander personage. The reeded angles, sharp carving on the turned legs and the sophisticated twist in the concave-fronted shelf betoken a good, careful maker. A hinged flap on each side is able to take books and papers. Were they those of Sir Robert Peel?
Prov: Sir Robert Peel; by descent.

3.   Library desk, mahogany, c1800. W57, H31, D34.
This desk is based on a typical Gillow model, and may well be by that distinguished firm. The top is lined with tooled red leather, and a heavy piece of furniture has been made easier to move by brass castors on the turned feet of the reeded, tapering legs.
Prov: H.R.H. the late Duke of Kent.

6.   *Canterbury, rosewood, c1835. W20.*
Able to take magazines, papers and music with ease between its five 'X'-shaped divisions, the Canterbury is given distinction by its lyre-shaped ends, and further use by the fitted drawer. It moves easily on gadrooned turned legs on castors.

5.   *Teapoy, mahogany, c1820. H32, W23.*
This attractive object contains four Chinese engraved zinc caddies enclosed by a rectangular hinged lid. Standing on ring-turned tapering legs, the caddies were easily available. The lock is stamped 'G R'.

7.   *Bedside steps, mahogany, 1820. W19.*
The high Regency bed needed steps to assist the elderly to mount into the enfolding sheets. This set doubles as a commode beneath the upper tread. All the treads are leather-lined. It has no castors, and so stood firmly *in situ*, sturdily practical.

8.   *Pole screen, giltwood, c1820. H66.*
This elegant screen, one of a pair, is in the manner of the distinguished designer C. H. Tatham (1772-1842), who exerted a considerable influence on the design of furniture in the early years of the nineteenth century. The support, formed as a splat, holds an oval banner covered with pleated green silk, centred by an ormolu classical head. The base of classical tripod form has winged lions' legs on a triangular base.
Prov: The 4th Earl of Powis, Berkeley Square, London.

Glossary of terms

The best source for terms used in the furniture trade is Thomas Sheraton's *The Cabinet Dictionary* of 1803 (reprinted, New York, 1970). Useful lists of terms used by Thomas Chippendale and William and John Linnell in the eighteenth century appear in Christopher Gilbert, *Thomas Chippendale: his Life and Work,* 2 vols., London, 1978 and Helena Hayward and Patricia Kirkham, *William and John Linnell,* 2 vols., London, 1980. An illustrated glossary is given by Robin Butler in his *Guide to English Furniture,* London, 1978, and reference can be made to Ralph Edwards (ed.), *Dictionary of English Furniture,* 3 vols., of 1954; shorter edn., London, 1964. 3 vols. reprinted Woodbridge (Antique Collectors' Club), 1983.

canthus Stylized leaf decoration derived from classical ornament. Found on the capitals of the Composite and Corinthian Orders — resembles the scalloped leaves of the acanthus plant.

ir-wood *See* harewood.

mboyna A warm, brown, honey-tone wood from the West Indies. Used for veneers as whole surfaces: it had a pronounced burr figure, making it attractive also for inlays and bandings.

nthemion A stylized plant motif derived from Greek art, based on the honeysuckle flower or the leaf of a date palm (known in the latter form, with inward pointing lobes, as a **palmette**.)

ntique An eighteenth-century term, often written *antick* in documents, to describe ancient Greek or Roman art or design.

pron An extension below the bottom edge of the seat of a chair, or frame of a table or cabinet.

umbry Medieval or Gothic cupboard, originally to house provisions given away as alms. Term soon applied to any closed cupboard or coffer.

aize A course, open woollen material with a long nap: used for drawer lining and **case-covers** (q.v.).

Baluster A short post or pillar, usually of circular section with a turned profile, as a table leg. Used in series to form a balustrade supporting a rail, as on a staircase.

Banding Ornamental or veneered borders around doors, panels, drawers or table tops. In **cross-banding** the grain runs at right angles to the edge; **feather-banding** and **herring-bone** bandings are set at an angle; **straight-banding** is cut along the length of the grain.

Batten(s) Square deal bar(s) used in the construction of packing cases, or against walls as a framework for hanging wallpaper or fabric.

Bead(ing) A narrow moulding, usually of semi-circular section.

Bevel Most commonly a slope cut at the edge of a flat surface, commonly seen on the edge of plate glass and mirrors.

Bole A type of clay used to achieve a smooth surface under gilding and in japanning. *See also* **French bole**.

Bombé A term adopted from the French to describe a curved or swelling form. Late eighteenth-century commodes were often of *bombé* form.

Bracket foot A shaped foot on **carcase furniture** (q.v.), which projects slightly at each corner. The bracket can be panelled with **beading** (q.v.).

Bun foot A flattened ball foot, used on furniture from the mid-seventeenth century.

Bureau A desk with a lid sloping at an acute angle (usually about 45°) that folds out as a writing surface, above drawers. If surmounted by a bookcase, titled a bureau-bookcase. The nomenclature of tables of French origin is very varied, e.g. *bureau-toilette,* a combined writing and toilet table.

Burnished gold Water gilding, highly polished or burnished.

Butler's tray   A tray of wood (or silver or japanned metal) mounted on a folding stand or legs—much used in the eighteenth century. Frequently has hinged side-flaps and pierced lifting handles.

Cabriole leg   A leg which curves outwards at the top or knee and tapers in an elongated 'S' towards the foot. Increased in popularity after its depiction in William Hogarth's *The Analysis of Beauty* (1753), as the form of the fashionable 'line of beauty'.

Canted   Obliquely faced, as in a canted corner.

Canterbury   A stand with deep open partitions, and a drawer between the legs, for holding sheet music. According to Thomas Sheraton, so-called because a 'bishop of that See first gave orders for these pieces'.

Carcase furniture   A term for furniture used for storage, as chest of drawers—**commode** (q.v.), as distinct from chairs or tables. **Carcase**—the body or main structure of furniture, to which veneers are applied.

Carlton House Table   A writing table with a low 'D'-shaped superstructure, usually in satinwood, of a type named after those at the Prince Regent's Carlton House, illustrated in Thomas Sheraton's *Drawing-Book* (1793).

Case   A loose cover for furniture.

Caster   A small, swivelling wheel of wood, metal, ivory, leather, etc., attached to the leg of a piece of furniture.

Chair rail   Horizontal timber mould affixed to wall at height of top chair rail to prevent damage to wall decoration when chairs are against it. Part of the **dado** (q.v.).

Chamfered   Describes a bevelled edge, or edge which has been smoothed off or cut away from the square.

Chasing   Tooling or surface modelling of metal—to raise patterns in relief on mounts, etc.

Chiffonier   Anglicized name from French for a small cupboard with a top, forming a **sideboard** (q.v.).

Claw-and-ball (foot)   A carved ornamental foot of (eagle) claws gripping a ball, in use during the eighteenth century.

Close stool   A movable latrine, superseded by the pot-cupboard or night-table—sometimes called a **necessary stool** (q.v.)—having a hinged top which opens to reveal a pan.

Club foot   Leg terminating in the form of a club.

Collared   Describes small, convex rings turned as decoration on the leg of a table or chair.

Commode (table)   French name for a chest of drawers, usually of elaborate appearance, serpentine in form, as in the production of Pierre Langlois. From the mid-nineteenth century the term was in use in England for a **close stool** (q.v)

Confidante   An upholstered settee with additional seats at each end. Illustrated in Hepplewhite's *Guide*, (1788), and said there to be 'of French origin . . .'

Console table   A table fixed to a wall, usually having a marble top, supported on shaped legs curving back to the wall; alternatively applied to tables with legs or supports (e.g., stylized eagle) at the front side only.

Court cupboard   A low cupboard (*court* = short) for the display of plate. Constructed in two stages, with an open base and central cupboard with canted sides in the upper stage.

Dado   A finishing of wood running along the lower part of the walls of a room having a base, panelling and a top projecting **chair rail** (q.v.).

Damask   A figured fabric: the term applies to the pattern formed by two faces of the same weave. The term is loosely applied to any silk fabric with a raised, usually floral, pattern.

Davenport   A small writing desk, often with a shallow-sloped top and several drawers.

Day-bed   A couch, often with a caned seat and an adjustable back, made in walnut or painted beech; popular from 1660 onwards.

Deal   Fir or pine, often used for the carcase of furniture intended to be veneered.

Dovetail   A wood joint in which wedge-shaped projections interlock with each other.

Drawing at large   A large-scale working drawing for use on the bench.

Dressing glass   A toilet mirror which stood on a **dressing table** (q.v.).

Dressing table   A table named after its function, usually with compartments for toilet requisites, and with a fitted, or separate **dressing glass** (q.v.).

Drum table   A circular table with drawers, usually on a tripod base; also called a capstan table or a rent table.

Dumb waiter   A wooden column with tripod foot carrying trays or shelves, one above the other, in diminishing circumference. Introduced in England about 1740, to set by dining tables to hold food, plates etc., for self-service.

Easy chair   A high-backed, upholstered, wing armchair.

Elbow chair   Term applied to armchairs, particularly those with open arms and padded rests.

En suite   Part of a series: matching.

Epergne   A silver or porcelain table centrepiece of elaborate design, incorporating dishes for fruit or sweetmeats.

Escutcheon   Ornamental brass or **ormolu** (q.v.) plate surrounding a keyhole opening.

Fall front   The drop front of a desk or cabinet, which forms a writing surface when lowered.

Fascia   Architrave of a window cornice.

Festoon   Ornament in the form of a garland of flowers, or foliage, suspended horizontally or vertically.

Field bedstead   A small, folding, four-post bed: also known as a 'tent bed'.

Fluting   Rounded, parallel grooves on friezes and pilasters.

Fly table   A small table with extending flaps supported on slender gate-legs, or hinged brackets.

Folding top   A top enclosed by hinged flaps.

French bole   The best quality **bole** (q.v.), of a blackish-red colour.

French elbow chair   A term used during the 1750s for

armchairs with upholstered seats and backs, carved frames and **cabriole legs** (q.v.).

Fret Geometrical ornament; e.g. as a key-pattern.

Fret table A tea table with a pierced trellis-work gallery.

'Furniture' The finger-plates, handles, locks, etc., of a door.

Fustian A rough cloth with a linen warp and cotton weft: usually brown in colour and made with many finishes and textures.

Fustic Yellow wood, which produced a yellow dye. Used by inlayers: Chippendale used it as a veneer. Sheraton (*Cabinet Dictionary*, 1803) noted that sun and air turned it a dead brown, and its use therefore declined.

Gadrooned A border ornament of radiating convex lobes of curved or straight form.

Garden mat A matting of a chequered weave, used as a packing material.

Gate-leg table A circular or oval table, whose flaps are supported by jointed gates which swing out from the central section.

Genoa damask/Genoa cut velvet Silk damask and velvet made at Genoa, *c*1670–*c*1750, but imitated in France and England (Spitalfields).

German stove Used for drying and heating in workshops.

Gesso A plaster-like composition, of gypsum, size and glue, usually gilded or painted.

Girandole A candelabrum. In the eighteenth century the word also described large rococo sconces, and mirror-backed wall brackets.

Girth web Woven hemp strips which support the stuffing of upholstered chairs.

Gros point Canvas embroidered in cross-stitch.

Guilloche A border moulding, composed of interlaced ribbon enclosing foliate rosettes, used as decoration from the sixteenth to eighteenth centuries.

Hair cloth A durable, dark fabric made from horse hair, used in upholstery for covering, in particular, dining and library chairs.

Harewood A veneer of sycamore wood dyed brownish-grey: used extensively in the late eighteenth century.

Harlequin table An elaborate form of small **Pembroke table** (q.v.) in which a central nest of drawers in a square or oval frame may be raised by weight or spring mechanisms, and pushed back flat with the table surface after use.

Hessian A strong, coarse brown cloth.

Hipped knee A **cabriole** (q.v.) chair leg with carved ornament on the knee.

Holland A linen fabric, usually dyed brown or green, and used for window blinds.

India paper Hand-painted oriental wallpaper.

Inlay Decorative technique, replaced by **marquetry** (q.v.). A pattern of different woods inset into the carcase wood.

Japanning Various methods of imitating oriental **lacquer** (q.v.) by using resins mixed with other materials, coloured, polished and gilded.

Kettle stand A small table to support a hot-water kettle or urn.

Knee The top of a **cabriole leg** (q.v.), sometimes carved.

Knife box A case fitted with slots in which knives would be stored blade-downwards; frequently of urn shape, or square with a sloping top.

Knole-settee A settee with high back and hinged arms which are held upright when not in use by rope loops. Popular in the 1920s after a seventeenth-century example at Knole Park, Kent.

Lacquer A water-resistant, clear varnish of oriental origin, having many variants (**shellac** [q.v.]) and imitations.

Library chair Armchair with padded, leather-covered, saddle-shape seat. The back has an adjustable hinged flap to hold a book, and compartments are located in the two padded arms for pens and ink, or for supporting candlesticks. The sitter usually straddles the seat facing the back. Incorrectly called a cock-fighting chair.

Linenfold Carved ornamentation on panelling or settee-backs imitating folded cloth — a popular decoration in the early sixteenth century.

Loo table A large oval or circular card table with a central support and tip-up top.

Loose seat A slip seat that fits into the frame of a chair or stool.

Lunettes Semi-circular panels or windows.

Lutestring A silk fabric, the surface dressed to give a sheen: often used for curtain linings.

Marquetry A pattern made by fitting together pieces of different coloured woods and other materials (ivory, thin metal, etc.) into one sheet, and applying this by heat, glue and pressure to the surface to be decorated.

Morocco leather A goat-skin leather, coloured, and used for surfacing library writing tables and for chair covers.

Mortise and tenon A joint in which the projecting tongue (**tenon**) is inserted into a rectangular cavity (**mortise**) in the adjacent piece of wood.

Mother-of-pearl A shiny substance from the lining of certain shells. Used as an inlay for furniture, particularly in the nineteenth century.

Moulding A shaped strip of wood, sometimes carved, applied to conceal joints, or as a decorative feature to panels and doors.

Muntin A vertical wooden member between two panels.

Necessary stool A **close stool** (q.v.) with a hinged top which opens to reveal a pan.

Night table A bedside pot cupboard, often with a tray top, and a **necessary stool** (q.v.) that pulls forward in the lower part.

Nonsuch chests Chests richly decorated with marquetry patterns of arches and fantastic architecture, reminiscent of Henry VIII's (vanished) palace of Nonsuch, but having no connection: the appellation means unequalled, 'non-such'. Probably made in north Germany, or by sixteenth-century German craftsmen settled in London at Southwark and elsewhere.

O's/oes/ows Round brass rings for hanging curtains.

Ogee curve A continuous double curve, convex above and concave below.

Oil gold A type of gilding in which linseed oil is used in preparing the ground. It cannot be burnished.

Ormolu Gilt bronze, used for furniture mounts and door 'furniture' (q.v.). The term is also applied, less precisely, to gilt brass.

Paling The fret, or lattice pattern, of straight diagonal bars, used by English makers in the 1750s to decorate furniture made in the Chinese style. Such decoration was held to be typical of the Chinese originals.

Palmette *See* **anthemion**

Panel A shaped or rectangular member framed by stiles, rails and (often) **muntins** (q.v.).

Papier-mâché Mashed paper combined with binding substances, which hardens on drying and may be formed as furniture, lacquered and decorated.

Parcel-gilt Description of plate, decorated by the partial application of gilding. Applied to furniture in this context — of some gilding to a structural part.

Patera A neo-classical motif, oval or round, resembling a flower or rosette.

Pattern chairs Models from which to work, frequently with arms or legs showing alternative forms, and styles of decoration.

Pedestal table One supported on a single column or pillar. A pedestal desk stands on two side sections with a kneehole.

Pediment Originally the gable above the portico of a classical temple. Adapted in various forms for the tops of furniture, e.g., 'broken', with a central break in base, and sloping side members, to incorporate a bust. If the sides are segmentally curved and end in scrolls, they form **swan necks** (q.v.).

Pembroke table A drop-leaf table on four legs. The flaps at the sides are supported on hinged wooden brackets when in use. Sometimes titled **sofa table** (q.v.).

Pendant Ornament that hangs or is suspended: frequently a representation of flowers and fruit as a decorative feature.

Pie-crust A raised edge (to tables), resembling a pie-crust.

Pier table One designed to stand against a pier as between windows, often surmounted by a pier mirror.

Pilaster Applied decoration in the form of a flat-sided column.

Pole screen A firescreen mounted on a pole, with a tripod or platform base. The screen may be moved vertically and locked at various heights.

Press bedstead A folding bedstead built into a cabinet which outwardly resembles a press or chest.

Purpleheart A native wood of British Guiana, so-called from the colour when freshly cut. Employed in veneer banding, line inlay, etc. (occasionally confused with rosewood).

Rail Any horizontal timber member in cabinet-making.

Reeding Consecutive parallel convex curves formed for vertical or horizontal decoration on chair and table legs, borders and edgings. The opposite of **fluting** (q.v.).

Refectory table A large hall table.

Rocaille *See* **rococo**.

Rockwork Decoration reminiscent of the rock formations of grottoes: *see* **rococo.**

Rococo Word derives from the French *rocaille*; a term used to describe a decorative style based on shell and rock forms, foliage and flowers, 'C'-scrolls and sinuous curves.

Sconce A general name for a wall light of metal, gilt wood or cut glass, consisting of a back plate and either a tray or branched candleholders.

Seaweed marquetry A term used to denote a type of **marquetry** (q.v.) decoration, using woods with a richly-figured grain, recalling seaweed. Used in the late seventeenth century for the fronts of scriptors, long-case clocks, etc.

Secretary A writing desk or cabinet with a fall-front desk drawer.

Shellac Purified lac (a resinous secretion produced on certain trees in the East Indies by an insect) melted and formed in thin plates. Used as a varnish or substitute for true lacquer.

Shield-back Chair design made fashionable in the 1780s by George Hepplewhite. The rail and stile form the shape of a shield.

Sideboard A serving table, in the neo-classical period often *en suite* with pedestals and urns, wine cooler and knife boxes.

Side table Designed to stand by a wall, and frequently acting as a secondary serving table.

Siena marble An Italian marble, yellow streaked with grey, used frequently for table tops in the eighteenth century.

Slide A sliding panel fitted to chests of drawers between the upper drawers and the top; also to small trays above the slant flaps of bureau cabinets, to support candlesticks when withdrawn.

Splat A vertical member between the seat and top rail of a chair.

Sofa table Similar to a **Pembroke table** (q.v.), but with flaps at the ends. In the late Regency period the end-flaps disappeared and the term was used as an alternative for an occasional table.

Squab A removable stuffed cushion for a chair or stool.

State bed A grand, lavishly upholstered bed intended for princes and noblemen.

Stile A vertical timber member of the side of a frame. The frame is formed from stiles, **rails** (q.v.), and **muntins** (q.v.) to contain panels.

Strapwork Stylized representation of geometrically-arranged leather straps: copied from Renaissance decorations.

Stretcher Horizontal timber member connecting and supporting the legs of furniture.

Stringing Line or lines of inlay used as a decorative border, usually in contrasting woods or brass.

Stucco nails Nails with round brass heads and of varying lengths, necessary in fixing large looking glasses or pictures.

Stumpwork A form of embroidery, padded so as to be in relief. Popular in the seventeenth century.

Surbase The moulding above the base of a column.

Sutherland table A small, swing-leg, drop-leaf table; the central portion is very narrow.

Swan neck An ogee curve applied to handles and 'broken' pediments.

Tambour Narrow strips of wood glued side-by-side to a canvas backing to form a roll-top or a vertical sliding door to writing desks or cupboards.

Tammy A fine woollen or wool and cotton fabric. Popular for lining, bed 'furniture', curtains and for backing chairs.

Tea box A tea caddy, often compartmented for black and green tea.

Tea poy A small stand, on a column set frequently on a foot of four splayed legs. The top houses a hinged compartment for tea caddies, mixing bowls, etc.

Tent bed *See* **field bedstead.**

Term (therm) A free-standing tapering column of architectural form, or a pedestal merging at the top into a sculpted animal or human figure.

Tester A canopy over a bedstead. An 'angel' canopy is supported from the ceiling by chains, rather than by posts.

Turkey work Imitation of Persian and oriental pile carpets. The wool was drawn through a canvas and knotted to form a pile. Usually found on chair seats as upholstery.

Turning Decoration applied to wood by gouges and chisels as it rotates in a lathe.

Valance A border of drapery hangings around the canopy of a bed.

Varnish A clear, often waterproof, coating of shellac applied to protect wood and enhance its colour.

Veneer A thin sheet of wood applied to a timber base.

Verre églomisé A process of decorating glass by drawing and painting on the underside and backing the decoration with gold or silver leaf, or foil.

What-not A stand of square or rectangular shelves, sometimes incorporating a drawer.

Bibliography

Since 1964, a bibliography of books and articles on furniture has been published in *Furniture History*, the annual journal of the Furniture History Society. Volume XXII (1986) contains a retrospective bibliography, 1981–5.

Agius, Pauline, *British Furniture, 1880–1915.* Woodbridge, (Antique Collectors' Club), 1978.

Aslin Elizabeth, *Nineteenth Century Furniture.* London, 1962.

Beard, Geoffrey, *The Work of Robert Adam.* London, 1978.

Beard, Geoffrey, *The National Trust Guide to English Furniture.* London, 1985.

Butler, Robin, *The Arthur Negus Guide to English Furniture.* London, 1978.

Chinnery, Victor, *Oak Furniture: The British Tradition.* Woodbridge (Antique Collectors' Club), 1980.

Chippendale Thomas, *The Gentleman and Cabinet-Maker's Director,* facsimile of third edition of 1762. London, 1962. Ibid., with introduction by Edwards, Ralph. London, 1957.

Coleridge, Anthony, *Chippendale Furniture: The Work of Thomas Chippendale and his Contemporaries in the Rococo Style.* London, 1968.

Collard, Frances, *Regency Furniture.* Woodbridge (Antique Collectors' Club), 1986.

Cornforth, John and Fowler, John, *English Decoration in the Eighteenth Century.* London, 1974.

Dictionary of English Furniture Makers, 1660–1840. Furniture History Society with W.S. Maney, Leeds, 1986.

Eames, Penelope, *Medieval Furniture: Furniture in England, France and the Netherlands from the Twelfth to the Fifteenth Centuries.* Furniture History Society, 1977.

Edwards, Ralph, ed., *The Dictionary of English Furniture from the Middle Ages to the Late Georgian Period.* Reduced facsimile of the three-volume 1954 edition, Woodbridge (Antique Collectors' Club), 1983. A shorter, one-volume version of the *Dictionary* was published in 1964.

Edwards, Ralph and Jourdain, Margaret, *Georgian Cabinet-Makers.* Third edition, London, 1962.

Fastnedge, Ralph, *English Furniture Styles from 1500–1830.* London, 1962.

Fastnedge, Ralph, *Sheraton Furniture.* London, 1962; reprinted London, 1985.

Furniture History, annual journal, 1964– of the Furniture History Society; indexes for vols. 1–10 and 11–15.

Gilbert, Christopher, *Furniture at Temple Newsam and Lotherton Hall: A Catalogue of the Leeds Collection.* Two vols., London, 1968.

Gilbert, Christopher, *Late Georgian and Regency Furniture.* London, 1972.

Gilbert, Christopher, *The Life and Work of Thomas Chippendale.* Two vols., London, 1978.

Gilbert, Christopher, 'Furniture by Giles Grendey for the Spanish Trade'. *Antiques* (New York) XCIX, 1971, pp. 544–50.

Gloag, John, *English Furniture Makers.* London, 1945.

Gloag, John, *English Furniture.* London, 1946.

Gloag, John, *The Englishman's Chair: Origins, Design, and Social History of Seat Furniture in England.* London, 1964.

Harris, Eileen, *The Furniture of Robert Adam.* London, 1963.

Harris, John, *Regency Furniture Designs from Contemporary Source Books, 1803–1826.* London, 1961.

Harris, M. & Sons, *The English Chair.* London, 1946.

Hayward, Helena, *Thomas Johnson and the English Rococo.* London, 1964.

Hayward, Helena, ed., *World Furniture.* London, 1969.

Hayward, Helena and Kirkham, Patricia, *William and John Linnell: Eighteenth Century Furniture Makers.* Two vols., London, 1980.

Heal, Sir Ambrose, *The London Furniture Makers from the Restoration to the Victorian Era.* London, 1953 (facsimile edition, 1972).

Hepplewhite, A. & Co., *The Cabinet-Maker and Upholsterer's Guide,* 1788; reprinted, London, 1970.

Hinckley, F.L.A., *Directory of the Historic Cabinet Woods.* New York, 1959.

Honour, Hugh, *Cabinet-Makers and Furniture Designers.* London, 1969.

Hope, Thomas, *Household Furniture and Interior Decoration.* 1807; reprinted London, 1970; New York, 1971.

Ince and Mayhew, *The Universal System of Household Furniture.* 1762; reprint with preface by Edwards, Ralph, London, 1960.

Irwin, David, *Thomas Hope and the Neo-Classical Idea.* London, 1968.

Jervis, Simon, *Printed Furniture Designs Pre-1650.* Furniture History Society, London, 1975.

Jervis, Simon, *The Penguin Dictionary of Design and Designers.* London, 1984.

Jourdain, Margaret, *Regency Furniture 1795–1830.* 1948; revised and enlarged edition by Fastnedge, Ralph, London, 1965.

Jourdain, Margaret, and Rose, Frank, *English Furniture, The Georgian Period, 1750–1830.* London, 1953.

Jourdain, Margaret; *see also* **Edwards, Ralph and Jourdain, Margaret.**

Joy, Edward, *English Furniture, 1800–1851.* London, 1979.

Joy, Edward, *Pictorial Dictionary of British Nineteenth Century Furniture Design.* Woodbridge (Antique Collectors' Club), 1980.

Kelly, Alison, *Decorative Wedgwood in Architecture and Furniture.* London, 1965.

Lever, Jill, *Architects' Designs for Furniture.* London, 1982.

Lucie-Smith, Edward, *Furniture: A Concise History.* London, 1981.

MacQuoid, Percy, *A History of English Furniture.* 4 Vols, The Age of Oak, Walnut, Mahogany and Satinwood. London, 1938.

Manwaring, Robert, *The Cabinet and Chair-Maker's Real Friend and Companion.* 1765; facsimile, London, 1937.

Mercer, Eric, *Furniture, 700–1700.* London, 1969.

Molesworth, H.D. and Kenworthy-Browne, J., *Three Centuries of Furniture in Colour.* London, 1972.

Musgrave, Clifford, *Regency Furniture.* London, 1961.

Musgrave, Clifford, *Adam and Hepplewhite Furniture and other Neo-Classical Furniture.* London, 1966.

Pinto, E.H. and E.R., *Tunbridge and Scottish Souvenir Woodware with chapters on Bois Durci and Pyrography.* London, 1970.

Reade, B., *Regency Antiques.* London, 1953.

Riley, Nöel, ed., *World Furniture.* London, 1980.

Rogers, J.C. and Jourdain, Margaret, *English Furniture.* Second edition, London, 1961.

Roche, S., *Mirrors.* London, 1957.

Sheraton, Thomas, *The Cabinet-Maker and Upholsterer's Drawing Book.* 1793; reprinted New York, 1970.

Sheraton, Thomas, *The Cabinet Dictionary.* 1803; reprinted New York, 1970.

Sparkes, Ivan, *The English Country Chair.* London, 1977.

Sparkes, Ivan, *English Domestic Furniture, 1100–1837.* London, 1980.

Symonds, Robert Wemyss, *Masterpieces of Furniture and Clocks, Seventeenth and Eighteenth Centuries.* London, 1940; reprinted London, 1985.

Symonds, Robert Wemyss, *Veneered Walnut Furniture, 1660–1760.* London, 1946.

Symonds, Robert Wemyss, *Furniture Making in Seventeenth and Eighteenth Century England.* London, 1955.

Symonds, Robert Wemyss, *English Furniture from Charles II to George II.* 1929; reprinted Woolbridge (Antique Collectors' Club), 1981.

Thornton, Peter, *Seventeenth Century Interior Decoration in England, France and Holland.* London, 1978.

Thornton, Peter and Tomlin, Maurice, *Ham House and its Furnishings.* Furniture History Society, London, 1980.

Toller, J., *Antique Miniature Furniture in Great Britain and America.* London, 1966.

Tomlin, Maurice, *Catalogue of Adam Period Furniture.* Victoria and Albert Museum, London, 1972.

Tomlin, Maurice, *English Furniture.* London, 1972.

Tomlin, Maurice, *see also* **Thornton, Peter and Tomlin, Maurice.**

Ward-Jackson, Peter, *English Furniture Designs of the Eighteenth Century.* London, 1958.

Wills, Geoffrey, *English Looking Glasses. A Study of the Glass, Frames and Makers, 1670–1820.* London, 1965.

Wills, Geoffrey, *English Furniture, 1550–1760.* London, 1971.

Wills, Geoffrey, *English Furniture, 1760–1900.* London, 1971.

Wolsey, S.W., and Luff, R.W.P., *The Age of the Joiner.* New York, 1969.

PRICE LIST

In some cases it has not been possible to give dates or prices for the objects illustrated. The prices shown below refer to the final bids at the time of sale, inclusive of any local taxes or premium. They are in pounds sterling, with the dollar equivalent at the exchange rate current on the day of the sale. Guineas have been converted to pounds. While every care has been taken in compiling this list, accuracy cannot be guaranteed.

The place of sale is indicated as follows:

(1) *Salerooms*

KS	Christie's, King Street, London
NY	Christie's, New York
SK	Christie's, South Kensington, London

(2) *House sales*

B	Belton, Lincs.
Ca	Charleville, Enniskerry, Co. Wicklow
CB	Childwick Bury, St. Albans
Co	Cornbury House, Oxon.
Cu	Cullen House, Banffshire
Cx	Croxteth Hall, Liverpool
E	Elveden Hall, Norfolk
FH	Fonthill House, Wilts.
GP	Godmersham Park, Kent
L	Luttrellstown, Ireland
NM	North Mymms Park, Herts.
NP	Northwick Park, Gloucs.
P	Powerscourt, Ireland
W	Wateringbury Place, Kent
WD	West Dean Park, Sussex

T	Top
B	Bottom
L	Left
R	Right

Page		Place	Date	Price	Price (US $)
Frontispiece		KS	7.7.32	485	1,698

OAK AND WALNUT 1500 – 1700

Page		Place	Date	Price	Price (US $)
8		KS	25.4.68	273	652
10		NY	29.10.83	11,656	17,600
11		KS	21.11.85	25,920	37,584
12		KS	22.5.67	420	1,151
13		KS	29.10.81	–	–
14		KS	17.3.77	27,500	48,015
15		–	–	–	–
16	1	KS	3.11.83	–	–
16	2	KS	16.4.64	683	1,904
16	3	KS	19.11.81	23,100	46,662
17	4	KS	3.11.83	6,480	9,785
17	5	KS	27.1.77	825	1,435
17	6	KS	4.5.78	1,100	2,112
17	7	KS	22.2.73	1,627	3,987
18	1	W	31.5.78	2,520	4,838
18	2	KS	21.3.68	3,360	8,030
18	3	KS	21.3.68	577	1,380
18	4	Cu	22.9.75	420	932
19	5	NY	12.3.83	13,113	19,800
19	6	NY	26.6.82	–	–
20	1	KS	24.2.83	3,024	4,566
20	2	KS	27.6.85	7,560	9,828
20	3	KS	21.3.68	3,150	7,528
20	4	KS	27.6.85	17,280	22,464
21	5	KS	12.6.80	836	1,940
21	6	KS	17.2.66	840	2,344
21	7	KS	12.6.80	550	1,276

Page		Place	Date	Price	Price (US $)
22	1	–	17.5.	700	–
22	2	KS	20.7.78	1045	2,006
22	3	KS	1.3.79	902	1,912
23	4	KS	19.7.79	1430	3,032
23	5	–	–	–	–
23	6	KS	12.6.80	605	1,404
23	7	KS	8.10.70	189	452
24	1	KS	28.2.80	3,080	7146
24	2	–	–	–	–
24	3	KS	21.11.68	1,260	3,011
24	4	KS	4.5.78	3,300	6,336
25	5	KS	18.11.71	420	1,025
25	6	KS	19.7.79	2,090	4,431
25	7	KS	8.7.71	1,155	2,818
26	1	KS	4.5.72	735	1,837
26	2	KS	21.10.81	2,200	4,444
26	3	KS	18.7.74	525	1,228
27	4	KS	30.10.69	787	1,882
27	5	KS	12.6.80	2,860	6,635
27	6	KS	26.6.75	–	–
28	1	KS	12.6.80	2,200	5,104
28	2	KS	11.3.71	315	769
28	3	KS	15.1.70	997	2,384
28	4	KS	26.6.86	10,800	16,416
29	5	KS	1.4.76	4,400	7,920
29	6	Ca	23.1.78	2,860	5,491
29	7	KS	29.3.84	41,040	59,508
30	1	NY	12.3.83	12,384	18,700
31	2	KS	27.6.85	19,440	25,272
32	1	KS	5.12.85	4,860	7193
32	2	KS	25.6.70	–	–
32	3	KS	19.11.81	11,000	22,220
32	4	KS	19.11.81	50,600	102,212
33	5	KS	27.11.69	252	602
33	6	KS	19.11.81	–	–
33	7	KS	11.10.62	294	823
33	8	KS	19.11.81	5,500	11,110
34	1	–	–	–	–
35	2	NY	14.4.84	–	–
36	1	–	–	–	–
36	2	KS	21.11.84	454	563
36	3	KS	27.6.85	2,160	2,808
36	4	KS	15.10.87	8,256	16,677
37	5	KS	30.10.69	6,825	16,312
37	6	NM	24.9.79	15,400	32,679
37	7	KS	28.6.62	–	–
38	1	NY	25.10.85	26,338	37,400
39	2	NY	29.10.83	10,927	16,500
40	1	KS	22.2.68	472	1,129
40	2	KS	22.11.73	1,470	3,601
40	3	KS	7.4.83	10,260	15,493
41		FH	1.11.73	1,155	2,818

QUEEN ANNE AND EARLY GEORGIAN 1700 – 1727

Page		Place	Date	Price	Price (US $)
42		NY	15.10.80	53,879	125,000
45	1	KS	28.6.84	20,520	28,112
45	2	GP	6.6.83	4,536	6,849
46		GP	6.6.83	81,000	122,310
47		NY	12.3.83	33,509	50,600
48		KS	7.4.83	2,808	4,240
49		GP	6.6.83	11,880	23,998
50		NY	31.1.81	86,634	175,000
51		NY	30.1.82	22,759	39,600
52	1	GP	6.6.83	6,480	9,785
52	2	KS	29.11.79	6,820	14,458
52	3	KS	29.3.84	9,180	13,311
53	4	KS	17.11.83	18,360	27,724
53	5	KS	29.11.79	3,300	6,996
53	6	KS	24.4.69	1,107	2,634
53	7	KS	15.1.78	7,700	14,784
54	1	NY	12.3.83	5,828	8,800
55	2	KS	27.6.85	–	–
55	3	KS	18.11.82	21,060	36,644
56	1	KS	1.4.76	7,480	13,464
56	2	GP	6.6.83	12,960	19,570
56	3	CB	15.5.78	4,950	9,504
57	4	KS	12.3.81	11,550	23,331
57	5	KS	18.11.82	1,404	2,443
57	6	KS	19.6.80	17,600	40,832
58	1	NY	23.10.82	17,701	30,800
59	2	NY	20.4.85	7,097	8,800
59	3	–	–	–	–
59	4	NY	20.4.85	–	–
60	1	Co	22.5.67	577	1,582
60	2	KS	20.4.78	9,900	19,008
60	3	KS	29.3.84	62,640	90,828
60	4	KS	22.11.73	7,350	18,007
61	5	NP	28.9.64	483	1,347
61	6	KS	16.3.78	3,520	6,758
61	7	KS	21.5.70	336	803
61	8	KS	11.5.67	336	921
62	1	KS	29.11.84	41,040	50,890
63	2	NY	14.4.84	15,493	22,000

Page		Place	Date	Price	Price (US $)		Page		Place	Date	Price	Price (US $)
64	1	KS	22.7.65	735	2,051		92	2	KS	11.5.67	3,150	8,631
64	2	KS	22.11.73	7,350	18,007		92	3	KS	17.11.83	11,880	17,938
65	3	KS	15.7.37	830	4,103		93	4	KS	23.11.72	1,102	2,756
65	4	KS	17.11.83	66,960	101,110		93	5	KS	24.11.60	735	2,058
65	5	GP	6.6.83	38,800	58,588		93	6	KS	26.6.80	22,000	51,040
66	1	NY	31.1.81	125,247	253,000		94-5	1	KS	11.4.85	32,400	40,176
66	2	KS	18.11.82	29,700	51,945		94	2	KS	7.4.83	11,340	17,123
67	3	NY	12.3.83	–	–		95	3	KS	21.11.85	91,800	131,274
67	4	KS	7.4.83	64,800	97,848		96	1	W	1.6.78	37,400	71,808
68	1	KS	5.4.73	4,200	10,290		96	2	KS	25.9.80	7,480	17,354
68	2	KS	18.11.82	5,400	9,396		96	3	–	–	–	–
68	3	KS	24.9.81	3,740	7,555		96	4	KS	28.6.84	41,040	56,225
68	4	KS	28.6.73	3,780	9,261		97	5	KS	29.6.78	10,450	20,064
69	5	–	–	–	–		97	6	KS	30.5.85	1,296	1,646
69	6	CB	15.5.78	5,500	10,560		97	7	KS	21.3.68	735	1,757
69	7	NM	24.9.79	1,760	3,731		97	8	KS	15.5.78	10,450	20,064
70	1	KS	17.3.66	472	1,318		98	1	NY	30.1.82	22,126	38,500
71	2	KS	21.3.68	472	1,129		98	2	NY	14.4.84	9,296	13,200
71	3	NY	–	–	115,500		98	3	NY	23.10.82	–	–
72	1	KS	29.11.79	10,450	22,154		98	4	NY	12.3.83	20,397	30,800
73	2	W	1.6.78	8,250	15,840		99	5	–	–	–	–
							100	1	W	1.6.78	37,400	71,808
							100	2	L	26.9.83	22,000	33,220

MAHOGANY AND GILDED PINE 1727 – 1754

Page		Place	Date	Price	Price (US $)		Page		Place	Date	Price	Price (US $)
74		NY	2.2.80	125,000	290,000		100	3	KS	21.4.66	472.5	1,318
76		KS	24.2.83	3,780	5,707		101	4	KS	17.11.83	6,480	9,785
77	T	KS	20.5.82	3,672	6,389		101	5	KS	19.11.70	1,470	3,513
77	B	KS	17.7.80	–	–		101	6	KS	19.11.70	4,410	10,540
78		KS	28.6.84	34,560	47,347		102	1	NY	14.4.84	9,296	13,200
79		KS	4.10.67	1,260	3,452		103	2	KS	26.6.86	12,960	19,699
80		KS	16.3.72	3,780	9,450		103	3	KS	30.11.78	2,750	5,280
81		KS	23.5.68	3,150	7,528		104	1	–	–	–	–
82		KS	7.4.83	10,260	15,492		104	2	KS	27.3.52	1,708	4,765
83		NY	29.10.83	6,556	9,900		105	3	KS	29.11.79	8,800	18,656
84		KS	10.4.75	2,205	4,895		105	4	SK	25.6.80	120	278
85		–	–	–	–		105	5	KS	24.6.65	378	1,055
86		NY	14.4.84	58,098	82,500		106	1	NY	23.10.82	13,908	24,200
87		KS	27.6.85	124,200	161,460		106	2	KS	28.6.84	20,520	28,112
88	1	W	31.5.78	11,000	21,120		107	3	NY	30.1.82	–	–
88	2	KS	23.5.68	2,520	6,022		108	1	KS	29.6.78	1,320	2,534
88	3	GP	6.6.83	20,520	30,985		109	2	KS	26.5.60	3,780	10,584
89	4	L	26.9.83	32,400	48,924							
89	5	W	31.5.78	8,140	15,628							
90	1	KS	19.11.81	9,900	19,998							

CHIPPENDALE AND THE ROCOCO 1754 – 1765

Page		Place	Date	Price	Price (US $)
91	2	KS	27.6.85	19,440	25,272		110		KS	19.6.80	39,600	91,872
91	3	–	–	–	–		112		P	24.9.84	IR£2,200	–
92	1	KS	23.5.68	–	–		113	T	KS	16.11.55	1,323	
							113	B	E	21.5.84	14,040	19,516

Page		Place	Date	Price	Price (US $)
114		NY	20.4.85	17,742	22,000
115		–	–	–	–
116	1	KS	26.5.60	1,890	5,292
116	2	–	–	–	–
117		KS	17.1.80	1,650	3,828
119		NY	14.4.84	9,296	13,200
120	1	KS	24.6.76	–	–
120	2	KS	23.6.60	–	–
121	1	KS	26.1.84	3,780	5,292
121	2	KS	22.5.69	966	2,309
121	3	KS	30.11.78	11,000	21,120
122	1	NY	19.4.86	146,666	220,000
123	2	KS	19.11.81	28,600	57,772
124	1	B	30.4.84	4,320	6,134
124	2	KS	22.11.73	4,200	10,290
124	3	KS	15.5.78	3,960	7,603
124	4	KS	15.4.82	1,404	2,442
125	5	CX	17.9.73	2,100	5,145
125	6	KS	29.11.84	34,560	42,854
125	7	KS	11.11.71	735	1,793
126		NY	20.4.85	–	–
127		–	–	–	–
128	1	KS	17.11.83	3,456	5,218
128	2	KS	21.3.68	399	954
128	3	KS	29.3.84	–	–
129	4	KS	20.3.75	2,730	6,061
129	5	GP	6.6.83	48,600	73,386
129	6	CX	17.9.73	892	2,187
129	7	KS	15.5.78	10,450	20,064
130	1	NY	6.10.85	–	13,200
131	2	KS	27.11.80	48,400	112,288
132	1	KS	17.11.83	3,240	4,892
132	2	KS	22.2.79	660	1,399
132	3	KS	12.5.55	606	1,690
132	4	KS	24.9.81	3,190	6,444
133	5	KS	29.11.84	30,240	37,498
133	6	KS	25.11.79	5,060	10,727
134	1	KS	21.10.81	7,700	15,554
134	2	KS	29.11.84	8,640	10,714
134	3	KS	29.11.85	5,940	8,791
135	4	–	–	–	–
135	5	–	–	–	–
136	1	KS	21.11.85	75,600	109,620
136	2	KS	28.11.84	4,536	5,625
136	3	KS	30.6.77	9,900	17,226
137	4	KS	18.11.82	–	–
137	5	KS	18.11.82	–	–

Page		Place	Date	Price	Price (US $)
138	1	KS	29.11.84	41,040	50,890
138	2	L	26.9.83	14,040	21,200
139	3	KS	9.10.69	756	1,807
139	4	KS	21.5.81	990	2,000
139	5	KS	25.11.65	483	1,347
140	1	KS	4.4.74	189	442
140	2	KS	22.11.73	13,650	33,442
140	3	KS	23.6.84	24,840	34,031
140	4	KS	24.4.58	–	–
141	5	KS	7.4.83	5,400	8,154
141	6	KS	26.4.82	2,160	3,758
141	7	KS	31.5.78	17,600	33,792
142	1	–	–	–	–
142	2	–	–	–	–
143	3	KS	27.6.85	–	–
144	1	KS	20.5.71	–	–
144	2	KS	20.5.71	–	–
145	3	CB	15.5.78	104,500	200,640
145	4	KS	1.6.61	2,415	6,762
146		KS	1.12.77	28,600	49,764
147		NY	30.1.82	31,609	55,000
148	1	KS	17.4.80	10,450	24,244
148	2	KS	27.11.80	17,600	40,832
148	3	CX	17.9.73	577	1,415
149	4	KS	11.5.67	2,310	6,329
150	1	KS	26.6.80	70,400	163,328
150	2	KS	12.3.81	88,000	177,760
151	3	KS	28.6.79	18,700	39,644
152	1	KS	27.1.83	4,536	6,849
152	2	KS	27.11.80	9,020	20,926
152	3	KS	15.5.75	23,100	51,282
153	4	W	31.5.78	–	–
153	5	KS	15.4.82	2,900	5,046
153	6	KS	27.11.69	829	2,133

CLASSICAL ORIGINS 1765 – 1790

Page		Place	Date	Price	Price (US $)
154		KS	28.6.79	33,000	69,960
156		KS	25.5.72	–	–
157		KS	18.11.82	7,020	12,215
158		NY	17.10.81	23,762	48,000
159		NY	20.4.85	5,766	7,150
160		KS	23.5.68	6,510	15,559
161		KS	–	–	–
163		KS	7.4.83	194,400	293.544
164	1	KS	4.6.68	–	–
164	2	KS	1.7.65	6,300	16,740

Page		Place	Date	Price	Price (US $)	Page		Place	Date	Price	Price (US $)
165	3	KS	26.6.75	–	–	186	1	NY	30.1.82	60,057	104,500
165	4	KS	20.5.76	825	1,485	186	2	KS	24.4.80	121,000	280,720
166	1	KS	23.11.72	17,325	43,312	187	3	KS	28.6.51	661	1,852
166	2	NY	28.3.81	34,653	70,000	187	4	KS	25.6.81	71,500	144,430
167	3	NY	25.10.85	–	–	188	1	–	–	–	–
167	4	NY	25.10.85	–	–	188	2	–	–	–	–
168	1	KS	29.3.84	9,180	13,311	188	3	–	–	–	–
168	2	NY	25.10.85	54,225	77,000	189	4	KS	19.5.80	71,500	165,880
169	3	KS	23.6.83	38,880	58,709	189	5	KS	19.6.80	71,500	165,880
169	4	KS	23.11.67	3,570	9,782	189	6	KS	22.3.79	1,375	2,915
169	5	W	1.6.78	5,060	9,715	190	1	KS	1.7.65	43,050	120,109
170	1	NY	20.4.85	66,532	82,500	190	2	KS	1.7.65	43,050	120,109
171	2	NY	14.4.84	10,845	15,400	191	3	NY	12.3.83	23,311	35,200
172	1	KS	9.10.69	546	1,305	192	1	KS	17.4.80	12,100	28,072
172	2	KS	30.6.77	1,375	2,392	192	2	KS	21.4.66	6,825	19,042
173	3	KS	30.6.77	1,375	2,392	193	3	KS	9.4.81	–	–
172	4	KS	30.11.78	418	802	193	4	KS	4.10.84	4,536	6,532
173	5	E	21.5.84	10,260	14,261	193	5	KS	29.6.78	352	676
173	6	KS	4.10.84	4,536	5,715	193	6	KS	28.6.84	4,752	6,510
174	1	KS	29.11.84	20,520	25,444	194	1	NY	2.2.80	–	–
174	2	NY	28.3.81	34,653	70,000	195	2	–	–	–	–
175	3	NY	12.3.83	13,112	19,800	196	1	KS	17.11.83	10,800	16,308
175	4	NY	14.4.84	5,810	8,250	196	2	GP	6.6.83	5,940	8,969
175	5	NY	30.1.82	8,534	14,850	196	3	KS	20.4.67	609	1,669
176	1	KS	25.5.72	–	–	194	4	W	1.6.78	12,650	24,288
176	2	NY	29.9.71	6,557	16,000	197	5	B	30.4.84	48,600	69,012
176	3	–	–	–	–						
176	4	KS	23.6.83	34,560	52,186						
177	5	KS	17.11.83	7,560	11,416	**SHERATON AND ELEGANT TASTE 1790 – 1805**					
177	6	KS	17.4.80	15,400	35,728	198		NY	14.4.84	7,359	10,450
177	7	KS	31.5.78	935	1,795	200	1	KS	19.11.81	6,050	12,221
177	8	KS	19.11.81	1,705	3,444	201	3	KS	23.7.81	2,310	4,666
178	1	NY	28.3.81	33,663	68,000	202		NY	30.1.82	9,483	16,500
179	2	–	–	–	–	204	T	W	31.5.78	825	1,584
179	3	W	31.5.78	704	1,352	204	B	W	31.5.78	1,375	2,640
179	4	–	–	–	–	205	L	W	31.5.78	440	845
180	1	KS	25.6.81	2,640	5,333	205	R	KS	11.4.71	399	973
180	2	KS	1.12.77	14,300	24,882	206	1	KS	10.4.86	4,320	6,329
181	3	KS	29.11.79	3,740	7,928	207	2	KS	10.10.85	6,480	9,137
181	4	KS	5.11.81	7,035	14,211	208	1	KS	18.11.82	2,160	3,758
181	5	KS	29.3.84	14,580	21,141	208	2	KS	28.6.84	8,640	11,837
182	1	NY	25.10.85	10,845	15,400	208	3	KS	7.4.83	10,260	15,493
183	2	–	–	–	–	209	4	KS	20.5.82	2,700	4,698
184	1	KS	25.6.81	7,150	14,443	209	5	KS	29.11.84	7,560	9,374
184	2	KS	21.5.70	2,835	6,776	209	6	KS	21.6.75	945	2,098
185	3	KS	15.4.82	–	–	210	1	KS	27.6.85	8,748	11,372
185	4	KS	29.3.84	140,400	203,580	210	2	NY	25.10.85	50,352	71,500

Page	Place	Date	Price	Price (US $)	Page	Place	Date	Price	Price (US $)
211 **3**	KS	27.6.85	–	–	229 **6**	KS	9.12.71	7,350	17,934
211 **4**	KS	21.11.85	9,180	13,127	230 **1**	KS	20.11.86	7,560	10,735
212 **1**	KS	23.5.68	6,000	14,340	231 **2**	KS	22.3.79	11,000	23,320
212 **2**	KS	12.3.81	6,600	13,332	232 **1**	KS	30.11.78	2,970	5,702
212 **3**	KS	31.1.85	12,960	14,515	232 **2**	KS	21.9.78	2,310	4,435
212 **4**	KS	24.6.76	–	–	232 **3**	KS	17.11.83	10,800	16,308
213 **5**	KS	9.4.81	4,180	8,444	232 **4**	KS	27.6.85	–	–
213 **6**	KS	12.3.64	1,365	3,808	233 **5**	KS	22.11.73	1,470	3,601
213 **7**	KS	19.6.80	6,600	15,312	233 **6**	KS	26.6.86	3,456	5,253
213 **8**	–	–	–	–	233 **7**	KS	25.6.81	6,600	13,332
214 **1**	KS	27.6.85	118,800	154,440	233 **8**	KS	7.4.83	1,728	2,609
215 **2**	WD	2.6.86	37,800	55,566					
216 **1**	KS	13.2.75	2,520	5,594	**THE REGENCY STYLE 1805 – 1840**				
216 **2**	KS	18.11.82	5,616	9,772					
216 **3**	GP	6.6.83	21,600	32,616	234	KS	21.11.85	145,800	211,410
217 **4**	KS	23.5.68	6,300	15,057	236	GP	6.6.83	14,040	21,200
217 **5**	KS	20.5.71	420	1,025	237	GP	6.6.83	10,800	16,308
217 **6**	–	–	–	–	238	NY	20.4.85	–	–
218 **1**	–	–	–	–	239	NY	25.10.85	–	–
218 **2**	KS	26.6.86	4,320	6,566	240 **T**	KS	1.12.77	10,450	18,183
219 **3**	KS	27.6.85	48,600	63,180	240 **B**	KS	29.6.78	770	1,478
219 **4**	–	–	–	–	241	KS	7.7.83	8,100	12,231
220 **1**	KS	28.6.84	40,000	54,000	242	NY	26.6.82	27,816	48,400
220 **2**	–	–	–	–	243	NY	25.10.85	–	–
220 **3**	KS	29.6.78	1,980	3,802	244 **1**	KS	12.3.81	28,600	57,772
221 **4**	KS	14.12.67	–	–	244 **2**	KS	4.7.85	15,120	19,958
221 **5**	KS	22.3.79	1,760	3,731	244 **3**	KS	22.9.75	1,470	3,263
221 **6**	KS	7.4.83	2,808	4,240	245 **4**	KS	26.6.75	504	1,119
221 **7**	KS	28.6.79	–	–	245 **5**	KS	15.4.82	1,134	1,973
222 **1**	KS	28.6.84	49,680	68,062	245 **6**	KS	29.3.84	8,640	12,528
222 **2**	–	–	–	–	246 **1**	NY	30.1.82	6,954	12,100
223 **3**	–	–	–	–	246 **2**	B	30.4.84	10,800	15,336
223 **4**	KS	10.4.86	5,616	8,199	247 **3**	NY	25.10.85	5,422	7,700
224 **1**	KS	28.5.64	682	1,904	247 **4**	KS	29.11.84	3,456	4,285
224 **2**	KS	7.11.85	9,720	13,705	248 **1**	KS	12.2.81	1,980	4,000
224 **3**	GP	6.6.83	18,360	27,724	248 **2**	KS	22.2.79	3,190	6,763
225 **4**	KS	26.5.66	231	644	248 **3**	KS	24.6.82	5,940	10,336
225 **5**	KS	30.11.78	2,750	5,280	249 **4**	KS	29.3.84	8,100	11,745
225 **6**	KS	1.12.77	2,420	4,211	249 **5**	KS	26.10.78	–	–
225 **7**	KS	11.5.67	1,050	2,877	249 **6**	KS	16.10.72	2,310	5,775
226	KS	24.10.85	5,184	7,361	250 **1**	KS	29.11.84	8,100	10,044
227	–	–	–	–	250 **2**	NY	17.10.81	28,713	58,000
228 **1**	KS	30.6.77	11,550	20,097	251 **3**	NY	23.10.82	8,850	15,400
228 **2**	KS	25.6.81	–	–	251 **4**	NY	14.4.84	–	–
228 **3**	KS	16.4.70	381	913	252 **1**	KS	24.6.76	2,090	3,762
229 **4**	KS	25.6.81	47,520	95,990	252 **2**	KS	23.2.84	9,720	13,997
229 **5**	KS	19.11.59	4,410	12,348	252 **3**	KS	3.2.72	997	2,494
					253 **4**	KS	22.11.73	5,250	12,862

Page		Place	Date	Price	Price (US $)	Page		Place	Date	Price	Price (US $)
253	5	KS	29.6.78	2,420	4,646	264	1	KS	14.5.81	–	–
253	6	W	31.5.78	3,080	5,914	264	2	KS	25.5.72	–	–
253	7	KS	22.3.79	2,860	6,063	265	3	KS	28.6.79	880	1,866
254	1	KS	25.11.76	4,400	7,920	265	4	KS	13.2.75	735	1,632
254	2	KS	17.11.83	8,640	13,046	266	1	–	–	–	–
254	3	KS	17.11.83	4,320	6,523	267	2	KS	18.12.82	4,860	8,456
254	4	KS	24.4.69	147	351	267	3	KS	29.11.84	16,200	20,088
255	5	KS	1.12.77	2,090	3,637	268	1	KS	12.3.70	399	954
255	6	KS	29.11.79	2,200	4,664	268	2	KS	29.4.65	420	1,172
255	7	W	31.5.78	6,050	11,616	268	3	KS	19.11.70	1995	4,768
255	8	KS	25.9.80	770	1,786	268	4	–	–	–	–
256	1	KS	1.12.77	1,320	2,297	269	5	KS	17.11.83	15,120	22,831
256	2	KS	26.6.79	880	1,866	269	6	KS	28.6.84	–	–
256	3	KS	21.12.77	330	572	269	7	KS	28.6.84	20,520	28,112
256	4	KS	17.11.83	4,104	6,177	270		–	–	–	–
257	5	KS	16.7.81	990	2,000	271		–	–	–	–
257	6	KS	28.6.51	231	647	272	1	KS	1.12.77	8,250	14,355
257	7	KS	25.2.71	1,995	4,868	272	2	KS	10.5.73	2,835	6,946
258		–	–	–	–	272	3	KS	14.12.67	378	1,036
259	2	KS	27.6.85	21,600	28,080	273	4	KS	26.6.69	315	735
260	1	W	1.6.78	1,430	2,746	273	5	B	30.4.84	15,120	21,470
260	2	CL	1.11.76	1,760	3,168	273	6	KS	15.10.81	825	1,666
260	3	B	30.4.84	7,560	10,735	274	1	WD	2.6.86	51,840	76,205
260	4	KS	21.11.74	1,250	1,550	274	2	KS	28.11.63	357	1,000
261	5	KS	29.3.84	75,600	109,620	275		KS	28.11.84	5,400	6,696
261	6	KS	18.11.82	9,180	15,973	276	1	KS	15.4.82	8,100	14,094
261	7	KS	1.4.76	1,540	2,772	276	2	KS	16.7.81	770	1,555
261	8	KS	15.1.70	–	–	276	3	KS	25.6.81	30,800	62,216
262	1	KS	10.4.86	7,020	10,249	276	4		–	–	–
262	2	KS	26.6.86	12,960	19,699	277	1	KS	1.5.79	440	933
263	3	KS	16.5.85	5,940	7,425	277	2	KS	28.6.73	157.5	386
263	4	KS	20.3.75	367	816	277	3	KS	17.11.83	2,808	4,240
263	5	KS	21.11.74	441	1,032	277	4	KS	6.12.73	577	1,415

INDEX